Identity and Communication

Identity and Communication offers an innovative take on traditional topics of intercultural communication while promoting new ideas and progressive theories.

With essays by emerging voices in identity communication, volume contributors discuss the ways that racial, cultural, and gender identities are perceived and relayed within those communities and the media. The text's essays are structured into four parts, each highlighting different themes of identity communication, from general approaches to racial perceptions to female and adolescent identities. Originating from the University of Texas at Austin's New Agendas in Communication symposium, this volume represents some of the latest and most forward-looking scholarship currently available.

Dominic Lasorsa is an associate professor in the School of Journalism, University of Texas at Austin, where he teaches courses in social science theory, writing, and reporting.

América Rodriguez, formerly a correspondent for National Public Radio (NPR), is an associate professor of Communication in the Departments of Radio-TV-Film and Journalism at the University of Texas at Austin.

New Agendas in Communication
A Series from Routledge and
the College of Communication
at the University of Texas at Austin

Roderick Hart and Stephen Reese, Series Editors

This series brings together groups of emerging scholars to tackle important interdisciplinary themes that demand new scholarly attention and reach broadly across the communication field's existing courses. Each volume stakes out a key area, presents original findings, and considers the long-range implications of its "new agenda."

Identity and Communication
edited by Dominic Lasorsa and América Rodriguez

Political Emotions
edited by Janet Staiger, Ann Cvetkovich, and Ann Reynolds

Media Literacy
edited by Kathleen Tyner

Communicating Science
edited by LeeAnn Kahlor and Patricia Stout

Journalism and Citizenship
edited by Zizi Papacharissi

The Interplay of Truth and Deception
edited by Matthew S. McGlone and Mark L. Knapp

Identity and Communication

New Agendas in Communication

Edited by
Dominic Lasorsa
América Rodriguez

NEW YORK AND LONDON

First published 2013
by Routledge
711 Third Avenue, New York, NY 10017

Simultaneously published in the UK
by Routledge
2 Park Square, Milton Park, Abingdon, Oxon OX14 4RN

Routledge is an imprint of the Taylor & Francis Group, an informa business

© 2013 Taylor & Francis

The right of Dominic Lasorsa and América Rodriguez to be identified as the authors of the editorial material, and of the authors for their individual chapters, has been asserted in accordance with sections 77 and 78 of the Copyright, Designs and Patents Act 1988.

All rights reserved. No part of this book may be reprinted or reproduced or utilised in any form or by any electronic, mechanical, or other means, now known or hereafter invented, including photocopying and recording, or in any information storage or retrieval system, without permission in writing from the publishers.

Trademark notice: Product or corporate names may be trademarks or registered trademarks, and are used only for identification and explanation without intent to infringe.

Library of Congress Cataloging in Publication Data
Identity and communication : new agendas in communication / edited by
 Dominic L. Lasorsa and America Rodriguez.
 pages cm. — (New agendas in communication)
 Includes bibliographical references and index.
 1. Communication—Social aspects. 2. Mass media—Social aspects. 3. Communication and culture. 4. Identity (Psychology) and mass media. 5. Group identity. 6. Intercultural communication. I. Lasorsa, Dominic L. II. Rodriguez, America.
 P95.54.I32 2013
 302.2—dc23
 2012038736

ISBN: 978-0-415-63279-9 (Pbk)
ISBN: 978-0-415-63273-7 (Hbk)
ISBN: 978-0-203-55710-5 (Ebk)

Typeset in Sabon and Gill Sans
by EvS Communication Networx, Inc.

Dominic Lasorsa dedicates this volume to his partner Richard Scroggins who suffered gracefully through the book production process and whose untiring support made it a better book than it otherwise would have been.

Contents

Figures ix
Contributors xi
Preface xv
Introduction xvii

1 Mass Media and Social Identity: New Research Agendas   1
 DOMINIC LASORSA AND AMÉRICA RODRIGUEZ

2 Media Influences on Adolescent Social Identity   6
 MEGHAN BRIDGID MORAN

3 Biased Optimism, Media, and Asian American Identity   22
 DAVID C. OH

4 Same News, Different Narrative: How the Latina/o-Oriented Press Tells Stories of Social Identity   43
 CAROLYN NIELSEN

5 The New Role of Bilingual Newspapers in Establishing and Maintaining Social Group Identities among Latinos   62
 ARTHUR D. SANTANA

6 Prehistory of a Stereotype: Mass Media Othering of Mexicans in the Era of Manifest Destiny   82
 MICHAEL J. FUHLHAGE

7 Overview of Research on Media-Constructed Muslim Identity: 1999–2009   107
 AMMINA KOTHARI

8 Mass Media and African American Identities: Examining
  Black Self-Concept and Intersectionality 126
  MEGHAN S. SANDERS AND OMOTAYO BANJO

9 Rebooting Identities: Using Computer-Mediated
  Communication to Cope with a Stigmatizing Social Identity 149
  KATIE MARGAVIO STRILEY AND SHAWN KING

10 Conceptualizing the Intervening Roles of Identity in
   Communication Effects: The Prism Model 168
   MARIA LEONORA (NORI) G. COMELLO

Index 189

Figures

9.1	Identity cues enmeshed within text	154
10.1	Identity as a moderator of the effect of communication on behavior	174
10.2	Identity as a mediator of the effect of communication on behavior	174
10.3	Communication as a moderator of the effect of identity on behavior (statistically equivalent to Figure 10.1)	176
10.4a	Prism model—version a	180
10.4b	Prism model—version b	180

Contributors

Omotayo Banjo is an assistant professor in the Department of Communication at the University of Cincinnati, where she studies the social and psychological effects of ethnic media, raising questions about how media can be used to further the conversation surrounding diversity.

Maria Leonora (Nori) G. Comello is an assistant professor in the School of Journalism and Mass Communication at the University of North Carolina at Chapel Hill. Her research lies at the intersection of strategic communication, identity, and health. In particular, she studies the potential for messages to frame health and other issues in terms of valued identities and, in so doing, to activate identities consistent with issue support. Her publications have appeared in refereed journals, including a sole-authored piece on identity in *Communication Theory*. Comello earned her doctorate at the School of Communication at The Ohio State University. Prior to her doctoral work, she worked on grant-funded research projects testing the effectiveness of media campaigns aimed at preventing youth substance abuse. In addition, she has worked in public relations for both nonprofit and for-profit organizations.

Michael J. Fuhlhage is an assistant professor of journalism in the Department of Communication and Journalism at Auburn University. He earned his doctorate in mass communication at the University of North Carolina at Chapel Hill and his master's in journalism at the University of Missouri-Columbia. With a Mexican American mother, a German American father, and an upbringing in both urban and rural environments, he became fascinated with cultural difference at an early age. He earned his bachelor's degree in news-editorial journalism at the University of Kansas. He then worked as an editor, designer, and writer at several newspapers, including the *Santa Fe New Mexican*, the *Des Moines Register*, the *Desert Sun* of Palm Springs, and the *Lawrence Journal-World*. While at the University of Missouri, he served as news editor at the *Columbia Missourian* while working on his master's degree. His research examines the development of stereotypical media representations of Mexican Americans and the ways cultural identity shaped journalists' perception and representation of Latinos in the nineteenth century.

Shawn King is a doctoral student in communication at the University of Oklahoma. He received both a bachelor of science degree in communication and a master of arts degree in communication from Missouri State University. His research explores the connection between communication, identity, and relational and mental health.

Ammina Kothari is an assistant professor in the Department of Communication at the Rochester Institute of Technology. She received her doctorate from the School of Journalism at Indiana University in 2012. She received her bachelor's degree in English and print journalism from North Central College in Illinois in 2006 and master's degree in mass communication from the University of Oregon in 2008. Her research interests include media representations of Islam, Africa, race and gender, implications of the Internet and new media for journalism, research methodologies, and health and development communication. She has published articles in *Journalism Studies* and the *Global Media Journal*.

Dominic Lasorsa is an associate professor in the School of Journalism, University of Texas at Austin, where he teaches courses in social science theory, writing, and reporting. He coauthored *How to Build Social Science Theories* (Sage, 2004) and the three-volume *National Television Violence Study* (Sage, 1997–1998). He has published in the *International Journal of Public Opinion Research, Journal of Media Economics, Journalism Practice, Journalism Studies, Journalism & Mass Communication Educator, Journalism & Mass Communication Quarterly, Newspaper Research Journal*, and other research journals. He has written entries for the *Encyclopedia of International Media & Communications, Encyclopedia of Political Communication, International Encyclopedia of Communication*, and *Historical Dictionary of Political Communication*. He served as book review editor of *Journalism & Mass Communication Quarterly*. He holds a bachelor's degree in journalism from St. Bonaventure University, a master's degree in journalism from the University of Texas, and a doctoral degree in communication from Stanford University. Before entering academe, he worked as a reporter and editor for newspapers in New York, Kansas, and Texas.

Meghan Bridgid Moran is an assistant professor in the School of Communication at San Diego State University. Until recently, she was a postdoctoral fellow in the Department of Preventive Medicine at the University of Southern California, funded by the Tobacco-Related Disease Research Program (TRDRP). Her research focuses on the role of identity in health behavior and its effectiveness for health communication campaigns. She received her doctorate from the Annenberg School for Communication, where she studied the influence of media on health behavior. Her current research on the intersection of everyday culture and health behavior focuses specifically on how social identity influences adolescent risk-taking behaviors. Specific research activities include work to better illuminate the mechanisms through which adolescent social identity affects behavior, as well as studies to develop and test identity-targeted antismoking advertising. She also conducts research involving the design and testing of campaigns to increase cervical cancer screening.

Carolyn Nielsen is an assistant professor in the Department of Journalism at Western Washington University, where she teaches news writing, reporting, feature writing, advanced reporting, ethics, and a course she developed called "Diversity, Mass Media, and Social Change." She also has served as the adviser for the campus newspaper. Her primary area of research is Spanish-language news media, especially as their coverage compares to that of major issues featured in general-market newspapers. She was recently published in the *Journal of Spanish Language Media*. She earned a bachelor degree in journalism from Cal Poly, San Luis Obispo, and a master's degree in journalism from Northwestern University. Prior to teaching, she spent nearly a decade as a reporter and editorial page editor at daily newspapers in California and Washington.

David C. Oh is a visiting assistant professor at Villanova University, where he has taught courses in research methods, visual communication and culture, media criticism, and public speaking. He previously taught a variety of media theory courses as an assistant professor at Denison University and as a lecturer at the University of Rhode Island. He received a bachelor of arts degree in psychology and journalism from Baylor University in 1996, a master of arts degree in broadcast journalism from Syracuse University in 2000, and a doctorate in mass communication from Syracuse University in 2007. His research interests are in the representations of Asian Americans in dominant media, Asian American representation in ethnic media, Asian American identity and media, and the Korean diaspora in the United States and transnational media reception. Increasingly, he has become interested in the ways these interests find expression in cyber spaces.

América Rodriguez, formerly a correspondent for National Public Radio (NPR), is an associate professor of communication in the Departments of Radio-TV-Film and Journalism at the University of Texas at Austin. She has published articles on the history and marketing of the U.S. Hispanic audience and on U.S. Latino journalism in *Critical Studies of Mass Communication, Communication Review, Aztlan: A Journal of Chicano Studies,* and other scholarly journals, as well as mass communication anthologies. She received a bachelor's degree in English and Spanish Literature from Swarthmore College, and a master's and doctorate in communication from the University of California at San Diego.

Meghan S. Sanders is an assistant professor at the Manship School of Mass Communication at Louisiana State University. Since 2001, she has conducted experimental and survey research specializing in the impact of media stereotypes and cognitive processing of and emotional responses to entertainment media. She received her doctorate in mass communication from The Pennsylvania State University.

Arthur D. Santana is an assistant professor at the University of Houston. He graduated from the University of Texas at Austin in 1993 with a bachelor's degree in English. He earned his master's degree in journalism from Columbia University in 1996 and his doctorate from the University of Oregon's School of Journalism and Communication in 2012. His areas of interests include newspapers, online journalism, user-generated content, and minorities in the media. He is a member of Kappa Tau Alpha and has twice been awarded top paper at the Association for Education in Journalism and Mass Communication (AEJMC) annual conference. His published articles have appeared in *Newspaper Research Journal.* Before entering academe, he spent 14 years as a reporter and editor, including at the *San Antonio Express-News,* the *Seattle Times,* and the *Washington Post.* He is a member of the National Association of Hispanic Journalists.

Katie Margavio Striley is a doctoral candidate in the Department of Communication Studies at Ohio University. She received her master's degree from Missouri State University and her bachelor's degree from Truman State University. Her primary research interests include social identity, marginalized and underresourced populations, ostracism, and social exclusion. She has the distinction of receiving the Distinguished Thesis award in 2008, the Donald P. Cushman award for top-ranked overall student paper at the National Communication Assoication in 2011, and the Outstanding Doctoral Student award in 2012.

Preface

When the idea was first proposed for a series of books on new agendas in communication research, we jumped at the chance to contribute a volume on the role of the mass media in establishing and maintaining social identity. We were especially intrigued by the idea that each volume would consist of chapters written by promising new scholars who would be instrumental in setting tomorrow's research agenda on this increasingly important topic.

Even though we knew of some of these up-and-coming stars, we decided to send out a broad call for chapter proposals to relevant divisions and interest groups in scholarly associations such as the International Communication Association and the Association for Education in Journalism and Mass Communication. To our delight, we received an amazing number of responses, with many superb ideas for chapters. Our first task was to whittle down the possibilities to a manageable number of potential chapters. The authors of the selected proposals then were invited to submit a chapter draft which was sent to all the other prospective authors. Each author then read and critiqued all the other chapter drafts. We then had at least the first author of each selected proposal attend a working conference on the proposed book, which was held at our host institution, the University of Texas at Austin, August 15–17, 2010. At the conference, the chapter authors presented a draft of thei,r chapters and the rest of us offered recommendations for improving each chapter. We are convinced that these interactions among the different authors helped strengthen the book considerably. Based on the feedback they received, the chapter authors then were invited to submit a final chapter draft. Ultimately, we accepted 10 chapters for publication.

A project like this has many moving parts and requires the help of many able persons. We want to acknowledge the assistance of those who helped make this book a success. We wish to thank the coeditors of the New Agendas book series, Rod Hart and Steve Reese, who agreed that our book was a good idea and who supported wholeheartedly our efforts to bring it to fruition. They also gave us valuable tips on how to organize both the Austin conference and the book itself.

We also want to thank Anne Reed, Candice Prose, and Kat Yerger of the College of Communication administrative staff, each of whom helped us immeasurably with the Austin conference. Their attention to detail (and patience with our lack of it) we greatly appreciated.

We also would like to thank LeeAnn Kahlor, a colleague of ours in the University of Texas Advertising Department, who organized one of the earlier conferences and books in this series. She graciously shared her experiences with us, helping make our conference and book better than they otherwise would have been.

Finally, we want to thank publisher Linda Bathgate of Routledge, who oversaw the production of the book and whose sage advice helped make it stronger. The book is in your hands now largely thanks to her.

Dominic Lasorsa
School of Journalism
América Rodriguez
Department of Radio-Television-Film
University of Texas at Austin

Introduction

Roderick P. Hart and Stephen D. Reese

We are happy to present this latest volume in the New Agendas in Communication series. Through this conference and publication initiative of the College of Communication at the University of Texas at Austin we hope to advance our goal of defining communication education in the 21st century. Selected college faculty members identify an interdisciplinary topic of broad appeal to the field of communication and then convene a group of the most promising emerging scholars to share and develop their ideas. Following this working conference in Austin, the faculty conveners edit a volume that brings the work together in a way intended to speak to a wide audience. We hope each volume will provide a new and fresh perspective on the crucial questions of concern to the field.

In this volume, *Identity and Communication*, coeditors Dominic Lasorsa, of the School of Journalism, and América Rodriguez, of the Department of Radio-Television-Film, track new directions in the study of identity. In the past, the vague concept of "diversity" covered a host of social categories from which people derived their identity, but increasingly these traditional designations no longer have the same predictive power. We must reexamine them, as do the contributors, to better explore the complexities of identity formation in networked society.

Chapter 1

Mass Media and Social Identity
New Research Agendas

Dominic Lasorsa and América Rodriguez

As this book's main title implies, the book is about how identity and media relate to each other and, in particular, the role of the mass media in establishing and maintaining social identity. As its subtitle implies, however, the book is not designed to describe or even to critique the existing body of literature but instead primarily to point to new and exciting directions for future research. To accomplish this goal, we turned to bright, young, enthusiastic scholars who have been recognized early in their academic careers for having already promoted promising and innovative ways for advancing knowledge on some aspect of this increasingly important topic. Even in their still-budding careers, these junior scholars have helped shift our attention in forward-looking ways toward productive scholarship that we believe will have a lasting effect on social identity research. This book is a testament to their groundbreaking ideas.

What do we mean by "social identity"? While each of us has a unique personal identity, we also possess a social identity, an identity shared with other members of a social group. Individuals recognize the social groups to which they belong, as well as other social groups to which they do not belong. Persons also learn to characterize these social groups and their members. Each chapter in this book takes the position that the mass media are integrally implicated in the construction of a social identity. While the chapters look back at what we already know, the focus of each chapter is on the future, to draw attention to promising directions for future research and to show how and why this research agenda is the way to go. It is relatively easy to make (and therefore common to see) suggestions that future research should replicate an existing study in a different context. So, an article on newspaper coverage suggests that future studies should examine television coverage, and an article on coverage of one marginalized group suggests that future studies should examine coverage of other marginalized groups, and so on. Each chapter here, however, attempts to do much more than that. These chapters point to future studies that are novel in the ways they theorize, conceptualize, and measure. The result is a cornucopia of fresh ideas both appetizing and nutritious, and ripe for the picking. Those interested in identifying new research projects that will advance our thinking about the relationship between social identity and mass media will find a variety of opportune ideas in each of the chapters here.

All but two of the chapters in this book examine the role of the mass media in the formation of the social identity of the members of a specific social group, with chapters focusing on adolescents, African Americans, Asian Americans, Latinos, Mexicans, and Muslims. One chapter deals with marginalized social groups generally in a new media landscape, and one chapter deals with ways to build theory regarding all social groups. Obviously, not all social groups are covered here, nor was that our intention. We selected chapters for inclusion in the book because they broke new ground and exemplified the research of the future, regardless of what social groups happened to be the objects of study. However, we did include chapters that represented an array of theoretical and methodological perspectives.

The chapter authors take a variety of both qualitative and quantitative approaches to their work, including activist, critical, cultural, economic, historical, humanistic, and technical frameworks, utilizing a variety of methods from content analysis to in-depth interviews. The chapters are not presented in any precise order, except that we put chapters on the same social group together and we end the book with the chapter that deals with marginalized groups generally, followed by the chapter dealing with all social groups.

In her chapter, Meghan Bridgid Moran (San Diego State University) examines how peers, specifically peer crowds and subcultures, act as sources of social identity for adolescents, focusing specifically on the role of the media in the process of connecting peers through their media use. Moran shows how the mass media play powerful roles in promoting specific social identities which adolescents experiment with and ultimately adopt (e.g., jocks, emos, preppies, nerds). The chapter also explores how the media can be used to reach a specific adolescent social group in order to attempt to influence the behavior of its members. Moran explains how the role of the media in the formation of social identity is unique among adolescents because adolescence is often a time of experimentation with a variety of social identities. Adolescents use the media to help them recognize and explore social identities; the media can also be used to reach and influence the adolescent who identifies with different social groups.

In his chapter, David C. Oh (Villanova University) explores how Asian Americans "read" the media in ways that allow them simultaneously to accept the mainstream media on one level while rejecting them on another. In doing so, he encourages audience reception studies to begin to address directly the influence of popular media on identity construction. He investigates how audience members make sense of the influences of popular media and the tactics they use to incorporate or insulate themselves from dominant ideologies or, at least, to convince themselves they are doing so. Guided by grounded theory, Oh uses the technique of in-depth interviews to explore Asian Americans' views of their racial identity, their perceptions of popular media representations of Asian Americans, and their beliefs about the media's impact on their own self-identity. He finds that Asian Americans often engage in what he calls "biased optimism," which allows them to believe in media effects on their own self-identity, including negative effects, while still allowing them to feel positive about their consumption of mainstream media.

In her chapter, Carolyn Nielsen (Western Washington University) marshals three narrative framing studies to illustrate the important role played by the Spanish-language press in the formation of a positive Latino social identity. Nielsen builds her work on the notion of the "counternarrative," an idea derived from critical race theory, one tenet of which is that interests of nonmajority social groups are addressed by the mainstream media when and in terms of how those interests are perceived to affect society's dominant social group. Nielsen examines how the mainstream press, such as the *New York Times* and the *Los Angeles Times,* covered the same three important news events in a systematically different way than did the Latino-oriented press in the same cities, such as *La Opinion* and *El Diario-La Prensa*. Nielsen shows how the counternarratives that these Spanish-language daily newspapers provide begin with a different set of assumptions and that, unlike the narratives provided by the mainstream media, these counternarratives reinforce and shape a positive Latino social identity.

In his chapter, Arthur D. Santana (University of Houston) introduces readers to an important yet almost completely ignored facet of the role of the media in the construction of social identity. Santana focuses on the growing number of Spanish-English bilingual newspapers in the United States and the roles these newspapers play in language development, acculturation, and identity. Santana maintains that the bilingual newspaper is a product of cultural contradictions that permeate the "neither-nor" cultural identity of later-generation Latinos. As such, Santana argues, the bilingual newspaper has become an increasingly important part of the acculturation process that plays such a critical role in the establishment and maintenance of social identity.

In his chapter, Michael J. Fuhlhage (Auburn University) advances our understanding of the historical development of the negative stereotyping of Mexicans in the early American press. Fuhlhage shows how leading communication scholars meticulously have traced media stereotypes about Latinos back to the start of the 20th century. Fuhlhage, however, has located negative representations in the press dating back a half-century earlier. He shows how the U.S. media in the 1800s "brewed" stereotypes about Mexicans which developed over decades. Fuhlhage uses a method of analysis called "cultural contrapuntal reading" which considers not only authorial presence and intent in determining the extent to which media sources reflect reality but, in addition, elaborates upon the influence of an author's social identity on his or her portrayals of an outgroup. By probing into the education, travels, and other experiences of those who wrote historical accounts of borderland inhabitants, Fuhlhage shows the mentality behind many of these writings which so influenced for so long others' understandings of these remote and therefore "exotic" people. One aspect of these 19th-century writings that is particularly remarkable is the extent to which religious differences permeate the conclusions drawn by these early writers. Fuhlhage's account of the extent to which anti-Mexican sentiments were connected to anti-Catholic sentiments raises a whole host of new questions about the role of the media in establishing and maintaining social identities—which is exactly the intention of this book.

In her chapter, Ammina Kothari (Indiana University) examines how communication scholars have envisioned and contextualized Muslim identity. She exhaustively reviewed all research on Islam and Muslims published in peer-reviewed journals between 1999 and 2009 and identified 31 studies that focused on how media construct Muslim/Islamic identity. She finds that the research is limited to text-based analyses of traditional media and that research predominantly uses the framework of Orientalism. Kothari concludes that the lack of diversity in the geographic location of research, the scarcity of scholarship on the topic, and the exclusion of multiple Muslim voices all work together to impede understanding of how media-constructed identities of Muslims and Islam influence both non-Muslim audiences and Muslims themselves. As with all of the chapters in this volume, this one culminates with a clear agenda for future research on this important contemporary topic.

In their chapter, Meghan S. Sanders (Louisiana State University) and Omotayo Banjo (University of Cincinnati) emphasize understudied aspects of the role of the media in establishing and maintaining the social identity of African Americans. Instead of examining the media's impact solely from the perspective of majority audiences, Sanders and Banjo focus as well on the impact from the perspective of the marginalized group itself. In addition, they draw attention to the impact of Black-oriented media on establishing and maintaining social identity. Furthermore, and importantly, they stress the importance of recognizing the interaction of characteristics and traits that make up a person's complete identity, rather than just one dominant characteristic, such as ethnicity or gender alone. It is the study of the "intersectionality" of marginalized groups' characteristics, Sanders and Banjo maintain, that offers the most productive and rewarding way to move research on social identity forward.

In their chapter, Katie Margavio Striley (Ohio University) and Shawn King (University of Oklahoma) look beyond the vast majority of research on computer-mediated communication by focusing on how marginalized individuals use it. Not only do Striley and King thereby broaden the context of computer-mediated communication research itself but they also demonstrate how those in marginalized groups, unlike more "typical" users, utilize CMC for a specific type of identity formation and maintenance. Furthermore, Striley and King broaden the theoretical understanding of CMC generally by recognizing a critical shift in the nature of computer-mediated communication. Earlier, CMC was utilized primarily to filter out identification; it was precisely the potential of being anonymous that made CMC alluring to many users for many years. Thanks to technological developments, however, CMC is now being utilized in other ways that encourage users to avoid anonymity and instead to provide more and more relevant personal information about themselves in their online communications. Striley and King show how this "filtering in" perspective has important ramifications for the role of computer-mediated communication in the construction and maintenance of social identity.

In her chapter, Maria Leonora (Nori) G. Comello (University of North Carolina) draws upon the metaphor of a prism to introduce a general model for the study of social identity which draws attention to two possible intervening roles that identity can play in explaining any causal relationship between communication and behavior. Identity can influence the effect of communication on behavior, thus serving as a moderator of communication effects (i.e., altering the impact of communication). Identity also can be a conduit for the effects of communication on behavior, thus serving as a mediator of communication effects (i.e., explaining the impact of communication on behavior). Since these two intervening roles can occur simultaneously, Comello observes, they can add to the complexity—and richness—of any analysis of the impact of communication on behavior. Ultimately, Comello demonstrates how her prism model can be used to help build theory about the role of the mass media in fostering social identity.

As can be seen from these brief descriptions, the chapters in this book do not form a closely knit tapestry in which all of the threads are woven together to spell out a single message. Perhaps the metaphor of a quilt is a more apt metaphor. In this book, we have attempted to stitch together a remarkable set of chapters, each of which in its own unique and fresh way draws attention to promising directions for future research on the role of the media in the cultivation of social identity. We hope you agree.

Chapter 2

Media Influences on Adolescent Social Identity

Meghan Bridgid Moran[1]

Adolescence can be a turbulent and uncertain time in an individual's life. Adolescents are learning how to negotiate any number of situations on their own for the first time and often look outside their family and home lives for guidance. At the same time, adolescents are developing their own identities, figuring out who they are as individuals independent of their families. As such, peers, in the form of individual friends, cliques of friends, and more amorphous crowds and subcultures, play an important role in the lives of adolescents. The following chapter details the nature of how peers—specifically, peer crowds and subcultures—act as sources of social identity for adolescents, with the focus being specifically on the role of the media in this process.

The Importance of Social Identity in the Lives of Adolescents

Adolescence is the time during which children, making the transition to young adulthood, learn to function in the world independently of their parents (Gavin & Furman, 1989). In the adolescent years, parents often give their children new freedoms (staying out later, getting a driver's license); as such, adolescents are facing new and unfamiliar situations that they must deal with on their own. For example, the adolescent years are often the period when teenagers attend their first parties alone (where there may or may not be drinking and drugs), have their first job, and enter into their first romantic relationship. The myriad of new decisions, freedoms, and experiences that teenagers face make adolescence a time riddled with ambiguity (Eichorn, Mussen, Clausen, Haan, & Honzik, 1981).

In addition to uncertainty over how to negotiate these new situations, adolescents also face uncertainty over their identity.[2] Adolescence is a time for individuals to explore and eventually form stable identities (Erikson, 1968; Marcia, 1966). As children enter the teen years, they must determine who they are outside of their family and how to fit into the larger world of their peers (Blos, 1975; Seltzer, 1982). As a part of this process, teenagers will often "try on" a series of identities before finally committing to one or more that can be used as a framework to understand the self (Erikson, 1959; Marcia, 1966). For many adolescents, this process is filled with false starts: teenagers may experiment with a number of identities (punk, jock, goth, etc.) before settling on a stable and enduring one.

Over the course of the teenage search for identity, many adolescents look to their peers for support and guidance (Brown, Mory, & Kinney, 1994; Erikson, 1968; Newman & Newman, 1976; Palmonari, Pombeni, & Kirchler, 1989, 1990). Whereas during the childhood years, the family was often the prime resource for this kind of support, adolescents now look toward peers as a resource for identity formation and for a source of guidance as to how to behave in uncertain situations (Brown et al., 1994; Stone & Brown, 1998). More specifically, adolescents often identify with peer crowds as a way to find stability during the teenage years because they can provide teens with clear identities complete with behavioral scripts.

Peer Crowds and Social Identity as Coping Mechanisms

A significant body of research has documented the phenomenon commonly known as *peer crowd identification* (Sussman, Pokhrel, Ashmore, & Brown, 2007), the process through which adolescents affiliate with a certain group, subculture, or social category to explore and manage their developing independent identities. While adolescents often have groups of friends with whom they interact and spend time, a peer crowd is more than just a collection of friends. Rather, a peer crowd is a "reputation-based collective" of adolescents who are united by common values, norms, and styles (Sussman, Pokhrel, et al., 2007). Peer crowds are "more cognitive than behavioral, more symbolic than concrete and interactional" (Brown, 2004, p. 365). Members of a peer crowd may share similar attitudes and beliefs, but they may not necessarily spend time together or even share the same geographic location. For instance, both a 14-year-old in Portland, Maine and a 14-year-old in San Diego, California may identify with the same peer crowd (for example, jocks)—sharing the same preference for athletic activities, style of dress, and so on—even though they have never met. Thus, the values, norms, and taste preferences of a peer crowd can generally be said to transcend geographic boundaries. Although adults often do identify with peer crowds, the phenomenon is studied primarily among adolescents due to the increased importance of peer crowd identification in adolescent life. Peer crowds, it has been argued, provide adolescents with a concrete resource through which they can navigate their social worlds, acting as guides for behavior (Brown et al., 1994; Stone & Brown, 1998).

It must be noted that, while adolescents do have a certain amount of agency over which crowds they identify with, there is occasionally a discrepancy between the crowd an adolescent identifies with (or wishes to identify with) and the crowd others perceive him or her as belonging to. For example, Brown, von Bank, and Steinberg (2008) asked adolescents to place their classmates into crowds and compared each adolescent's placement with his or her self-placement. There was a low level of concordance when an adolescent's peers placed him or her into a "low-status" group, such as outcasts. Specifically, although an adolescent's peers perceived him or her as identifying with a low-status group, the adolescent did not share this perception (Brown, von Bank, & Steinberg, 2008). Thus, while an adolescent may self-identify with a group, he or she may not be fully accepted by others who identify with the group, leading to potential cognitive dissonance over the individual's social identity.

Social identity theory (Tajfel, 1978; Tajfel & Turner, 1979) provides an important theoretical context to the role of peer crowd identification in an adolescent's transition to adulthood, as research indicates that these peer crowds act as an important source of social identity for an adolescent (Tarrant et al., 2001). According to social identity theory, the social groups to which an individual belongs provide that individual with a source of identity, self-esteem, and behavioral guidance (Hogg & Abrams, 2003). An adolescent peer crowd, then, can be viewed as a social category with which an individual identifies. According to social identity theory, individuals portray the group to which they belong (the in-group) positively, so a sense of esteem and belonging is derived from being a member of the group, which helps to combat one source of uncertainty for the adolescent (Abrams & Hogg, 1999; Tajfel, 1978; Tarrant, 2002; Turner, Brown, & Tajfel, 1979). And, these social categories have corresponding prototypes that provide cues for how to engage in the social world. This helps to combat another source of identity for the adolescent.

Social Identity and Adolescent Behavior

Consequently, an adolescent's social identity as a member of a crowd can have a pronounced impact on behavior. At a basic level, an adolescent may choose to dress the way that is prescribed by the crowd's prototype and, accordingly, *not* dress the way that is prototypical of another crowd. For instance, an adolescent who identifies with the preppy crowd may choose to wear clean-cut clothes from Abercrombie & Fitch but not wear black, edgier clothes that may be typical of the goth crowd. However, peer crowds can also influence more risky behavior, such as substance use. For example, adolescents who identify with the "deviant" crowd are significantly more likely to consume cigarettes, drugs, and alcohol, while those who identify as academics are considerably less likely to engage in alcohol or drug use (Sussman, Pokhrel, et al., 2007).

The mechanisms through which the behavioral influence of social identity occurs are contested (Dickson & Scheve, 2006). The theoretical explanation of why and how social identity shapes behavior hinges upon the premise that behavioral motivations vary on a continuum from interpersonal to intergroup (Tajfel, 1974, 1978). At the interpersonal extreme, behavioral motivation is located at the person-to-person level, determined by individual personality and idiosyncratic quirks. At the intergroup extreme, behavioral motivation is located at the group level, such that individuals are motivated to act in accordance with their group's prototype. At the same time, these individuals are acting in a way that distinguishes them from members of other groups. For instance, when adolescents who identify as punk wear Mohawks and Doc Marten boots, they are actively differentiating self from other groups, such as jocks who might dress in more athletic clothing. Thus, during the adolescent years, when teenagers are still determining an individual identity, they most often look to peer crowds for guidance, thus acting as members of the crowd at the intergroup end of the spectrum. According to social identity theory, when individuals act according to the prototype for one of their social identities, they are doing so because they are acting out who they are as a member of a group. In other words, the individual's social identity served a "self-definitional function" (Hogg & Reid, 2006, p. 12), and the group prototype acted as a framework for organizing behavior according to who one is as a member of a social category.

There are several mechanisms that influence the extent to which social identities are adopted and consequently impact on behavior (Hogg & Turner, 1987; Reed & Forehand, 2003). The following text details four main behavioral mechanisms of social identity, explaining the processes that must occur for individuals' social identity to influence their behavior.[3]

- First, a crowd must be recognized as existing and then contrasted as different from other crowds. In other words, adolescents must recognize that one crowd, for instance, emo,[4] exists and is different from other crowds.
- Second, adolescents must actually identify with a specific peer crowd. That is, adolescents must cognitively think of themselves as belonging to the emo crowd, but not to the jock or hippie crowd. This is influenced by the perceived desirability of the social category—the adolescent must perceive belonging to the "emo" crowd as preferable to the "jock" crowd. Because identification with a specific crowd is a cognitive as well as a social process, adolescents consequently

can identify or cease to identify with social categories traditionally thought of as "fixed," such as race or gender. In other words, a biological female can cognitively identify or cease to identify with the gender female or male and manifest those group prototypes as she chooses (even though others may perceive her gender identification differently).

- Third, individuals must be aware of that crowd's corresponding prototype. This prototype must be clear and relevant to the social category. Reed and Forehand (2003) argue that a social identity will only influence behavior for which it is diagnostic. For example, self-categorizing as emo might influence music purchase (e.g., Dashboard Confessional but not Dave Matthews Band), but may have no relevance to and influence on preference for pizza as opposed to Chinese takeout. So, in order for adolescents' emo social identity to influence behavior, they must possess knowledge that this crowd's prototype includes wearing tight jeans, Chuck Taylor sneakers, and listening to bands like Taking Back Sunday.
- Fourth, the identity must be salient or accessible for adolescents. Hogg and Reid (2006) argue that "[p]eople use accessible categories to make sense of their social context" (p. 12). For adolescents' emo social identity to influence their behavioral decision in a given situation, they must be thinking of themselves as emo. For example, if a young woman identified both as emo and as female, the salience of these two social identities might vary based upon her situation. In a room full of males, as the only female, her female social identity might become more salient and consequently be the basis upon which she acts. Alternately, in a room full of jocks, her emo social identity might become most salient.

The influence of social identity on behavior is even more pronounced in adolescence than during other life stages, precisely because of the uncertain nature of these teen years when adolescents are constantly being confronted with new situations they must handle on their own. Social identities offer prototypical ways of behaving for these new environments and experiences. Peer crowds provide a stable source of identity, complete with corresponding prototypes that offer prescribed norms, values, and taste preferences to help guide adolescents' behavior in new and ambiguous situations.

The Role of the Media in Peer Crowds

Because social identity has such an important impact on an adolescent's life and behavior, it is important to understand how the behavioral mechanisms of social identity are influenced. Directly relating to these four behavioral mechanisms, four questions arise:

- How do adolescents learn about and distinguish the myriad social categories from which they adopt social identities?
- How do adolescents perceive one social category as more desirable than another?
- How do adolescents learn the prototype for a social category?
- How are social identities made salient in the mind of an adolescent?

While a certain proportion of influence on the behavioral mechanisms of social identity is due to day-to-day contact with other adolescents (Hogg & Reid, 2006), adolescent peer crowds and their prototypes remain relatively stable through time and across geographies (Sussman et al., 2010). Direct contact with others who share the same social identity is not a necessary reason for an adolescent to adopt a social identity and consequently act according to the group's prototype. It has been hypothesized that the media play a crucial role in this process (Slater, 2007). Specifically, responding to the questions above, the media are a major influence on the behavioral mechanisms of social identity in four ways. First, the media can construct or create social categories and can provide individuals with access to social categories about which they might not otherwise have known. Second, the media can influence the desirability of a social identity. Third, media can define prototypes of social categories. Fourth, the media can influence the salience of a particular social identity in the mind of an adolescent.

Creating and Providing Access to Social Categories

The first way in which the media may affect social identity is in the creation of social categories with which one may identify (Huntemann & Morgan, 2001). Individuals may be categorized into groups on the basis of almost anything, and the media—particularly through advertising—are responsible for offering many of the social categories with which we choose to identify. Jenkins (2003) argues that individuals cannot become subjects until they are subjectified and, as such, cannot have identities until identities are created for them. This seemingly simple point—one cannot identify as a jock, nerd, or skater if those social categories do not exist—is deserving of significant analysis. Quite often, the media are a key player in this process. Identity has long been a popular vehicle for selling consumer goods, whereby certain products are aligned with certain social categories; for example, the classic case of Sprite aligning its soda as a natural extension of hip-hop culture (Walker, 2002). In the increasingly cluttered media environment, media practitioners, especially marketers, have turned to narrowcasting in order to hail specific audiences. This often means creating new identity categories, such as the tween, so that individuals will feel a product is "for them." Thus, the media are constantly providing individuals with more and new social categories (the metrosexual, the technosexual, and so on) with which they may choose to identify.

The designation of "teenager" itself is a prime example of a social category seemingly "invented," or at least propagated, by the media (Sivulka, 1998). The term *metrosexual* might be a more current example relating to young adults. Tuncay (2006) traces the evolution of this social category to Mark Simpson, who used the term both in his book *Male Impersonators: Men Performing Masculinity* (1994) and also in a later published Salon.com article, "Meet the Metrosexual" (2002). Upon publication of this article, other popular press outlets such as the *New York Times* picked up on the term, publishing their own articles. By 2003, advertising firm Euro RSCG Worldwide had picked up on the phenomenon—after all, Simpson (2002) described metrosexuals as "the most promising consumer market of the decade." The metrosexual group prototype traditionally is a young, single White male with a large disposable income to spend in a major metropolitan city, concerned with fashion, grooming, and consumer products. Certainly, before the introduction of this social category by advertisers and media, many men fit the metrosexual prototype. However, it was not until this term was widely pushed through media vehicles that these prototypical behaviors were distilled into a prototype and "metrosexual" became available to men as a social identity.

In addition to creating and promoting social categories, media can also provide individuals with access to existing social identities they might not have otherwise known. The world to which adolescents have physical access is particularly limited by geography (or by parents). Many adolescents are not allowed to or do not have the means to travel beyond a small area. Thus, their ability to discover new subcultures, cliques, and crowds via direct contact is limited. For this reason, media play a particularly important role for adolescents to learn about, and subsequently adopt, social identities to which they would not otherwise have access. Kitwana (2006) writes about a young White man living in Eugene, Oregon, a city with a large White majority, who identified with the hip-hop subculture. His access to hip-hop as a social identity was facilitated entirely through the media. With Eugene, Oregon, not having much of a hip-hop scene, this young man, as an adolescent, relied on MTV and local radio as key resources through which he could develop and maintain this social identity. In particular, the changing media landscape and evolution of the Internet and social media afford adolescents access to a world they might not otherwise have known about and, perhaps more importantly, contact with individuals who they might not otherwise have known. Without access to both traditional and new media, which transcend geographies, an adolescent would have no way of learning about the existence of social categories prominent in other locations.

Influencing the Desirability of Social Categories

The media also influence the desirability of a social identity. Mass media tend to characterize social groups, portraying certain groups positively and others negatively. Take, for example, the classic teenage sitcom *Saved by the Bell*. Certain social categories (jocks, preppies) are celebrated: Zach (who represents the preppy category) and Slater (who represents the jock category) are the most popular guys in school, with no shortage of friends or dates. On the other hand, the nerds who excel academically are constantly mocked. These sorts of patterns persist throughout other programs and other forms of media, wherein specific social groups are portrayed as "cool" while others are not. Perhaps more importantly, though, is that beyond portraying certain groups as undesirable, the media have the ability not to portray certain groups at all. This "symbolic annihilation" (Gerbner, 1972; Gerbner & Gross, 1976) of social categories conveys an important message to adolescents about what type of person counts in society. This has an obvious effect on the extent to which an adolescent perceives a specific group as desirable, consequently adopting that social identity and behaving in accordance with its prototype.

Content Defining

Third, the media play an important role in defining what it means to be a member of a social category (Huntemann & Morgan, 2001). In other words, the information gotten from the media can be crucial in the formation of a group prototype. The power of mass media to influence the public's perceptions of specific groups or categories of individuals has long been recognized; Coleman and Yochim (2008) note that films such as *Scarface* and *The Godfather* have disclaimers indicating that the films are not meant to represent any ethnic group. Kleine, Kleine, and Kernan (1993) similarly suggest that media are resources that teach individuals how to perform identities. Thus, in the specific context of social identity theory, media can be important influences in defining the exact nature of a group's prototype. Obviously, interpersonal communication between group members plays an important part in the creation of group prototypes, but the influence of the media here should not be overlooked—especially for those individuals who may not have direct contact with group members.

Warnick, Dawson, Smith, and Vosburg-Bluem (2010) argue that popular American cinema consistently portrays "peer communities" among adolescents, offering the film *The Breakfast Club* as an illustration. In this movie, five adolescents from five crowds are represented: the brain, the athlete, the basket case, the princess, and the criminal. Over the course of the film, the prototype for each crowd is clearly illustrated. The brain is smart, unpopular, and has a strong desire to please his teachers and parents. His stature is small and he wears a sweater and pants that are slightly too short. The jock plays sports, is popular, goes to parties, and bullies those he sees as weak. This sort of prototype defining occurs perpetually and across various media forms. For example, in 2002 *Seventeen* magazine ran a piece describing the emo prototype, including guidance to any adolescent on how to act and dress in accordance with the emo crowd. Media choices often are important components of a social category's prototype. As argued by Huston, Wartella, and Donnerstein (1998), media choices often serve as a performance of identity. The media not only act as informational resources, whereby people learn how to enact social identities—learning how to dress emo from reading Seventeen magazine—but can also act as resources for the performance of social identities (Kleine, Kleine, & Kernan, 1993). Greenwald (2003) cites the example of a young woman who says she wears band T-shirts because she wants people to know what bands she likes and, consequently, the type of person she is. The *Seventeen* magazine article notes that certain media serve as markers of the emo social identity, such as Sunny Day Real Estate albums and J. D. Salinger's *Franny and Zooey*.

It is important to note that because the role of media in defining a group prototype is likely to be most pronounced when an individual does not have direct contact with group members, the media may be particularly important in the formation of out-group prototypes. If we are to assume that the media have more influence over the content of prototypes of groups with which one does not have much direct contact, then this may be the area where the most influence may be seen. Consequently, because an in-group prototype is dependent upon perceptions of the relevant out-group, we may see media affecting perceptions of group prototypes both directly (influencing the perception of the in-group prototype) and indirectly (influencing the perception of the out-group prototype, which in turn spurs individuals to reconceptualize the relevant criteria through which to define their in-group).

Increasing Salience

Finally, media portrayals of social identity can affect the salience of a social identity. Research on social identity posits that which identity is salient depends upon the individual's social context (Forehand,

Deshpande, & Reed, 2002; Reed & Forehand, 2009). As nearly ever-present companions in the lives of adolescents, media can be important factors in determining which social identity is primed in the adolescent's mind. For example, ads that contain gender-related cues could prime a gender-related social identity, thus making that social identity more salient. Thus, this social identity will be readily accessible and consequently is expected to influence cognitive processing and subsequent behavior (Maldonado, Tansuhaj, & Muehling, 2003). Forehand et al. (2002) found that students who viewed ads that primed their Asian ethnicity showed higher levels of identity salience than those not exposed to identity-related primes. Slater (2007) pushes this further, arguing that media influence on the salience of a social identity can have a "reinforcing spirals" effect, whereby individuals choose media relevant to a salient social identity, and those relevant media, in turn, increase the salience of that social identity, thus priming the individual to again spend time with media relevant to that social identity.

Consequences of Media Influence on Social Identity

The previous section detailed the mechanisms through which media influence social identity in adolescents. This section offers examples of how the media, via their influence on social identity, have had tangible behavioral impact. Health behavior is one realm through which this influence has been most widely studied. Although social identity has been identified as a useful tool to promote a myriad of healthy behaviors, this section focuses on cigarette use because it is a realm where some of the most cutting edge research in this field is being done.

For decades, cigarette manufacturers have used identity-targeted appeals to sell cigarettes to groups of individuals. For example, Lucky Strike branded its cigarette as fashionable, respectable, and classy—ideal for a woman who could smoke with style (Sivulka, 1998). On the other hand, the creation of the Marlboro man by Philip Morris effectively associated Marlboro cigarettes with masculinity. This brand image was created in the 1950s, with the goal of rebranding Marlboro (a cigarette previously associated with women) as manly, tough, and rugged. The identity of the Marlboro Man—a handsome yet tough cowboy figure— was the personification of this identity and Marlboro cigarettes were his brand of choice (Kellner, 1991). Clearly, this sort of appeal was successful, as thousands of American teenagers tried and consequently became addicted to cigarettes.

In recent years, however, in order to persuade adolescents *not* to smoke, antismoking campaigns have used an identity-targeting approach. The truth® campaign is an example of a national antismoking campaign that targets edgy and cutting-edge youth aged 12 to 17 years. The campaign was developed in Florida, where formative research found that adolescents viewed cigarettes and smoking as a way to express their identity and show their rebelliousness and control over their lives (Hicks, 2001). Thus, the truth® brand was created, representing a "cool" alternative to smoking meant to appeal to those kids "outside the mainstream ... not prone to joining the most establishment groups" (e.g., student council, football team). To appeal to these youths, ads were created that exposed the tactics tobacco companies used to manipulate teens. For example, one early campaign ad featured a public display of body bags representing people who had died from tobacco use. In another ad, young adults entered a tobacco company's headquarters and tried to get the marketing department to take a lie detector test. Additionally, the truth® campaign has been able to leverage social media to increase the effectiveness of its messages. For example, adolescents can upload videos of themselves dancing to the truth® website for a chance to win a video game. Tactics such as these allow the campaign to engage its target audience better, and also allow that audience to communicate with each other, reinforcing the notion that smoking is not something people in this crowd do. The response to the truth® campaign has been marked: the truth® campaign was found to have produced significant increases in anti-smoking attitudes and behavior among teens (Farrelly, Davis, Haviland, Messeri, & Healton, 2005; Farrelly Nonnemaker, Davis, & Hussin, 2009).

The Virginia Healthy Youth Culture Initiative takes a similar approach, identifying at-risk crowds to develop targeted campaigns designed to promote healthy behaviors. One such campaign, known as 2UP2DOWN attempts to reduce cigarette use by targeting adolescents who identify with the hip-hop subculture. One way this is done is through social events featuring DJs and dancing. In this campaign, media and cultural events are used to promote the brand. A flyer promoting a 2UP2DOWN campaign event contains no reference to the campaign's antismoking purpose, and instead contains several stylistic cues that align it with the hip-hop subculture. This illustrates the campaign's approach to establishing the 2UP2DOWN brand (and corresponding antismoking stance) as an essential component of the hip-hop social identity's prototype.

These examples highlight the power of the media in influencing behavior via social identity. Because individuals, adolescents in particular, tend to behave in accordance with the prototypes of the groups with which they identify, a useful way to influence the behavior of adolescents who identify with those groups is to position certain positive behavior as prototypical of the in-group (edgy, nonmainstream youth in the case of the truth® campaign, and the hip-hop subculture in the case of the 2UP2DOWN campaign).

Conclusion and Future Directions

It is clear that social identification with peer crowds plays a crucial role in the lives of adolescents, and that media are an important influence on how adolescent social identity is constructed and enacted. As research continues in this area, several questions deserving of further consideration arise. First, future research is needed to address the intersectionality, or overlap, of adolescent social identities. It has been found that adolescents identify with multiple groups (Verkooijen, de Vries, & Nielsen, 2007), supporting the notion that an individual's biography and lived experience are the product of their various identities and how these identities intersect and overlap. Future research should address how the media affect the ways in which an adolescent negotiates these multiple social identities to produce a coherent sense of self, specifically in regard to how media marginalize or value certain social categories. Second, research is needed to further investigate the extent to which mass media, social media, and interpersonal contact interact to influence an adolescent's perceptions of a group prototype. How do geographically linked individuals use mass media and social media content to produce specific group prototypes? Another area that could be further developed is the study of the adoption, maintenance, and stagnation of social identities. Adolescents often cycle through several social identities during their teen years. Although a considerable body of research has studied identity status change among adolescents (see Kroger, Martinussen, & Marcia, 2009), there is less research focusing on social identity specifically. The research that does exist indicates that adolescents do indeed cycle through several social identities during adolescence (Kinney, 1993). A better understanding is needed of how media influence the various social identities an adolescent chooses to cycle through and eventually settle upon.

Ultimately, the complex relationship between adolescents, social identity, and mass media deserves the attention of communication scholars and psychologists alike. The bulk of the research on adolescents and the media focuses on how media influence what an adolescent does; perhaps now attention should be focused on how media influence who an adolescent is.

Notes

1. This chapter was supported by funding from the Tobacco-Related Disease Research Program (18FT-0175).
2. Identity in this chapter is used to refer to the concept of social identity or how one views oneself as a member of a social group.
3. Although these are not the only processes that must occur for social identity to influence behavior, they are four major components given considerable attention in the literature.

4. "Emo" is a crowd originally evolving from the punk rock subculture. Traditionally, it revolves around a certain style of rock music with emotional lyrics.

References

Abrams, D., & Hogg, M. A. (1999). *Social identity and social cognition*. Malden, MA: Blackwell.

Blos, P. (1975). The second individuation process of adolescence. In A. Esman (Ed.), *The psychology of adolescence: Essential readings* (pp. 156–176). New York: International Universities Press.

Brown, B. B. (2004). Adolescents' relationships with peers. In R. M. Lerner & L. D. Steinberg (Eds.), *Handbook of adolescent psychology* (2nd ed., pp. 363–394). Hoboken, NJ: Wiley.

Brown, B. B., Mory, M. S., & Kinney, D. (1994). Casting crowds in a relational perspective: Caricature, channel, and context. In R. Montemayor, G. Adams, & T. Gullotta (Eds.), *Advances in adolescent development, Personal relationships during adolescence* (pp. 123–167). Newbury Park, CA: Sage.

Brown, B. B., von Bank, H., & Steinberg, L. (2008). Smoke in the looking glass: Effects of discordance between self- and peer rated crowd affiliation on adolescent anxiety, depression and self-feeings. *Journal of Youth and Adolescence, 37*, 1163–1177.

Coleman, R. R. M., & Yochim, E. C. (2008). The symbolic annihilation of race: A review of "blackness" literature. *African American Research Perspectives, 12*, 1–10.

Dickson, E. S., & Scheve, K. (2006). Social identity, political speech, and electoral competition. *Journal of Theoretical Politics, 18*(1), 5–39.

Eichorn, D. H., Mussen, P. H., Clausen, J. A., Haan, N., & Honzik, M. P. (1981). Overview. In D. H. Eichorn, J. A. Clausen, N. Haan, M. P. Honzik, & P. H. Mussen (Eds.), *Present and past in middle life* (pp. 414–444). New York: Academic Press.

Erikson, E. H. (1959). *Identity and the life cycle: Selected papers*. New York: International Universities Press.

Erikson, E.H. (1968). *Identity: Youth and crisis*. New York: Norton.

Farrelly, M. C., Davis, K. C., Haviland M. L., Messeri, P., & Healton, C. G. (2005). Evidence of a dose-response relationship between "truth" antismoking ads and youth smoking prevalence. *American Journal of Public Health, 95*(3), 425–431.

Farrelly, M. C., Nonnemaker, J., Davis, K. C., & Hussin, A. (2009). The influence of the national truth® campaign on smoking initiation. *American Journal of Preventive Medicine, 36*(5), 379–384.

Forehand, M. R., Deshpande, R., & Reed, A. (2002). Identity salience and the influence of differential activation of the social self-schema on advertising response. *Journal of Applied Psychology, 87*(6), 1086–1099.

Gavin, L. A., & Furman, W. (1989). Age differences in adolescents' perceptions of their peer groups. *Developmental Psychology, 25*, 827–834.

Gerbner, G. (1972). Violence in television drama: Trends and symbolic functions. In G. A. Comstock & E. Rubinstein (Eds.), *Television and social behavior: Vol. 1. Content and control* (pp. 28–187). Washington, DC: U.S. Government Printing Office.

Gerbner, G., & Gross, L. (1976). Living with television: The violence profile. *Journal of Communication, 26*(2), 172–194.

Greenwald, A. (2003). *Nothing feels good: Punk rock, teenagers, and emo.* New York, NY: Macmillan.

Hicks, J. J. (2001). The strategy behind Florida's "truth" campaign. *Tobacco Control, 10*, 3–5.

Hogg, M. A., & Abrams, D. (2003). Intergroup behavior and social identity. In M. A. Hogg & J. Cooper (Eds.), *Handbook of social psychology* (pp. 407–431). Thousand Oaks, CA: Sage.

Hogg, M. A., & Reid, S. A. (2006). Social identity, self-categorization, and the communication of group norms. *Communication Theory, 16*, 7–30.

Hogg, M. A. & Turner, J.C. (1987). Social identity and conformity: A theory of referent informational influence. In W. Doise & S. Moscovici (Eds.), *Current issues in European social psychology* (Vol. 2, pp. 139–182). Cambridge, England: Cambridge University Press.

Huntemann, N., & Morgan, M. (2001). Mass media and identity development. In D. G. Singer & J. L. Singer (Eds.), *Handbook of children and the media* (pp. 309–322). Thousand Oaks, CA: Sage.

Huston, A. C., Wartella, E., & Donnerstein, E. (1998). *Measuring the effects of sexual content in the media.* Menlo Park, CA: Kaiser Family Foundation.

Jenkins, R. (2003). *Rethinking ethnicity: Arguments and explorations.* London: Sage.

Kellner, D. (1991). Reading images critically: Toward a postmodern pedagogy. In H. A. Giroux (Ed.), *Postmodernism, feminism, and cultural politics: Redrawing educational boundaries* (pp. 60–82). Albany, NY: SUNY Press.

Kitwana, B. (2006). *Why white kids love hip-hop: Wiggers, wannabes and the new reality of race in America.* Cambridge, MA: Basic Civitas Books.

Kleine, R. III, Kleine, S., & Kernan, J. (1993). Mundane consumption and the self: A social-identity perspective. *Journal of Consumer Psychology, 2*(3), 209–235.

Kroger, J., Martinussen, M., & Marcia, J. E. (2009). Identity status change during adolescence and young adulthood: A meta-analysis. *Journal of Adolescence, 33*, 683–698.

Maldonado, R., Tansuhaj, P., & Muehling, D. (2003). The impact of gender on ad processing: a social identity perspective. *Academy of Marketing Science Review, 2003*(3). Retrieved from http://www.amsreview.org/articles.htm

Marcia, J. (1966). Development of validation of ego-identity status. *Journal of Personality and Social Psychology, 3*, 551–558.

Newman, B. M. L., & Newman, P. R. (1976). Early adolescence and its conflict: Group identity versus alienation. *Adolescence, 11*, 261–274.

Palmonari, A., Pombeni, M. S., & Kirchler, E. (1989). Peergroups and evolution of the self-system in adolescence. *European Journal of Psychology of Education, 4*(1), 3–15.

Palmonari, A., Pombeni, M. S., & Kirchler, E. (1990). Adolescents and their peer groups: A study on the significance of peers, social categorization processes and coping with developmental tasks. *Social Behaviour, 5*(1), 33–48.

Reed, A., & Forehand, M. (2003). *Social identity and marketing research: An integrative framework.* Unpublished manuscript. Retrieved from http://faculty.washington.edu/forehand/documents/ResearchStuffUnderReview/SocialIdentity(JM).pdf

Reed, A., & Forehand, M. (2009). *Linking brands to consumer social identity: A theoretical analysis and roadmap for strategies, tactics and insights* (Working Paper). University of Pennsylvania, Philadelphia.

Seltzer, V.C. (1982). *Adolescent social development: Dynamic functional interaction.* Lexington, MA: Lexington Books.

Simpson, M. (1994). *Male impersonators: Men performing masculinity.* New York: Routledge.

Simpson, M. (2002). Meet the metrosexual. Retrieved from http://www.salon.com/2002/07/22/metrosexual/

Sivulka, J. (1988). *Soap, sex and cigarettes: A cultural history of American advertising.* Belmont, CA: Wadsworth.

Slater, M. (2007). Reinforcing spirals: The mutual influence of media selectivity and media effects and their impact on individual behavior and social identity. *Communication Theory, 17,* 281–303.

Stone, M. R., & Brown, B. B. (1998). In the eye of the beholder: Adolescents' perceptions of peer crowd stereotypes. In R. Muuss (Ed.), *Adolescent behavior and society: A book of readings* (5th ed., pp. 158–169). Boston, MA: McGraw-Hill College.

Sussman, S., Dent, C. W., McAdams, L. A., Stacey, A. W, Burton, D., & Flay, B. R. (1994). Group self-identification and adolescent cigarette smoking: A 1-year prospective study. *Journal of Abnormal Psychology, 10*(3), 576–580.

Sussman, S., Dent, C. W., & McCullar, W. J. (2000). Group self-identification as a prospective predictor of drug use and violence in high-risk youth. *Psychology of Addictive Behaviors, 14*(2), 192–196.

Sussman, S., Dent, C. W., Simon, T. R., Stacy, A. W., Burton, D., & Flay, B. R. (1993). Identification of which high-risk youth smoke cigarettes regularly. *Health Values, 17*(1), 42–53.

Sussman, S., Dent, C. W., Stacy, A. W., Burciaga, C., Raynor, A., Turner, G. E., ... Flay, B. R. (1990). Peer group association and adolescent tobacco use. *Journal of Abnormal Psychology, 99*(4), 349–352.

Sussman, S., Pokhrel, P., Ashmore, R. D., & Brown, B. B. (2007). Adolescent peer group identification and characteristics: A review of the literature. *Addictive Behaviors, 32*(8), 1602–1627.

Sussman, S., Simon, T. R., Stacy, A. W., Dent, C. W., Ritt, A., Kipke, M. D., ... Flay, B. R. (1999). The association of group self-identification and adolescent drug use in three samples varying in risk. *Journal of Applied Social Psychology, 29*(8), 1555–1581.

Sussman, S. Sun, P., Gunning, M., Moran, M. B., Pokhrel, P., Rohrbach, L. A., ... Masagutov, R. (2010). Peer group self-identification in samples of Russian and U.S. adolescents. *Journal of Drug Education, 40,* 203–215.

Sussman, S., Unger, J., & Dent, W. (2004). Peer group self-identification among alternative high school youth: A predictor of their psychosocial functioning five years later. *International Journal of Clinical and Health Psychology,* 4(1), 9–25.

Tajfel, H. (1974). Social identity and intergroup behaviour. *Social Science Information/sur les sciences sociales,* 13(2), 65–93

Tajfel, H. (1978). Social categorization, social identity, and social comparisons. In H. Tajfel (Ed.), *Differentiation between social groups* (pp. 138–151). London: Academic Press.

Tajfel, H., & Turner, J. (1979). An integrative theory of intergroup conflict. In W. G. Austin & S. Worchel (Eds.), *The social psychology of intergroup relations* (pp. 33–147). Pacific Grove, CA: Brooks/Cole.

Tarrant, M. (2002). Adolescent peer groups and social identity. *Social Development,* 11(1), 110–123.

Tarrant, M., North, A. C., Edridge, M. D., Kirk, L. E., Smith, E. A., & Turner, R. E. (2001). Social identity in adolescence. *Journal of Adolescence,* 24(5), 597–609.

Tuncay, L. (2006). Conceptualizations of masculinity among a "new" breed of male consumers. *Gender and Consumer Behavior,* 8, 312–327.

Turner, J. C., Brown, R. J., & Tajfel, H. 1979. Social comparison and group interest in in-group favouritism. *European Journal of Social Psychology,* 9, 187–204.

Urberg, K. A. (1992). Locus of peer influence: Social crowd and best friend. *Journal of Youth and Adolescence,* 21(4), 439–450.

Urberg, K. A., Degirmencioglu, S. M., Tolson, J. M., & Halliday-Scher, K. (2000). Adolescent social crowds: Measurement and relationship to friendships. *Journal of Adolescence Research,* 15(4), 427–445.

Verkooijen, K. T., de Vries, N. K., & Nielsen, G. A. (2007). Youth crowds and substance use: The impact of perceived group norm and multiple group identification. *Psychology of Addictive Behaviors,* 21(1), 55–61

Walker, R. (2002). Ad report card: Instant nostalgia from Sprite. *Slate.* Retrieved from http://www.slate.com/id/2060452.

Warnick, B. R., Dawson, H. S., Spencer, D., & Vosburg-Bluem, B. (2010). Student communities and individualism in American cinema. *Educational Studies: Journal of the American Educational Studies Association,* 46(2), 168–191.

Chapter 3

Biased Optimism, Media, and Asian American Identity

David C. Oh

Identity is salient for many Asian Americans because of cultural marginalization (Song, 2003), and popular media are powerful sites in creating racist and marginalizing discourses about Asian Americans (Espiritu, 2004). Popular media consistently exclude Asian Americans, and when Asian Americans are represented, these media rely on stereotyped tropes to represent them. The invisibility of Asian/Americans[1] in popular media damages Asian Americans' self-image by withdrawing popular legitimation (Yamada, 2003), and stereotyped representations of Asian/Americans weaken identity and self-esteem. This is evident in the literature in both psychology and critical cultural studies. Though not specifically writing about media, Tajfel (1978) pointed out that ethnic minorities are at greater risk for lower self-esteem. Asian Americans, in particular, have been found to have the lowest ethnic identity scores and the lowest self-esteem of all major racial groups in the United States as a result of societal stereotyping (Martinez & Dukes, 1997). Kohatsu et al. (2000) argue that as "middlemen minorities," Asian Americans experience increased internalized racism because of the pressure to identify with Whites.

Societal stereotypes also limit the assertion of individual identity in favor of racially defined ones (Phinney, 1990; Tuan, 1998). As critical cultural scholars note, stereotypes are not innocently created but were formed with political intentions to dominate. Teun van Dijk (1993) maintained that racial stereotypes have their roots in European colonial history, and Edward Said (1978) made clear that the colonial perceptions of the "Orient" served to construct a positive self-image for colonizing nations. The politics of race continues to privilege Whites (Song, 2003), causing harm to Asian American self-esteem and identity (Kibria, 2002; Song, 2003; Tuan, 1998). The purpose of this study is to explore with Asian Americans themselves their understandings of the influences of popular media on their identity and how they negotiate dominant influences in the media.

Considering the near consensus on the problematic representation of Asian Americans in U.S. popular media (Espiritu, 2004; Feng, 2002;

Hamamoto, 1994; Kang, 2002; Kawai, 2005; Lee, 1999; Marchetti, 1993; Oehling, 1980; Orbe, Seymour, & Kang, 1998; Shim, 1998; Wilson, Gutierrez, & Chao, 2003; Wong, 2002), it is hardly surprising that Asian Americans might struggle with identity and self-esteem. Yet, the media attitudes and behaviors of Asian American audiences, particularly U.S.-born or raised Asian Americans, are largely absent in the audience reception literature. This is consistent with a more widespread lack of inclusion of Asian Americans in academic research generally (Almaguer, 1994, pp. 1–16; Kohatsu et al., 2000; Mansfield-Richardson, 2000; Omi & Winant, 1994). Therefore, through its investigation of the ways Asian Americans understand popular media to interact with their racial identities, this study builds on audience reception literature, complicating the simplistic Black–White paradigm of race (Omi & Winant, 1994; Wu, 2002).

Audience Reception, Race, and Identity

Mass media are the dominant means of social signification and thus are powerful in constructing cultural meaning (Hall, 2003). They shape our semiotic systems (Lewis, 1991) and provide the discourses into which identities are articulated (Hall, 2003). Because identity is constructed and constrained within cultural discourses, identities are not value-free; they are not free of the relations of power (Woodward, 1997). Therefore, the racialized cultural subject creates her identity within or in reaction to racist stereotypes in popular culture, utilizing existing cultural discourses in which to embed identity. Persons of color "read" media from the standpoint of their racial identity (in intersection with multiple social identities). Though Morley (1980) was writing about class, he noted that social location matters because it increases the likelihood of an ideological response consistent with members of the interpretative community. Key to understanding the role of race in audience reception, this has been confirmed in studies that demonstrate that readings are structured (though not determined) by race. For example, Innis and Feagin's (2002) research on middle-class African American viewers' reception of *The Cosby Show* found that viewers watch the sitcom series with ambivalence because of their concern that the program promotes new racism, a fear rooted in their social experience. Research has found that African American and White viewers interpret media texts in widely different ways (Jhally & Lewis, 1992; Squires, 2002). The differences are not only interracial but also intraracial. Among African American viewers, there are no single uniform readings of media texts around race but gradations of interpretations (Means Coleman, 2000). Despite the importance of these findings, the research needs to be extended further to include other marginalized racial groups, including Asian Americans, because these groups' social locations and lived experiences differ in meaningful ways, which may lead to different reception practices.

Likewise, there are few audience reception studies that directly address the influence of popular media on identity construction, likely because of fears that this line of inquiry moves too closely to a social scientific inquiry of "effects." Despite such concerns, it is worth investigating how audiences make sense of the influences of popular media and the tactics they use to incorporate or insulate themselves from dominant ideologies, or at least to convince themselves they are doing so. In the handful of studies that address this question, audiences consistently point to their ability to filter out unwanted influences and to filter in wanted influences. For instance, Bobo (2002) observed that marginalized groups learn to ferret out beneficial representations and put up "blinders" against the rest because not to do so would require they not use media at all. This view is consistent with optimistic views that audiences can pick and choose what "raw materials" of culture they want to use to construct their identities. Likewise, Means Coleman's (2000) interviews of African American viewers of Black sitcoms demonstrate that African Americans are acutely aware of stereotyped representations but, because they are unwilling to give up the shows that provide them with representational pleasure, they say they attempt to filter out the "negative" influences and try to find "positives" to redeem the shows and justify their viewing of them. Similarly, Mayer (2003) found that Mexican American teenage girls also believe they are unaffected by unwanted representations, but Mayer approaches this more critically, pointing out that if her participants did not adopt this view of media influence then it would require that they have to diminish institutions that provide everyday joys in an otherwise bleak social world, specifically the girls' fantasies of romantic relationships and escape with idealized pop idols. In these studies, however, understanding how participants negotiate their relationship with dominant media is not the central focus of the work and therefore does not theorize their participants' use in context with their participants' concerns about undesirable media representations.

Biased Optimism

To make sense of racialized ethnic minorities' optimistic belief in their ability to be affected only in ways that they desire, I draw on work outside of the critical and cultural traditions to better elaborate and name the phenomenon. In research on perceptions of health risks, Weinstein (1980) proposed the concept of *unrealistic optimism*, finding that participants were less likely to believe that they would be affected by future health risks than others and were more likely to experience positive health outcomes. In the realm of media effects, Davison (1983) found that individuals tend to believe that others are more influenced by mass media than they themselves are, which he called the third-person effect. To elaborate the mechanism of the third-person effect, scholars have turned to unrealistic optimism, also called biased optimism, as an explanation (Chapin, 2008; Gunther & Mundy, 1993; Gunther & Thorson, 1992; Perloff, 2002). In their attempt to reconceptualize the third-person effect, Hoorens and Ruiter (1996) observed that individuals respond to media in ways that they believe are optimal in relation to imagined others (e.g., believing themselves more influenced by "positive" media messages) rather than a generalized belief that they are less influenced. Similarly, Gunther and Thorson (1992) found that individuals claim they are more influenced than others for "positive" public service announcements but less influenced when messages are judged neutral or negative.

Partly because the third-person effect only accounts for a generalized belief in others' naiveté toward media, Wei, Lo, and Lu (2007) argue that the third-person effect and optimistic bias are parallel but distinctly unrelated processes that lead to different outcomes (e.g., third-person perception acts as a motivator for behavior change whereas optimistic bias acts as an inhibitor). In a study of body image among Singaporean women magazine readers, Chia (2007) found that her participants manifested *biased optimism*, reducing their sense of activist urgency. Similarly, it is arguable that the participants in the studies on racial identity mentioned earlier exhibit biased optimism because they recognize the undesired influences of media while being unwilling to give it up. Like Wei, Lo, and Lu (2007), this chapter views biased optimism to be similar yet conceptually different from the third-person effect because biased optimism is not a generalized belief about media influence but shifts in relation to the perceived valence of the media message and because biased optimism acts to inhibit behavioral intention (e.g., turn off the television).

In-Depth Interviews with Asian American Young Adults

The observations reported here were based on in-depth interviews with Asian American young adults about their social identity, and their media perceptions and use, in order to determine the extent to which they engage in biased optimism. At a private university in the Northeast, an Asian American campus organization called Asian Students in America (ASIA) was utilized to help recruit study participants, including 17 traditional students, ranging in age from 18 to 22, and representing a variety of ethnic groups, including Japanese, Korean, Filipino, Vietnamese, Chinese, and multiethnic Americans, from a number of states across the United States, including Alabama, California, New York, New Jersey, and Texas. Interviews were held in public areas on campus and lasted between 30 minutes and 2 hours, depending on the level of investment and interest of the participant. Because this area of investigation is still relatively unexplored, the study employed a grounded theory approach, which allows theory to emerge from the data (Glaser & Strauss, 1967; Strauss & Corbin, 1994).

Views on Racial Identity

To add depth and context to participants' reflections on media, it is informative briefly to describe their beliefs about racial identity. Their responses indicate that racial identity is not uniformly understood. One axis of difference is their understanding of racial identity as a nonpolitical identity. Espiritu (2004) maintained that Asian American identity is constructed in response to the experiences of racialization in the United States. However, among participants in this study, only Jane actively constructs "Asian American" as a politically activist identity that is rooted in collective resistance. Instead, the few participants who allude to resistance limit the scope to individual reactions to perceived racism or ignorance. For instance, Cindy says, "It's everyday life, too. Like if other people make racial remarks or stereotypes, then you come out and are like that's wrong, and it's not right. Let them know that it's offensive." For Bob, his experiences with racism have motivated him to seek larger pan-ethnic connections. He says, "As an Asian American, I understand that I have faced similar stereotypes with other Koreans and Japanese because a lot of people generalize Asian Americans as, oh, you're all Chinese or something, and it's just … we basically face the same problems, and our cultures are somewhat similar."

Instead of understanding racial identity as a political identity, the participants generally believed that being Asian American means being imbued with a "fundamental essence" or that it is an identity formulated by cultural similarity (see Kibria, 2002). To illustrate the former, Emily and Jack imply that their racial identity is a passive identity that does not require work. It is simply who they are. Emily says:

> I've always realized I'm Asian. It's not like I looked in the mirror one day, and I was like whoops, I'm Asian. I've always known that I had that culture and that background. I guess like in terms of identifying myself as Asian American. I'm not sure exactly where to put that. I'm not sure, what does that mean?

For Emily, the question itself is confusing because to her and several other participants, being Asian American is obvious to the point that elaboration is unnecessary. For Jessica, being Asian American is not defined by engaging in perceived cultural practices but simply one's heritage. She says, "It's not about the music you listen to, or the people you hang out with. It's about who you are as an individual, where your parents came from, the heritage, the culture. It's knowing how you got here individually."

Kibria (2002) noted that Asian Americans often understand their racial identity through an ethnonational lens. Bob, for example, is confused when asked the difference between being Asian American and being ethnically Chinese. In response, Bob says:

> I'm not sure quite what to say to that. I'm not, I don't quite understand the question. I know I'm like I don't know, you're going to have to, I just don't get the gist of the question. You're going to just have to, I mean I hear what you're saying, but just [does not continue his thought].

Katie, on the other hand, differentiates but favors her ethnic identity, saying, "I guess I'd put them, um, my culture comes first, then it's like the Asians, then it'd be everyone else." The fact that they prefer their specific ethnic identities is consistent with research on pan-ethnic Asian friendships that demonstrate that ethnicity is often preferred to race and is sometimes used as a strategy to defy racialization and the assumptions of intra-Asian affinity (Kibria, 2002; Song, 2003).

Most other participants defined Asian American as an amalgam of their American cultural identity and their specific Asian ethnic heritage. This can take two forms, either a belief in a fundamental Asianness that is supplemented by an American cultural identity or a bicultural identity. The former perspective is epitomized by Dan, who says, "Basically, I believe the definition goes as like you were born from America and that you're Asian, and that's what I think is Asian American." The latter perspective, a bicultural identity, is the one held by most participants. Characteristic of this viewpoint is Diana, who says, "I guess to be an Asian American is to understand the culture and to know the American culture and being kind of like balancing both of them, to be Asian and American." Their varying views of racial identity could very well affect how different participants perceive the media and negotiate their use of it.

Perceptions of Media Representations

These thoughts about Asian American identity provide a context with which to understand the participants' responses to popular portrayals of Asian Americans, which every one of the participants said is problematic. Because of their apolitical identity (with the exception of Jane), their responses are also largely apolitical. There is a relationship between a strong sense of racial identification and the conviction that media representations are problematic, but this rarely leads to political action or even individual-level decisions about media use. Regardless of the participants' views of their racial identity, their concern with representation, or their childhood and neighborhood experiences, all participants say they are active fans of media. Only Jane reluctantly avoided media because of its perceived psychological harm. All others not only used media frequently but found satisfaction in it. Yet, interestingly, they listed almost exclusively White entertainers and media texts with predominantly White casts as their favorites. The only exceptions are Halle Berry and Jackie Chan, who were each mentioned once. This pattern holds for their media choices, too, as only Meghan mentioned a favorite film that did not feature a predominantly White cast, the Korean film, *My Sassy Girl*. Clearly, participants' media experiences are largely with dominant racial representations. I argue that participants are able to rationalize their primarily White media choices by believing in optimistic bias, thinking they are largely unaffected by representations they dislike and are only affected by representations they prefer.

Before describing their optimistic bias, it is first informative to understand participants' views of popular cultural representation. As mentioned earlier, the participants in this study nearly uniformly say that representations of Asian/Americans are problematic. One major complaint is that media underrepresent them. For instance, April said:

> I think they're not portrayed. Period. They're not portrayed at all. Am I supposed to take the three times I've seen [Asian Americans in media] and say this is how they're portrayed? They're not portrayed. That's the problem. Give me a couple of 10, 100s, and then I'll tell you how they're portrayed. But I don't really see them.

Dan also was dissatisfied, but he moderated his criticism somewhat through his understanding of the industry's economic logic and the intersection of his own experiences growing up in a predominantly White, affluent neighborhood in New York City, saying:

> I don't think they're being portrayed enough in the, like, media, but I guess in some ways I can kind of understand why they're not particularly, but I don't know, I see the movie industry especially as so money driven. They want to make the most amount of money, and the only way they can do that is to have the top actors and the top actresses be in all these movies, and I think that, you know, they're excluding. It makes sense why they're excluding minorities. We're pretty much in a dominantly White society.

For most participants, underrepresentation was salient, and they wished for increased cultural representation in media.

Seeking a Humanizing Range of Representations

Interestingly, the participants' primary concern with stereotypes is not that they are consistently undesirable but that they present Asian Americans in ways that are inconsistent with the lived realities they know. This reflects a nuanced understanding learned through their experiences with the "model minority" stereotype. Because they perceive that the stereotype is culturally portrayed as "positive" but feel victimized by it nonetheless, they do not articulate a simple desire for good versus bad representations but rather a more diverse, humanizing representational range. Like Dan above, Emily acknowledged corporate motivations but was more hostile to the implications of stereotyped representation:

> If you look around the city, Asian Americans are just like any other city people. Basically, everybody dresses alike. We're all pretty much mixed and stuff like that in my experience. We act like normal people. I think it's hard to kind of pinpoint exactly what, how the movie would do it, but you would hope that it would be fair and accurate, and not something completely stereotypical or ridiculous or something like that. I think that is important because the only way for people to get a fair image is to see the real Asian Americans, not some executive's idea of an Asian American.

James also made an appeal to fair, humanized representations, pointing to the harm stereotypes create, constraining his individuality and self-image:

> But, I guess, it's a bad thing. Asians don't want to be portrayed like that. We can be portrayed as anything. We're not all smart. We're not all hard-working. I don't know. We just want to be looked upon as people. I think a lot of times most people want to be looked upon as just people. Everybody has their own story.

Fleeting Frustration, Lasting Pleasure

It should be pointed out that these are among the strongest expressions of dissatisfaction with Asian American representation. Though the belief that Asian Americans are not portrayed fairly was supported by all participants, they generally did not express outrage or a desire for resistance. This is because very few thought representations have had an undesired long-term impact. Some participants said watching stereotyped representations leads to frustration, but, like James, they said it is fleeting:

> That I'm not like that, that that's not entirely true, that I'm a little angry about it, but what can I do? Then, I forget about it. Sometimes, these things happen so often and so frequent that you ... it just numbs you. It's just another stereotype. Okay. It's not like I consciously try to tough it out, but it's just a natural thing to do to just get past it, so initially I'm a little angry about that stereotype, but pretty soon, I just forget about it.

His inability to change representations leads to the belief that the impact of the images is short-lived because not to do so would mean that his frustrations could become despair or because he would have to give up media to avoid frustrations borne out of a lack of agency in changing unwanted representations. As Means Coleman (2000) pointed out, audiences of color are unwilling to give up media because of the pleasures media provide in their everyday lives.

For Dan and April, frustration was a rare reaction reserved only for the most problematic representations. Dan said:

> Only when I'm looking at it, analyzing it at depth do I realize that it kind of pisses me off that why is he being portrayed in, like, that way, why is he portrayed as an Asian geek or something like that because that just continues to perpetuate the stereotype, and, um, that's the only time that it would piss me off.

What is striking about Dan's quote is that it demonstrates how often participants respond with a justifiable sense of anger but only for fleeting moments. Likewise, April said:

> I will be very upset if they put such an extreme thing out. You have to understand I'm talking about extreme. I'm not talking about accents. I'm not talking about people working in stores.... I don't know personally it's just I don't have my foot up my ass, and I don't get offended at everything, you know. But I do get offended, and I feel very strong[ly] about a lot of issues.

April's quote reveals a contradiction as she is competing against her values of finding stereotypes offensive and cultural values of not being too serious, which is then manifest in an uneasy negotiation of being both passionate but yet nonchalant about her attitudes toward stereotyped representations. The contradiction allows her space to respond with both resentment and pleasure.

Concerns about Lasting Impacts

This is not to deny that a small number of participants are concerned with lasting impacts to their racial identity and self-image. With some reluctance, Bob said, "I guess absence of Asian Americans in the mainstream entertainment media has left me kind of disappointed and [does] not act ... as a damper on my confidence in myself." The cause for perceived harm to self-image is not only the stereotyped representations but the favorable representations of Whites. Ann says that because of the exclusion of Asian American images, she felt more comfortable with Whites than Asian Americans:

> If there were more groups of Asians hanging on TV, I'd be more leaning towards hanging out with Asians here, but I don't. I guess TV doesn't really do that. I haven't really had a whole group of girl Asian friends to hang out with. That would seem really weird to me. I don't even know how to deal because I figure it'd be different than White.

In addition to the underrepresentation of Asian Americans, another reason for Asian Americans to identify with White actors is because of White media norms and standards. Jane said, "This [the media structure] caters to Western ideals of beauty, and if you don't fit that mold, you're going to dislike yourself regardless of what race you are, and it's particularly important to Asian Americans because it's like an entire race." She added:

> By now, I've probably internalized all that stuff that I've been absorbing through the media, so I'm sure it affected me and how you grow up if you absorb a lot of movies, you basically get the feeling that you're lesser as a minority. I've never really seen a definitive Asian American portrayal that made me feel empowered, that made me feel good about myself. I guess that's why I don't really participate in the popular media so much. I don't go to the movies, and I don't watch a lot of TV, so that's basically my reaction to it because I do try to preserve my own self-worth.

Jane's self-reflexivity about the long-term impact and her choice to avoid media are unique among the participants. Perhaps it is this self-reflexivity that prompted her activist political identity.

An Optimistic Cultural Logic

Instead, other participants who pointed to media's impact on their self-identity referred to the impact largely in the past tense, as a part of their development that no longer influences them. This is a more characteristic response for the minority of participants who said media have shaped their racial identification and self-image. Katie and Samantha both pointed to the ways they were affected as young girls because of the lack of role models but they pointed to this as limited to their childhood. Samantha said, "I guess because I had no one to look up to, nobody to say they're really cool, and they're Asian, too, and I can do that, too. People are too impressionable, and I was one of them." It is instructive to note her use of the past tense to indicate that she no longer identifies herself as an impressionable person, implying that she has overcome its effects. Katie, as well, referred to possible impact on her self-image as being in the past:

> When I was younger, when all the girls were getting into makeup and stuff like that, and when I was trying to shape my ideas of what beautiful was, like, it was hard to imagine a product on me if none of the models are Asian. Like how I want to cut my hair, and there are no Asians, and obviously I want to look for someone like me, so I could see if the haircut would look good, and there were like none, so how will I know if the haircut will look good on me? I don't know. It affected me that way.

Amy more clearly delimited the influences on self-identity as part of her past by pointing to her ability in the present to empower her own self-identity in spite of the portrayals:

> Yeah, when I was little like I told you, when you're made fun of because of the way you look, you become ashamed of who you are, like, oh my god, I want to be like everybody else. I don't want these eyes; I don't want this color on me. But then, I guess, as I grew up, I learned to have more pride in myself. Like it's okay to be Asian. It's okay to be different. You're not White, so what can you do about it, so accept yourself for who you are.

A belief in their own agency to resist and ignore the elements of programming they dislike and to incorporate elements they like was characteristic of most participants, even those who recognized the undesired influences of media images on their own self-image. The cultural logic appears to be that U.S. media represent Asian Americans poorly, if at all, and that it has led to short-term impact or to resolved identity concerns they had as adolescents. Again, this is an optimistic appraisal of their ability to overcome undesired representation, which shields them from cognitive dissonance that might arise from believing the media they use and enjoy harm their self-image, which, in turn, allows them to use media unproblematically.

Resistance Strategies

Participants cited a wide variety of sometimes contradictory reasons that allowed them to resist undesirable media representations of Asian Americans. Though each response alone appears plausible, in context with the other responses, the lack of consistency points to the possibility that the varied rationales are as much about finding reasons to watch media they characterize as problematic as they are actual defenses against media influence. Meghan said:

> I think I'm at a point where it doesn't matter to me because I feel like I have a pretty good idea of who I am, but I know you're trying to ask questions about me, but if a certain person was not very aware of who they are, then I'm sure they would have some struggling issues, but I have a pretty good idea of who I am, so I don't think it affects me.

Likewise, Bob explained that the impact of undesired media representations is a challenge to overcome, again pointing to developmental maturity and personal fortitude as a way to justify his choice to watch media that he had earlier stated could have impacted his self-confidence:

> It's discouraging. It puts me down somewhat, but I see it as more of a challenge to overcome. I may not be able to change the world, but I can change me and try to show to everybody I'm not like that, I'm not that guy. I'm not the one on TV who programs [computers] and do not fit the exact stereotype of an Asian American.

This explanation of overcoming an obstacle might be a specifically gendered one as Steve also used this metaphor, saying, "I've learned to overcome it. I've learned to become my own *man* [emphasis added] so to speak."

On the other hand, several participants pointed not to developmental maturity but rather to its near opposite: a casual, unserious attitude toward media representations. To demonstrate that media do not affect them, some participants did not draw from the cultural value of personal strength but of lightheartedness and the ability not to take life too seriously. Jessica, for example, said:

> They affect me, but in general I'm a very nonchalant person. I don't really get myself worked up and angry all the time, so I'm not a very good activist. I wouldn't make a good protester. Obviously, I'd be offended by negative portrayals. If it really bothered me to the point that I thought it was wrong, [but] I'm not going to sit around and talk about it. I'm just a lazy ass I guess you could say.

Similarly, Steve said he was not offended because he finds humor in the problematic representations. He said, "I just take a more humorous approach to it. Sort of like a joke. That's how I approach it most of the time, even though I think some of the stereotypes are true. I think a lot of them are out there for the humor."

Emily, on the other hand, went so far as to ridicule individuals who are actively critical, saying, "It's just a movie to us. I'd probably notice it and be like it has to be the Asian guy who's evil. We joke about it, I think. It's not like, oh my gosh, he's evil, so do you think I'm evil?" In Emily's quote, it is particularly revealing her construction of a favored in-group that does not take media seriously versus those who are critical of media representations. Therefore, there may be in-group pressure not to openly criticize media representations in serious ways.

Future-Directed Optimism

The desire not to be cynical also is manifest in several participants' future-directed optimism, which they pointed to as a shield against undesired images and a rationale to continue to watch media with which they are currently displeased. Bob said, "Um, I think in the future, we'll see more Asian Americans in movies. It's only a matter of time, basically. It's only a matter of time because as Asian Americans we're not only growing in population but we're also growing in power."

For Samantha, change in representations signals a more promising future:

> Because it's nice to know that there's a bit of me being represented. Just because we live in America, and it's supposed to be all racially diverse and equal. It's the kind of environment I feel like I'm walking around in. I guess it'd be closer to being more realistic. It'd be closer to feeling like there isn't as much racism as there was before. Things are going to be okay, things are going to be more equal, things are going to be more diverse.

April, who earlier expressed frustration about representation, also said she was optimistic about representations in the future, which for her renders concern in the present somewhat meaningless. She said, "I don't see why it [increased and desirable representations] wouldn't happen. There's no reason it shouldn't happen, so I feel and believe that it will happen. It doesn't bother me."

In addition to personal attitudes, participants pointed to their life experiences and their neighborhoods—multicultural, Asian American, or White—as protection against unwanted media influences. This is particularly interesting because any experience is thus perceived as guarding one's racial identity and self-image. The most logical belief is that living in multicultural and majority Asian American neighborhoods builds more resilient racial identities (Smith, 1991). April echoed this sentiment:

> Because I'm constantly surrounded by Asian American images, anyway, so it's not like I need it when I get home, and like I'm surrounded by Asian American people, and I live in New York City. I don't feel like I'm losing anything because I'm also educated, and I don't, I know that's not how they're supposed to be portrayed.

Emily, too, described her diverse neighborhood home as providing images and experiences that moderate influences media might have. Emily said:

> Taking my own experience, I find that New York City is so diverse that like you don't need media images to kind of reinforce what you already know in terms of Asian American culture. I don't know. You see the diversity; you don't need to see it on screen because you know it's there.

Yet, Asian Americans who grow up in the isolation of White neighborhoods also felt that their experiences in predominantly White spaces also have shielded them. These responses, especially, point to the ways Asian Americans guard their interests in media. Dan, for instance, said that it was precisely because he more strongly identified with Whites than with Asian Americans that he is protected against media:

> It's probably because I don't think it bothers me as much because it goes back to my background and who I hang out with. It's all the time with a bunch of White people, and I guess in some ways it doesn't bother me because I'm so ... I guess in some ways I feel that I am White, too. I don't really see myself as Asian or bearing Asian qualities that like my parents or other people say I should have. Um, but, I guess when it does bother me is like I guess it's only when I think about it or when I see myself as Asian.

His quote contradicts his belief in the importance of his racial identity by claiming he is culturally White. It also might contradict his belief that media do not adversely affect his racial identity or self-image if his identification as White is understood not only through his experiences in his neighborhood and school but also with the interaction of media in legitimating this choice. Ann also said her experiences in White spaces protected her sense of racial identity, although her rationale was not because she did not identify as Asian American but, rather, for her, because her regular experiences with marginalization in White society meant she was less affected by problematic representations than those who live in multicultural neighborhoods:

> I think that because it's never, I guess, I guess it's something about the reason, people are used to like having Asian counteractions [sic] in everyday life. They counteract with a lot more Asians, and they're more used to it, so when they watch TV and don't watch any, they might feel like something's missing. But for me, TV's just about the same as my everyday life.

In other words, because she had already experienced marginalization, she was not affected by televised marginalization or alienation. Again, it is probable that multiple points of marginalization would have a greater impact than a singular one but, by believing that society is more marginalizing, she could discount the impact of media, thus justifying her choice to use it.

"Positive" Images and Racial Identity

Participants responded most enthusiastically to the part of the interview relating to the "positive" relationship with media and the "positive" impact of media on their racial identity. In fact, all participants enthusiastically expressed moments when media had legitimated their racial identity and helped generate racial pride. This is very different from their measured and perceived delimited influence of undesired media representation, and their twists of logic to explain why media do not affect them. Instead, participants responded with joyful emotion, recalling their favorable experiences with media. This is consistent with optimistic bias in that they are reluctant to suggest that media influence them in ways they do not want, and simultaneously they are enthusiastic in suggesting that media influence them in ways they do want.

The most commonly mentioned "positive" outcome was increased racial pride and cultural legitimation. When asked how she would feel about representations that resonated more closely with her life experience, April said:

> That'd make me feel great. I told you that'd make me feel great. Like the movies. These people have normal jobs. These people are like ... they're ... the race has nothing to do with it. I see he's Asian American, you know. Other people will see that, too. Besides that, there's nothing different, and that's going to make me happy, and that's going to continue to make me happy because I know that's going to continue to be the trend.

Likewise, Frances said she responds with joy when she sees affirming representations of Asian Americans in media. She said, "I have to say when I watch something, and an Asian person pops up, and I'm like Oh, my God, there's an Asian person. Like I would tell my roommate, my friend, whoever I'm sitting next to. Just because they're Asian." When asked why she responds with such enthusiasm, she replied, "Because I hardly see Asian Americans on TV. That's why I get excited just to see 1-2-3, as many. I get happy. I get excited simply because I see them, simply because there are so few movie shows that have them." For Dan, he recounted a show that legitimated him not only racially but also as a man, which acted as a source of pride:

> It was one of those martial arts films, and it was like kicking the ass of all the non-Asian people and stuff like that. See, Asians can go beat you up. We're not some nerd or something like that that studies all day and stuff like that. I don't know. That was younger, though, that made me kind of feel pride.

Therefore, for several participants, it acts as a source of pride to see Asian American representations that they find desirable because these representations act as evidence that the dominant culture values them.

In addition, some participants said they find hope in representations for improved racial relations and cultural legitimation that signal a step toward a fully inclusive culture. Ann shared her experiences of joy and connection with her mother when Vietnamese American comic Dat Pham won the reality program *Last Comic Standing*. After asking her why she responded strongly to his appearance and success on the show, she replied, "That, um, even if you are Asian American, if you're really good at what you do, you can step above the barriers, I guess. Usually, during competitions of anything, you don't see much Asians participating as other races."

Like other participants, Samantha responded with joy when discussing the representations she had enjoyed and found to be "realistic." The enthusiasm with which this is recounted suggests the importance of media in their lives and happiness for being able to justify their interests in it.

In addition to legitimation, seeing Asian Americans in media creates opportunities to relate to a character in more profound ways and from which they can build their own identities. Jane said:

> Because we're so underrepresented in the media, and I was interested in seeing a portrayal of people who were Asian American. Not a portrayal, but just seeing them, people who look like me are on this big screen. That in itself was cool to watch. It wasn't like I'm expecting justice or something. No.

Jane's comment is revealing because it is representative of other participants who do not intend to be activist but long for a cultural representation to which they could relate. Identity is argued to be drawn from elements of popular culture (Gauntlett, 2002), and, for Jane, she desired representation to be able to fold into her own sense of being Asian American.

Jessica made clear that for identification to happen, characters need to exhibit the full range of humanity:

> It's like Asian people having that portrayal of regular emotions, of having a love affair, or having fun, or being sad, that's because Asians give off that aura of being collected and very serious and stuff, and when it's the opposite, it's intriguing. It's interesting because you realize everyone can relate to somebody. It's relatable. Everyone's the same when it comes down to it. Everyone has flaws, everyone has imperfections.

It should be noted that one benefit of media for Jessica was the ability to identify in ways that validated her Asian American experience as "normal." In those times when media have represented Asian Americans "fairly" and nonstereotypically, participants argued that media allow for a meaningful connection.

Conclusions

Asian American participants in this study said that media consistently underrepresent them and portray them in ways that they find stereotypical and undesirable. Yet, because media provide everyday pleasures for Asian Americans and are an important part of their lives, they are unwilling to abandon media (see Bobo, 2002; Means Coleman, 2000). To ease the cognitive dissonance created by this tension, they are reluctant to believe media influence them in unwanted ways and that, to the extent that media have negatively influenced them, they say they have "overcome" these harmful influences, drawing upon a variety of sometimes contradictory reasons to explain their ability to resist such media messages.

Yet, at the same time, the Asian American participants in this study optimistically said they believe media influence them in desirable ways, leading to greater racial pride, cultural validation, and social identification. These attitudes enable Asian Americans to enjoy using the media while, at the same time, to resist the lack of Asian American media representations, to resist the stereotypical nature of what Asian American representations they do receive, and to resist their concerns about the effects of these Asian American representations on themselves and others. In a telling moment, Jack said, "If I let that [believing in unwanted media influences], things would be getting to me all the time. I guess that's who I am. I just don't let things get to me because I don't want to have a nervous breakdown or something." Also, Bob said that he watched "a good amount to keep in touch with mainstream culture" so that not watching media would symbolically mean that he was also breaking from popular culture, and the consequences of that are disconcerting. Therefore, participants engage in optimistic bias as a way of reconciling the cognitive dissonance that emerges at the intersection of their concern for media representations and their enjoyment and connection to media.

I approach the data from a critical audience reception approach that recognizes media power in shaping audiences' ideological systems. In this study, participants do not engage in active resistance such as reappropriating meanings in popular media, and only one expresses an activist approach to media, indicating that they were at best making negotiated readings if not preferred ones. Asian American audiences are likely influenced to some degree by dominant messages about racial difference, but because acknowledging so would change their relationship with media, they rationalize their use of media, overestimating desired influences and underestimating undesired ones, thus reflecting optimistic bias.

Future Directions

While these in-depth interviews yielded promising insights into the role of the mass media in establishing and maintaining social identity, the findings pertain only to a small group of young adults from one university who were self-selected from an organization already sensitized to think about racial membership. The extent to which these findings apply more generally is a question worth pursuing. Even within this rather narrowly defined group, we nonetheless observed considerable variations among study participants in a number of important ways, from their varying conceptions of their own racial identity, to their varying explanations of how they resist undesirable media images. The findings demonstrate once again the value of observing individual persons in some depth in order to uncover differences more superficial observations might miss. Even though only 17 persons were studied here, the case can be made that a number of valuable insights have emerged from observing them. Yet, even amid the various views observed here, the participants in this study all appear to have engaged in biased optimism. For Asian Americans, living in a predominantly White media world, optimistic bias appears to work as a cognitive coping device for holding two seemingly antithetical feelings about the media. From what is seen here, it is even possible that biased optimism is a *necessary* coping device for the members of this social group, and perhaps for members of other social groups, as well. That, however, remains to be seen.

Note

1. "Asian/American" refers to the conflation of Asian and Asian American. It is a term I borrow from Parreñas Shimizu (2007) to refer to representations in U.S. media that blur Asian and Asian American.

References

Almaguer, T. (1994). *Racial fault lines: The historical origins of white supremacy in California*. Berkeley, CA: University of California Press.

Bobo, J. (2002). *The color purple*: Black women as cultural readers. In R. R. Means Coleman (Ed.), *Say it loud!: African-American audiences, media, and identity* (pp. 205–227). New York: Routledge.

Chapin, J. (2008). Youth perceptions of their school violence risks. *Adolescence*, 43(171), 461–471.

Chia, S. C. (2007). Third-person perceptions about idealized body image and weight-loss behavior. *Journalism and Mass Communication Quarterly*, 84(4), 677–694.

Davison, W. P. (1983). The third-person effect in communication. *Public Opinion Quarterly*, 47(1), 1–15.

Espiritu, Y. L. (2004). Ideological racism and cultural resistance: Constructing our own images. In M. L. Andersen & P. Hill Collins (Eds.), *Race, class, and gender: An anthology* (5th ed., pp. 175–184). Belmont, CA: Wadsworth.

Feng, P. X. (2002). Introduction. In P. X. Feng (Ed.), *Screening Asian Americans* (pp. 1–18). New Brunswick, NJ: Rutgers University Press.

Gauntlett, D. (2002). *Media, gender, and identity: An introduction*. New York: Routledge.

Glaser, B. G., & Strauss, A. S. (1967). *The discovery of grounded theory: Strategies for qualitative research*. Chicago, IL: Aldine.

Gunther, A. C., & Mundy, P. (1993). Biased optimism and the third-person effect. *Journalism Quarterly*, 70(1), 58–67.

Gunther, A. C., & Thorson, E. (1992). Perceived persuasive effects of product commercials and public service announcements: Third-person effects in new domains. *Communication Research*, 19(5), 574–596. doi: 10.1177/009365092019005002

Hall, S. (2003). The whites of their eyes: Racist ideologies and the media. In G. Dines & J. M. Humez (Eds.), *Gender, race, and class in media: A text-reader* (2nd ed., pp. 89–93). Thousand Oaks, CA: Sage.

Hamamoto, D. Y. (1994). *Monitored peril: Asian Americans and the politics of TV representation*. Minneapolis, MN: University of Minnesota Press.

Hoorens, V., & Ruiter, S. (1996). The optimal impact phenomenon: Beyond the third person effect. *European Journal of Social Psychology*, 26(4), 599–610.

Inniss, L. B., & Feagin, J. R. (2002). *The Cosby Show*: The view from the Black middle class. In R. R. Means Coleman (Ed.), *Say it loud!: African-American audiences, media, and identity* (pp. 187–204). New York: Routledge.

Jhally, S., & Lewis, J. (1992). *Enlightened racism: The Cosby Show, audiences, and the myth of the American Dream*. Boulder, CO: Westview Press.

Kang, L. H.-Y. (2002). The desiring of Asian female bodies: Interracial romance and cinematic subjection. In P. X. Feng (Ed.), *Screening Asian Americans* (pp. 71–98). New Brunswick, NJ: Rutgers University Press.

Kawai, Y. (2005). Stereotyping Asian Americans: The dialectic of the model minority and the yellow peril. *The Howard Journal of Communications, 16,* 109–130.

Kibria, N. (2002). *Becoming Asian American: Second-generation Chinese and Korean American Identities.* Baltimore, MD: John Hopkins University Press.

Kohatsu, E. L., Dulay, M., Lam, C., Concepcion, W., Perez, P., & Euler, J. (2000). Using racial identity theory to explore racial mistrust and interracial contact among Asian Americans. *Journal of Counseling and Development, 78*(3), 334–342.

Lee, R. G. (1999). *Orientals: Asian Americans in popular culture.* Philadelphia, PA: Pennsylvania State University Press.

Lewis, J. (1991). *The ideological octopus: An exploration of television and its audience.* New York: Routledge.

Mansfield-Richardson, V. (2000). *Asian Americans and the mass media: A content analysis of twenty United States newspapers and a survey of Asian American journalists.* New York: Garland.

Marchetti, G. (1993). *Romance and the "yellow peril": Race, sex, and discursive strategies in Hollywood fiction.* Los Angeles: University of California Press.

Martinez, R. O., & Dukes, R. L. (1997). The effects of ethnic identity, ethnicity, and gender on adolescent well-being. *Journal of Youth and Adolescence, 26*(5), 503–516.

Mayer, V. (2003). *Producing dreams, consuming youth: Mexican Americans and mass media.* New Brunswick, NJ: Rutgers University Press.

Means Coleman, R. R. (2000). *African American viewers and the Black situation comedy.* New York: Garland.

Morley, D. (1980). *The nationwide audience: Structure and decoding.* London: British Film Institute.

Oehling, R. (1980). The yellow menace: Asian images in American film. In R. M. Miller (Ed.), *The kaleidoscopic lens: How Hollywood views ethnic groups* (pp. 182–206). Englewood, NJ: Jerome S. Ozer.

Omi, M., & Winant, H. (1994). *Racial formation in the United States: From the 1960s to the 1990s* (2nd ed.). New York: Routledge.

Orbe, M. P., Seymour, R., & Kang, M. (1998). Ethnic humor and ingroup/outgroup positioning: Explicating viewer perceptions of All-American Girl. In Y. R. Kamalipour & T. Carilli (Eds.), *Cultural diversity and the U.S. media* (pp. 125–136). Albany, NY: State University of New York Press.

Parreñas Shimizu, C. (2007). *The hypersexuality of race: Performing Asian/American women on screen and scene.* Durham, NC: Duke University Press.

Perloff, R. M. (2002). The third-person effect. In J. Bryant & D. Zillmann (Eds.), *Media effects: Advances in theory and research* (pp. 489–506). Mahwah, NJ: Erlbaum.

Phinney, J. S. (1990). Ethnic identity in adolescents and adults: Review of research. *Psychological Bulletin, 108*(3), 499–514.

Said, E. W. (1978). *Orientalism.* New York: Vintage Books.

Shim, D. (1998). From yellow peril through model minority to renewed yellow peril: Asians in popular media: Constructing (mis)representations. *Journal of Communication Inquiry, 22*, 385–410.

Smith, E. J. (1991). Ethnic identity development: Toward the development of a theory within the context of majority/minority status. *Journal of Counseling and Development, 70*(1), 181–188.

Song, M. (2003). *Choosing ethnic identity.* Malden, MA: Polity.

Squires, C. R. (2002), Rethinking the black public sphere: An alternative vocabulary for multiple public spheres. *Communication Theory, 12*, 446–468. doi:10.1111/j.1468-2885.2002.tb00278.x

Strauss, A., & Corbin, J. (1994). Grounded theory methodology. In N. K. Denzin & Y. S. Lincoln (Eds.), *Handbook of qualitative research* (pp. 273–285). Thousand Oaks, CA: Sage.

Tajfel, H. (1978). *The social psychology of minorities.* London: Minority Rights Group.

Tuan, M. (1998). *Forever foreigners or honorary Whites? The Asian ethnic experience today.* New Brunswick, NJ: Rutgers University Press.

van Dijk, T. A. (1993). *Elite discourse and racism* (Vol. 6). Newbury Park, CA: Sage.

Wei, R., Lo, V-H., & Lu, H-Y. (2007). Reconsidering the relationship between the third-person perception and optimistic bias. *Communication Research, 34*(6), 665–684. doi: 10.1177/0093650207307903

Weinstein, N. D. (1980). Unrealistic optimism about future life events. *Journal of Personality and Social Psychology, 39*(5), 806–820.

Wilson, C. C., Gutierrez, F., & Chao, L. M. (2003). *Racism, sexism, and the media: The rise of class communication in multicultural America.* Thousand Oaks, CA: Sage.

Wong, E. F. (2002). The early years: Asians in the American films prior to World War II (excerpt, with a new introduction). In P. X. Feng (Ed.), *Screening Asian Americans* (pp. 53–70). New Brunswick, NJ: Rutgers University Press.

Woodward, K. (1997). Concepts of identity and difference. In K. Woodward (Ed.), *Identity and difference* (pp. 1–6). Thousand Oaks, CA: Sage.

Wu, F. H. (2002). *Yellow: Race in America beyond Black and White.* New York: Basic Books.

Yamada, M. (2003). Invisibility is an unnatural disaster: Reflections of an Asian American woman. In C. R. McCann & S.-K. Kim (Eds.), *Feminist theory reader: Local and global perspectives* (pp. 35–40). New York: Routledge.

Chapter 4

Same News, Different Narrative
How the Latina/o-Oriented Press Tells Stories of Social Identity

Carolyn Nielsen

In spring 2006, as unprecedented immigration marches filled the nation's streets, entrepreneurs in the Los Angeles Olvera Street market saw their daily struggles and successes mirrored within the pages of *La Opinión*. But in the *Los Angeles Times,* they saw their sweat-and-toil contributions described not as a testament to the American Dream, but as a threat to the American Way (Nielsen, 2009a). In summer 2009, New York's *El Diario-La Prensa* readers saw a headline dubbing U.S. Supreme Court Justice Sonia Sotomayor "Santa Sonia," and read about the benefit of increasing diversity on the bench. *New York Times* readers, however, saw politicians calling Sotomayor a racist and reporters questioning whether she could be an impartial judge if she refused to check her ethnic identity at the door.

In these examples, the nation's two largest and oldest Spanish-language daily newspapers told counternarratives to "mainstream" coverage of the same events in the same cities. The counternarratives began with a different set of assumptions—chiefly that racism is an everyday occurrence and that diversity is beneficial. While that readership—from Mexicans to Peruvians to Puerto Ricans to Cubans, from new immigrants to third-generation (and beyond) U.S.-born Latina/os—is not monolithic, it shares a Latina/o identity that begins with knowing bigotry as a part of life, seeing the negative stereotypes about Latina/os that run deep and wide in U.S. society and media, and feeling that ethnicity and culture are points of pride and not things to be lost in a melting pot. In this way, Latina/o-oriented newspapers'[1] narratives reinforce and shape Latina/o social identity.

Critical race theory (CRT) is helpful in exploring the role of news media in informing social identity because it recognizes institutionalized racism that is often unseen or unacknowledged by those not directly affected by it. CRT sees racism as normative even when not overt, speaks to the importance of news media that give voice to the marginalized, and shows the role of the counternarrative as one that provides a different perspective from, contradicts, or challenges the narratives in general-market news.

This chapter explores the counternarrative through the examples of three recent narrative framing analyses of news coverage of iconic events centered on Latina/os. The three studies examine general-market and Latina/o-oriented newspaper coverage of: the 2003 release of 2000 U.S. Census data that showed Hispanics as the nation's largest minority group, the 2006 protests against immigration legislation, and the 2009 nomination of U.S. Supreme Court Justice Sonia Sotomayor as the first Latina on the high court. The studies are presented in chronological order, moving from broadest to narrowest. The chapter begins with a study examining framing in coverage of a large population (Latina/os), then moves to a study framing in coverage of a subgroup of that population (immigrants), and finishes with a study examining framing in coverage of an individual (U.S. Supreme Court Justice Sonia Sotomayor). Each study explores counternarrative through the lens of critical race theory.

General-Market News Mostly Ignores Latina/os

Although Latina/os are a large and growing population in the United States, most general-market news coverage ignores issues centered on their lives. A study of more than 34,000 news stories from 2009 found that only 2.9% contained substantial references to Hispanics, and only 0.16% of those stories focused directly on the lives of U.S. Hispanics. By media sector, newspapers carried the most coverage containing substantial references to Latina/os, 4.3%, compared to cable news networks' low of 1.9% (Pew Hispanic Center, 2009).

Spanish-language news media's role in influencing U.S. Latina/o identity goes beyond differences in language to provide different perspectives, sourcing, and context than general-market news coverage. As ethnic-media analyst Elena Shore wrote, "When I started working for the ethnic media news site 'New America Media' in San Francisco six years ago, I didn't fully understand how 'ethnic' and 'mainstream' media differed. What I have discovered since has taught me that the language is perhaps the least of what separates them" (Shore, 2008).

Spanish-language news media outlets have moved from their historic role of helping Latina/os assimilate to a modern role that serves a "dual role of acculturation and pluralism" (Subervi-Vélez, 2008, p. 59), to helping to preserve Latina/o identity while also empowering Latina/os with information necessary for participation in democracy. Latina/o-oriented media provide news from immigrants' homelands, news on key topics such as immigration, and a different narrative construction of U.S. Latina/o identity than the one portrayed in general-market media (Santa Ana, 2002; I. Rodriguez, 2007; Nielsen, 2009a, 2009b, 2010).

Latina/o-oriented newspapers enjoy strong reader loyalty. Latina/os consume ethnic newspapers more than African Americans, Native Americans, Asian Americans, or Arab Americans and are the only racial/ethnic group that prefers ethnic media to mainstream media for information about political affairs and government. Moreover, 82% of Latina/os rely more heavily on ethnic media than on "mainstream" media for news of their communities or their homelands; and 87% of all Latina/os adults use ethnic media (television, radio, or newspapers) on a regular basis (Bendixen & Associates, 2005, p. 39).

The contemporary growth of Latina/o-oriented newspapers began in the 1990s and coincided with Latina/o population growth. The number of Latina/o-oriented newspapers increased from 355 in 1990 to 652 in 2000, according to the Latino Print Network. During that same period, overall circulation of those daily newspapers more than tripled from 400,000 to more than 1,400,000 (Pew Project for Excellence in Journalism, 2004). This is particularly interesting when contrasted to general-market dailies, which lost about 6 million readers during that same period (Pew Project for Excellence in Journalism, 2004). The growth of Latina/o-oriented newspapers began to level out in 2005, and began to decline slightly in 2007 as the economy slowed. Despite that, they have been largely immune to the circulation decline that hit general-market dailies (Poynter Institute and Edmonds, 2007). Loyalty to and reliance on ethnic news media, coupled with the dearth of general-market news coverage about their lives show that Latina/o-oriented news media have a strong role to play in shaping U.S. Latina/o social identity.

Framing Creates the Counternarrative, CRT Explicates It

The findings of the three narrative framing studies presented in this chapter illustrate how the counternarrative permeates all types of coverage. The first study, by Ilia Rodríguez, examined coverage of the 2000 Census, which showed that, for the first time, Hispanics were the nation's largest minority group. On its face, that could be viewed simply as a trend story. But the general-market newspaper narratives presented population growth as a story of conflict, while the Latina/o-oriented newspapers presented population growth as a story about growth in Latina/o political capital (I. Rodríguez, 2007). The second study, conducted by the author, examined the spring 2006 marches for immigrants' rights. That news coverage could have been classified as event coverage, and the general-market newspaper presented it that way. But the Spanish-language newspaper's narrative presented it as a story about the beginning of a political movement (Nielsen, 2009a). The third analysis, also by the author, examined coverage of U.S. Supreme Court Justice Sonia

Sotomayor. This coverage represented a political story about a candidate facing a Senate confirmation vote. The general-market newspaper narrative portrayed Sotomayor's nomination as upsetting the Anglo status quo, while the Spanish-language newspaper narrative portrayed her nomination as opening the door for others who are marginalized (Nielsen, 2010). The Sotomayor coverage offered yet another layer for examination. As a Latina in the news, Sotomayor represented a departure from both the dominant gender and ethnicity on the court. This news story raised issues of intersectionality and represented a test for news media familiar with covering one element of diversity at a time.

The three studies presented in this chapter share a common definition of framing: the way in which news stories are organized to call attention to particular themes that shape readers' understanding based on what is included in the frame. Frames focus readers' attention on particular aspects or angles, especially in regard to causes and solutions of problems (Entman, 1993; Goffman, 1974; Iyengar, 1994; Pan & Kosicki, 1993).

These three studies represent a body of work that shows how the counternarrative of Latina/o-oriented newspapers can create a discourse that both portrays and reinforces U.S. Latina/o social identity.

Counternarrative Begins With Latina/o Lived Experience

"Counternarrative" as it is used here, is derived from critical race theory (CRT). CRT was developed in the 1980s by progressive legal scholars to describe and explain the power behind institutionalized racism and to expand the discussion about racism. CRT asserts that racism should be viewed as more than legal exclusion of people of color because it also exists in cultural beliefs and social constructions that aren't written into law (Crenshaw, 1995).

CRT acknowledges "major media" as "the cultural creators in our society" (Crenshaw, 1995, p. 194); and while it is relatively new to media-effects studies, it is a powerful tool for examining how news media reflect the interests of dominant groups and established power structures. CRT can help to further understanding of how dominant forces, including the news media, perpetuate beliefs and social constructions that help maintain societal divisions (Delgado, 1995).

Key principles of CRT as it applies to news media studies include:

1. Racism is a regular part of U.S. life; it is not aberrant. Racism is an "endemic facet of life in our society," and "neutrality, objectivity, colorblindness and meritocracy are all questionable constructs" (Pizarro, 1998, p. 62).

2. Telling the real stories of people who have experienced oppression, rather than those who can talk about it in theory, is an important part of the narrative. When narratives include the lived experience of people of color, told by those people, those narratives can "cast doubt on the validity of accepted premises or myths especially ones held by the majority" (Delgado & Stefancic, 2001, p. 144).
3. Whiteness is portrayed as normative and other racial/ethnic groups are described as nonwhite. They are shown as opposite, defined not by who they are, but by what they aren't. "Literature and the media reinforce this view of minorities as the exotic other" (Delgado & Stefancic, 2001, p. 76).
4. Interests of nonmajority racial groups are more likely to be addressed when those issues affect or are perceived to affect, the dominant group (Delgado & Stefancic, 2001, p. 16–20).

In each of the three studies presented in this chapter, general-market newspapers depicted Latina/os in their roles as non-Anglos, described how Latinos affect the dominant group, and equated "neutrality" with renouncing non-Anglo identity.[2] Most of what appeared in general-market coverage was rooted in a set of common assumptions: change in racial/ethnic demographics equals conflict and fear and can upset dominant power structures; immigration is a problem to be dealt with, rather than a benefit to the nation; the "melting pot" promotes harmony, and those who refuse to "blend in" by shedding their culture are un-American/racist and therefore a threat.

Framing Contributes to the Counternarrative

Although there is considerable scholarship exploring how general-market news media write about race/ethnicity, class, or gender, there are few studies that have compared coverage in Latina/o-oriented newspapers to coverage in general-market newspapers. Those studies have found sharp differences in framing that speaks to counternarrative (Nielsen, 2009a, 2010; I. Rodríguez, 2007; Santa Ana, 2002).

This is an important because framing can significantly influence public opinion. Entman wrote that frames "call attention to some aspects of reality while obscuring other elements, which might lead audiences to have different reactions" (1993, p. 55). Framing narrative, he writes, "has the ability to define the terms of a debate without the audience realizing it is taking place.... Framing also reflects the richness of media discourse and the subtle differences that are possible when a specific topic is presented in different ways. Those fine points are often lost in a crude pro-or-con bias approach" (p. 97). The study of framing "has the potential of getting beneath the surface of news coverage and exposing the hidden assumptions" (p. 96). This is particularly important when examining counternarratives, which are deeper and subtler than the use of bigoted language or obvious stereotypes. All three studies in this chapter used Gamson and Modigliani's (1989) concept of news packages, coding for specific topics within frames, including metaphors, exemplars, and catchphrases.

The three narrative frame analyses used in this chapter were chosen because they analyzed coverage of iconic events of the decade and because they used parallel methodologies. They also represent a substantial portion of the scholarship on narrative framing of political issues in general-market and Latina/o-oriented newspapers. The first study examined narrative framing of Latina/o population growth through the lens of CRT. The second study examined narrative framing and explored episodic versus thematic framing. The third study examined narrative framing through the lens of CRT and also explored intersectionality, which explains how modes of oppression act together to further discrimination.

The Counternarrative of Population Growth

In her 2007 study, "Telling Stories of Latino Population Growth in the United States," Ilia Rodríguez examined news coverage of the U.S. Census Bureau's 2003 report showing that Latina/os had surpassed African Americans as the country's largest minority group. Rodríguez conducted a framing analysis of 42 news articles in 20 general-market, nine Latina/o-oriented, and 10 African American newspapers.

She found general-market news media focused on themes of "conflict and competition as the preferred frame for the interpretation of population trends and their implications for inter-ethnic relations between Blacks and Latinos" (2007, p. 573). Latina/o-oriented newspapers emphasized Latina/o population growth as a key frame, but did not strongly emphasize the competition of Latina/os against African Americans. Rodríguez also found that the general-market newspapers "were more likely to open space for inter-ethnic dialogue by incorporating the opinions of Latino and African-American sources and thus opening room for questioning the competition frame" (p. 586). She found the Latina/o-oriented newspapers were more likely to "give more attention to the discussion of lingering challenges and opportunities posed by the new status as largest ethnic minority" (p. 586). In this way, she described the framing as a "closed and isolated dialogue" among Latina/os.

In this case, the Latina/o-oriented press presented a counternarrative, but did not directly challenge the general-market news narrative. Rodríguez wrote that, "the minority press, though not always counter-hegemonic, plays a key role in opening the public forum for richer discussions of racial and ethnic issues.... Likewise, in Latino papers, the analysis of challenges facing the Latino population offered a richer discussion of the implications of demographic trends" (p. 587).

She found general-market media, while providing space for Latina/o and Black voices, still framed the issue as one of conflict. Rodríguez concluded the "emphasis on conflict and hierarchy among minorities adds credence to the proposition of critical race theorists who maintain that interest convergence among minorities becomes a relevant topic in society only when the status of the dominant groups is perceived to be directly at stake. In this case, discussion of the significance of Latino population growth for European Americans, or any other group besides African Americans, is left outside public discourse" (p. 587).

La Opinión Shows Counternarrative in Coverage

Three years after the Census data were released, the news media turned their attention to another iconic event: the political debate over U.S. immigration policy that would have made it a felony, rather than a civil infraction, to be in the United States without authorization. HR4437, The Border Protection, Anti-Terrorism, and Illegal Immigration Control Act, spurred never-before-seen immigrant political action (Hing & Johnson, 2006). The bill also proposed increased penalties for businesses that hired undocumented workers, and sought to increase U.S.–Mexico border fortifications with an enhanced fence that became known simply as "the Wall."

During the Congressional debate, Los Angeles became "the epicenter of the resurgence of the immigrant rights movement" (Miller, 2006). The largest single demonstration in the country was the May 1 "Day Without an Immigrant" march in Los Angeles, which drew an estimated 500,000 people. Los Angeles is home to the nation's largest number of undocumented immigrants, most of them Latina/o. In 2006, there were 1 million unauthorized immigrants in the Los Angeles metropolitan area, which is nearly twice the number of any other major metropolitan area in the country and represents about 10% of that area's population (Fortuny, Capps, & Passell, 2007).

As a former Southern California newspaper reporter, I became interested in how the immigration debate was playing out in Congress, in the streets, and in Los Angeles' biggest newspapers. I conducted a narrative framing analysis of 303 articles that appeared in the *Los Angeles Times* and *La Opinión* beginning the week before the first march and ending the week after the immigration bills died in Congress. I restricted my study to news articles longer than 500 words and conducted close readings of 158 *Los Angeles Times* articles and 145 *La Opinión* articles. I examined word choice as a symbolic metaphor and a part of framing, narrative framing itself, news packages, and episodic versus thematic framing.

Language Shapes Social Identity

Language is an important part of framing, and has the power to create or reinforce stereotypes, or to debunk them. The words journalists use and the source quotations they choose to include in their articles help shape readers' thoughts, and also reveal the (often unconscious) biases of the journalists themselves (VanDijk, 1991). Word choice as a symbolic metaphor was especially important to this study because it stood to reveal so much connotative subtext with the narrative frame. Certain phrases have the power to frame coverage in a shorthand the audience often absorbs without questioning its slant (Gamson & Modigliani, 1989).

For example, in *Los Angeles Times* coverage of the 2006 immigration marches, the word *immigrant* was used interchangeably with the word *Mexican* in 49% of the articles, meaning "immigrant" became synonymous with "Mexican." In *La Opinión*, the word *inmigrante* was most often used as an umbrella term not tied to a specific country of origin 41% of the time. *La Opinión* used *inmigrante* as a synonym for *trabajadores* or "workers," but the *Los Angeles Times* did not (Nielsen, 2009a).

Words in texts can become linked in readers' minds (VanDijk, 1991). In *Los Angeles Times* coverage, "immigrant" most often appeared in text in conjunction with "illegal." "Illegal immigrant" appeared in 78% of the articles. By contrast, *La Opinión* primarily used the less menacing sounding *inmigrantes indocumentados* or "undocumented immigrants," which appeared in 80% of the articles. *La Opinión* also used the term *immigrant workers*, a construction that never appeared in *Los Angeles Times* coverage.

The language used by sources quoted in the articles also differed between publications. Quotations in the *Los Angeles Times* mostly modified "immigrants" with "illegal." *La Opinión* quotations most often used the construction "*inmigrantes indocumentados*/undocumented immigrants." However, *Los Angeles Times* sources' quotes also used the terms *illegal aliens* and *illegals*. Those terms never appeared in the *La Opinión* articles.

For immigrants who view nationality as a point of pride, and immigration as a quest for work rather than a crime, "undocumented worker" reflects a counternarrative to "illegal" and "Mexican." The standalone term *illegals* is used by anti-immigration groups as a hostile slur, and carries a threatening subtext associated with vigilantism.

Framing Narratives Center on Fear

Los Angeles Times coverage built a narrative of fear and otherness that illustrated the critical race theory concepts of describing immigrants as "nonwhite" and covering issues from the standpoint of how the minority would impact the majority. *Los Angeles Times* framing showed immigration as a source of crime, a force of change to "U.S. culture," and a source of job loss. In most cases, this was shown as concern over Latina/os taking jobs away from African Americans. This aspect mirrors the Black-Latina/o conflict frames seen in Rodríguez's work on Census coverage (I. Rodríguez, 2007). *Los Angeles Times* news packages portrayed immigrants as a source of fear and border fortification as part of the solution (Nielsen, 2009a).

La Opinión's counternarrative carried frames of multicultural solidarity and news packages that portrayed proposed legislation as the source of fear and pointed to political action against the bill as part of the solution. Only *La Opinión's* coverage reflected immigrants as contributors to U.S. culture and addressed U.S. Latina/o political mobilization as a rising power (Nielsen, 2009a).

The newspapers showed the potential implications of the legislation from vastly different standpoints—from one that would "keep us safe" to one that would "turn us into criminals." The difference was in defining "us" in a city that is half Latina/o (both U.S.-born and foreign born).

Thematic Immigration Coverage Furthers Counternarrative

This study also examined whether each newspaper's coverage was episodic or thematic, a dimension of framing that affects who society sees as responsible for problems and solutions (Iyengar, 1994). In previous studies, episodic framing of issues such as poverty and racial discrimination led the audience to believe individuals were responsible for their own misfortunes and also for finding their own solutions. Thematic framing, defined as exploring the root causes of the problems, led the audience to believe that society was responsible for both creating the problem and finding the solution (Iyengar, 1994). When general-market news covers Latina/o issues episodically, it ignores factors such as institutionalized racism and supports the myths of the "level playing field" and the "American Dream." It causes readers to believe individuals are responsible for their own problems and it fails to acknowledge that society plays a role. In this way, episodic framing works in conjunction with critical race theory. In this study, episodic framing would show the spring 2006 marches as a here-today-gone-tomorrow product of a political contest, whereas thematic framing would explore the causes and hardships of illegal immigration and frame the marches as the beginning of a new political movement.

Results showed *Los Angeles Times* coverage framed 83% of its immigration articles episodically, as events or contests, without any substantive focus on the issues behind the bill and the marches. By contrast, *La Opinión* provided thematic coverage 48% of the time. Its coverage portrayed the marches as a representation of something bigger—a growing political movement based in a past of oppression, injustice, and persecution; and a future in which the Latina/o voice could play a role in key policy decisions (Nielsen, 2009a).

A June 2006 Pew Hispanic Center survey showed that 63% of Latina/os nationwide viewed the marches as the beginning of a "new and lasting social movement" rather than a one-time phenomenon (Suro & Escobar, 2006). Further, 54% of respondents in that survey said they had experienced an increase in discrimination, which they believed to be a result of the 2006 legislative debate.

After the immigration legislation died in committee and before the 2010 Arizona immigration bills were written, the immigration debate all but disappeared from general-market coverage, but remained strong in Latina/o-oriented news. This bolsters the concept of episodic versus thematic framing of the issue. Immigration news, which is a prominent, standalone section alongside business, entertainment, and sports news in Latina/o-oriented newspapers, was rarely covered in general-market news after the marches and legislative debate subsided (Pew Hispanic Center, 2009). According to the Pew Hispanic Center report, "Immigration, which from 2006 through 2008 had been heavily debated in Congress and on the political campaign trail, was the subject of fewer than one in 10 stories involving Latina/os, a reflection of the degree to which the issue largely fell off the radar during the early months of the Obama Administration" (Pew Hispanic Center, 2009).

Then, in 2009, both presses turned their attention to U.S. Supreme Court nominee Sonia Sotomayor.

A Test of Framing Intersectionality

President Barack Obama's May 26, 2009, nomination to the U.S. Supreme Court of then-U.S. Court of Appeals Judge Sonia Sotomayor marked the first nomination of a Latina in the high court's 200-year history. It also launched the biggest story about Latina/os in 2009 and the first time a newsmaker had received more coverage than President Obama. Of the less than 2.9% of general-market news stories about Latina/os, 39% were about Sotomayor. The other most prominent topics included the Mexican drug war, 15%; the H1N1 virus, 13%; and immigration, 8.4% (Pew Research Center, 2009).

If confirmed, she would be the third woman and first Hispanic to sit on the U.S. Supreme Court. As the child of low-income Puerto Rican immigrants, Sotomayor stood at the intersection of what CRT scholars call "multiple forms of exclusion." She faced the potential for discrimination based on her gender, ethnicity, and social class.

It was that test of the news media's ability to interpret intersectionality in its coverage of a high-profile woman of color that sparked my interest in studying the Sotomayor coverage in both of her hometown papers, *The New York Times* and *El Diario-La Prensa*. I wanted to learn whether the general-market newspaper would portray her identity differently than the Spanish-language newspaper.

Intersectionality, where multiple forms of exclusion meet, is both a method and a theory. As a method, it guides study design, in this case, providing categories for content analysis to determine whether news coverage employed a unitary (e.g. focused solely on either race, gender, or class); a multiple (focused on more than one dimension of identity, but recognizing each separately); or intersectional approach (recognizing how dimensions of identity work together to form a collective identity in which no one aspect is more dominant than the others). Common to political science and sociology, intersectionality has rarely been examined in media studies, but has a valuable role to play because social identity is so often at the heart of news narratives.

Most identity-oriented studies of news coverage of candidates has used a unitary approach, choosing to examine one aspect of "difference" in candidates who don't fall into the middle- or upper-class, Anglo, male demographic.

As a theory, intersectionality shows how discourse that focuses on a unitary approach (e.g. only race, or class, or gender) is both inaccurate and unfair in presuming one aspect of someone's identity is most important or most explanatory (Hancock, 2007). This fits well with the long-held journalistic norms valuing accuracy and fairness. Intersectionality posits that because members of a group share one demographic characteristic, for example, ethnicity, does not make that group homogenous. When elites try to homogenize a particular identity based on a singular aspect of that identity, it marginalizes members of that group whose identity might differ in other aspects (e.g., in terms of gender, sexual orientation, or class) from the majority of that group (Hancock, 2007). In this case, a Latina from a poor family does not have the same life experiences as a Latina from a wealthy family or as any Latino. And the fact that she is Latina, or the fact that she comes from a poor family, cannot be separated out as if one of these is more important to her identity.

Intersectionality is frequently unseen or unacknowledged. This is particularly true in political narratives, where gender and race have not been scrutinized in tandem because the dominant culture has not willingly employed intersectional frames (Winter, 2008). In analyzing intersectionality, it is important to distinguish between individual and collective standpoints, for example, the fact that "no homogeneous Black *woman's* standpoint exists... [however] a Black *women's* collective standpoint does exist, one characterized by the tensions that accrue to different responses to common challenges" (Collins, 2000, p. 28). A Latina identity is yet more complex because of racial differences within the ethnicity, for example, defining a "black-Cubanwoman" or a "*Puertorriqueña trigueña*" (a Puerto Rican woman who is indigenous, African, and Spanish) (Hernández-Truyol, 1998, p. 29).

Just as struggles for women's rights have largely overlooked women of color, and as struggles for civil rights have largely relegated women to support roles, when women of color are portrayed in general-market media as a singular identity they have the potential to be marginalized at their intersections. From a journalistic standpoint, Sotomayor's race and ethnicity were newsworthy because they represented the breaking of barriers. Her class status, the "housing project to Ivy League" storyline, was one she shared with previous nominees, and therefore was less novel and less newsworthy. If the newspapers presented Sotomayor singularly, as either a woman or a person of color, rather than intersectionally, that would indicate a hegemonic narrative.

Framing Diversity as Burden or Benefit

My 2010 analysis examined narrative framing in a saturation sample of the 124 news articles about Sotomayor that appeared in *The New York Times* (76 articles) and *El Diario-La Prensa* (48 articles) between May 26, 2009, the day Sotomayor was nominated, and August 15, 2009, one week after she was sworn in. These two newspapers were chosen because they cover her hometown and because both represent the prestige press, which helps set the tone for coverage emulated by other news outlets. While the general-market newspaper is intended to reach a mass audience, and the Latina/o-oriented newspaper's audience is targeted, both newspapers operate under the same journalistic norms of accuracy, fairness, objectivity, and thoroughness.

This study found the narrative framing in the two newspapers to be directly opposite, revealing the strongest Latina/o-oriented news counternarrative of all three studies presented in this chapter. *The New York Times* narrative relied on themes of diversity as a burden, showing Sotomayor as biased toward Latina/os, and questioning whether she could "overcome" her ethnicity to be an impartial justice. *El Diario-La Prensa* narratives portrayed diversity as a benefit that would expand the court's worldview, and devoted entire articles to highlighting Sotomayor's impartiality while also showing her as a role model for Latina/os and as someone opening new doors for people who are marginalized.

This study also examined exemplars, metaphors, and catchphrases as a key component of framing (Gamson & Modigliani, 1989). *The New York Times* used the *Ricci v. DeStefano* racial discrimination case as an exemplar. It was newsworthy in that Sotomayor, as a member of a three-judge appellate panel, had ruled against the discrimination claims of white firefighters who were denied promotions, and because it was docketed to come before the Supreme Court. However, the focus on *Ricci* as an exemplar fed an anti-Anglo narrative and lacked a full exploration of her judicial record. As an appellate judge, Sotomayor upheld claims of racial discrimination (brought mostly by people of color) in only 10 of 97 cases. Nine of those decisions were unanimous. Her record did not support the assumption of anti-Anglo biases created by the use of this exemplar.

The metaphors in the *Times* coverage were affirmative action and Sotomayor's advocacy work with the Puerto Rican Legal Defense and Education Fund (PRLDEF). Affirmative action was a metaphor in the *Times* in two ways: coverage linked Sotomayor's success to affirmative action and it suggested how she might rule in regard to affirmative-action cases.

El Diario's coverage had no identifiable exemplars, but in a clear example of counternarrative, used her PRLDEF work as an exemplar with a tone of leadership rather than one of bias.

"Wise Latina" Reclaimed in Counternarrative

The catchphrase *wise Latina*, excerpted from a 2002 speech Sotomayor gave at the University of California Berkeley law school, became a prominent fixture in Sotomayor coverage and an illustrative example in this study. The catchphrase was a two-word descriptor from the oft-quoted line, "I would hope that a wise Latina woman with the richness of her experiences would more often than not reach a better conclusion than a white male who hasn't lived that life." Using that quotation in a vacuum removes necessary context. Removing the context speaks to the CRT principle of powerful institutions dealing only with racism when it appears to confront or affect the majority.

In general-market news, the out-of-context quote was largely referred to as a "gaffe" that "revealed" her sense of "fiery, Latina pride" (Stolberg, 2009). *The Washington Post, The Arizona Republic, The Seattle Times, The Houston Chronicle, The Associated Press* wire service, and others carried the headline "Sotomayor Refuses to Renounce 'Wise Latina'" remark, as though she were taking a stand in favor of personal bias. A *USA Today* editorial urged readers, "Beyond Sotomayor's 'Latina' Gaffe, Consider Her Record." Although the editorial supported her and denounced ideas that she was a "reverse racist," it also failed to understand that "wise Latina" was not a gaffe, nor was it something to renounce.

When placed in context (as it was in *El Diario*), the quotation was hardly inflammatory. The next part of that speech was intentionally inclusive:

> Let us not forget that wise men like Oliver Wendell Holmes and Justice Cardozo voted on cases which upheld both sex and race discrimination in our society. Until 1972, no Supreme Court case ever upheld the claim of a woman in a gender discrimination case. I, like Professor Carter, believe that we should not be so myopic as to believe that others of different experiences or backgrounds are incapable of understanding the values and needs of people from a different group. Many are so capable. As Judge Cedarbaum pointed out to me, nine white men on the Supreme Court in the past have done so on many occasions and on many issues including *Brown*. (Sotomayor, 2002, p. 92)

In a separate study, a computer analysis of 1.6 million media sites and blogs found the two-word phrase "wise Latina" was the fourth most commonly used phrase of all concepts in the news media between February 1, 2009 and July 3, 2009. It was repeated more than 2,500 times. The three phrases that outnumbered "wise Latina" all came from President Obama's public remarks (Pew Research Center, 2009).

My study found that the use of the "wise Latina" catchphrase in *The New York Times* was always in conjunction with someone asserting that Sotomayor was biased or bigoted. It was always taken out of context and used in a narrative of confrontation. Conversely, the use of the phrase in *El Diario* was positive, in keeping with the spirit of a speech in which her rhetoric embraced intersectionality while acknowledging that many of the Anglo men who have historically dominated the U.S. Supreme Court were capable of making decisions in favor of equality.

El Diario editors, apparently well aware of the term's misappropriation, put a spin on the phrase in the August 7, 2009 headline, "Sabia confirmación de Sotomayor para la Corte Suprema," (Cadiz, 2009) ("Wise confirmation of Sotomayor for the Supreme Court"). The headline takes direct aim at general-market news media portrayals of the term as a negative. In a different article, a reporter described "un festejo en El Bronx en honor a la 'sabia latina,'" or "a festival in the Bronx in honor of the 'wise Latina'" (Correal, 2009).

General-Market News Uses Unitary Approach to Identity

My study found *The New York Times* coverage took a unitary approach focused almost exclusively on Sotomayor's ethnicity and almost never delved into gender issues. *The New York Times* was not alone in this. A study of 55 general-market news outlets across the country showed that nearly half of the stories about Sotomayor made substantial references to her ethnicity with a particular focus on the role it would play in her confirmation. The study found, "The notion that race was too much a part of Sotomayor's legal thinking became a major talking point and dividing line in the media debate" (Pew Research Center, 2009).

Several *New York Times* articles in this study raised questions about whether she could "overcome" her ethnicity to be an impartial judge—never questioning whether she should be asked to check her ethnicity at the door, only asking whether she could. None of those articles explored whether Anglo judges could be impartial. No articles questioned her gender as either something to be overcome or portrayed her gender as an asset (Nielsen, 2010). That lack of intersectionality speaks to critical race theory because *The New York Times* coverage framed her primarily as non-Anglo, defining her by what she is not. It began with an assumption that Sotomayor should "melt in" to be capable of impartiality.

El Diario-La Prensa embraced intersectional frames that mirrored Sotomayor's speeches about the richness of her lived experiences as a Latina and how they could benefit her decisions as a judge. *El Diario* also presented the strongest counternarrative of the three studies in this chapter. While most of *The New York Times* articles framed diversity as a burden to be overcome in order to be "impartial," *El Diario* framed diversity as a benefit that would enhance the court's perspective and expand the worldview on the bench (Nielsen, 2010). In doing so, it directly contradicted the dominant narrative.

Conclusion

The three studies described in this chapter present an overview of the coverage of three iconic events involving U.S. Latina/os over the past decade. The analysis is presented both chronologically and in order of broadest to most specific topic of coverage—from Census group to subgroup to individual. Further, the examples show a progression in the level of the counternarrative in the individual studies. The counternarrative in the Census study shows how the Latina/o newspapers presented a different narrative, but not one that directly challenged the dominant messages. The immigration study showed a counternarrative that posed a challenge as to whether the marches were something bigger than singular events. Finally, the Sotomayor study showed how the Spanish-language newspaper presented a counternarrative that not only directly contradicted the general-market newspaper, but also reclaimed and redefined the catchphrase "wise Latina" as a term of pride rather than a gaffe.

In each study, the framing differences that formed the counternarrative bear out the key tenets of critical race theory: to show how frames of conflict and racial hierarchies dominate coverage, and how coverage of racial/ethnic minorities becomes relevant only in the context of the dominant group; to show how framing narratives "otherize" immigrants and create fear; to show how episodic coverage promotes a sense of individual responsibility while ignoring institutionalized racism; and to show how representing a singular identity as "something to be overcome" plays to the concept of the melting pot.

General-market media are supposed to cover all segments of their circulation areas "without fear or favor," as *The New York Times* founder Adolph S. Ochs famously said. As the studies highlighted in this chapter clearly show, that is not happening. William Gamson wrote that frames emerge not necessarily in response to what is most important about an issue, but in response to what elites feel is most important about an issue (Gamson, Crocteau, Hoynes, & Sasson, 1992).

Latina/o-oriented news media have an increasingly important role to play in reflecting the communities they serve, and also in continuing to shape U.S. Latina/o identity. As of this writing, the fourth major iconic event involving Latina/os as the nation's largest minority group is making headlines in both Latina/o-oriented and general-market newspapers. The state of Arizona is facing off with the federal government over who has the right to dictate immigration policy. Arizona's SB1070 requires law enforcement officers to request citizenship documents from anyone they suspect might be in the country illegally. On June 25, 2012, the U.S. Supreme Court ruled 5–3 to strike down some sections of SB 1070 that it ruled were pre-empted by federal law. The court upheld one of the law's most contentious provisions allowing Arizona law enforcement officers to investigate the immigration status of people they have stopped or arrested if there is reasonable suspicion those people are in the country illegally. Polls have shown widespread support for the law, and 17 states, chief among them Oklahoma, South Carolina, and Utah, have attempted to create similar legislation (Savage, 2010). Further, Arizona has banned the teaching of ethnic studies classes and has removed teachers with "heavy accents" from its classrooms (Jordan, 2010; Lewin, 2010). The news coverage of Arizona's policies is helping to shape readers' (and politicians') thoughts about those laws.

It is my hope that more media scholars will begin to examine intersectionality and will also expand the concept of news media to include more studies of Latina/o-oriented news media. Both the use of intersectionality and the broadening of the research domain could provide important contributions to the body of research examining how news media portray and inform social identity.

Notes

1. Latina/o-oriented news media encompasses Spanish-language, bilingual, and English-language media targeted toward the Latina/o consumer.
2. "Anglo" is used here to describe people who are racially White and ethnically European. Most U.S. residents who are ethnically Latina/o are racially White, therefore "Anglo" is a more precise descriptor than "White."

References

Bendixen & Associates. (2005, November). *The ethnic media in America: The giant hidden in plain sight*. Retrieved from http://www.ncmonline.com/polls/full_em_poll.pdf

Cadiz, A. (2009, August 7). Sabia Confirmación De Sotomayor [Wise confirmation of Sotomayor]. *El Diario-La Prensa*, pp. 2–4.

Collins, P. H. (2000). Gender, Black feminism, and Black political economy. *Annals, American Academy of Political and Social Science, 586*, 41–61.

Correal, A. (2009, August 7). Festejos En Nueva York. *El Diario-La Prensa*, p. 3.

Crenshaw, K. (1995). *Critical race theory: The key writings that formed the movement*. New York: New Press.

Delgado, R. (1995). *Critical race theory: The cutting edge*. Philadelphia, PA: Temple University Press.

Delgado, R., & Stefancic, J. (2001). *Critical race theory: An introduction*. New York: New York University Press.

Entman, R. (1993). Framing: Toward a clarification of a fractured paradigm. *Journal of Communication, 43*(4), 51–58.

Fortuny, K., Capps, R., & Passell, J. S. (2007). *The characteristics of unauthorized immigrants* (Vol. 8, Rev.). Washington, DC: Urban Institute.

Gamson, W. A., Crocteau, D., Hoynes, W., & Sasson, T. (1992). Media images and the social construction of reality. *Annual Review of Sociology, 18*, 373–393.

Gamson, W. A., & Modigliani, A. (1989). Media discourse and public opinion on nuclear power: A constructionist approach. *American Journal of Sociology, 95*(1), 1–37.

Goffman, E. (1974). *Frame analysis: An essay on the organization of experience*. New York: Harper & Row.

Hancock, A. (2007, March). When multiplication doesn't equal quick addition: Examining intersectionality as a research paradigm. *Perspectives on Politics, 5*(1), 63–79.

Hernández-Truyol, B. E. (1998). Building bridges: Latinas and Latinos at the crossroads. In R. Delgado & J. Stefancic (Eds.), *The Latino/a condition: A critical reader* (pp. 24–31). New York: New York University Press.

Hing, B. O., & Johnson, K. (2007). The immigrant rights marches of 2006 and the prospects for a new civil rights movement. *Harvard Civil Rights-Civil Liberties Law Review, 42*. Retrieved from http://ssrn.com/abstract=951268

Iyengar, S. (1994). *Is anyone responsible? How television frames political issues*. Chicago, IL: University of Chicago Press.

Jordan, M. (2010, April 30). Arizona grades teachers on fluency. *The Wall Street Journal*, p. A3.

Lewin, T. (2010, May 14). Citing individualism, Arizona tries to rein in ethnic studies in school. *The New York Times*, p. 13.

Miller, G. (2006, April 10). Immigration activists on march again. *Los Angeles Times*, p. A11.

Nielsen, C. (2009a, August). *Mi patria, mi país, mi periódico/my homeland, my country, my newspaper: Second-level agenda setting in the Los Angeles Times and La Opinión*. Conference paper presented at the Association for Journalism and Mass Communication Education annual conference, Boston, Massachusetts.

Nielsen, C. (2009b). The Spanish town crier: A case study of Radio Sol's grassroots programming in an era of Spanish-language radio consolidation. *Journal of Spanish Language Media*, 2, 126–141.

Nielsen, C. (2010, August). *Wise Latina: The framing of Sonia Sotomayor in the New York Times and El Diario-La Prensa*. Conference paper presented at the Association for Journalism and Mass Communication Education annual conference, Denver, Colorado.

Pan, Z., & Kosicki, G. M. (1993). Framing analysis: An approach to news discourse. *Political Communication*, 10(1), 55–75.

Pew Hispanic Center. (2009, December 7). *Hispanics in the news: An event-driven narrative*. Retrieved from http://www.journalism.org/analysis_report/hispanics_news

Pew Project for Excellence in Journalism. (2004). "Spanish Language Press." The state of the news media 2004: An annual report on American journalism. 2005. Retrieved March 2009 from http://stateofthemedia.org/2004/ethnicalternative-intro/spanish-language-press/

Pew Research Center's Project for Excellence in Journalism. (2008). *The state of the news media 2007*. Retrieved from http://www.stateofthemedia.org/2007/

Pew Research Center's Project for Excellence in Journalism. (2009). *Ethnic/alternative: Spanish language press*. Retrieved from http://www.stateofthemedia.org/2004/

Pizarro, M. (1998, January). "Chicana/o power!" Epistemology and methodology for social justice and empowerment in Chicana/o communities. *International Journal of Qualitative Studies in Education*, 11(1), 57–80.

Poynter Institute, & Edmonds, R. (2007). "Newspapers-intro." Pew Research Center, state of the news media 2007: An annual report on American journalism. Retrieved May 2009 from http://stateofthemedia.org/2007/newspapers-intro/

Rodríguez, I. (2007). Telling stories of Latino population growth in the United States. *Journalism*, 8(5), 573–590.

Santa Ana, O. (2002). *Brown tide rising: Metaphors of Latinos in contemporary American public discourse*. Austin: University of Texas Press.

Savage, M. W. (2010, July 8). Three other states weighing tough immigration bills. *The Washington Post*, p. A4.

Shore, E. (2008, Summer). The Spanish-language press delves into racial complexities. *Nieman Reports*. Retrieved fromhttp://www.nieman.harvard.edu/reportsitem.aspx?id=100029

Sotomayor, S. (2002). A Latina judge's voice. *Berkeley La Raza Law Journal, 13*(1), 87–94.

Stolberg, S. G. (2009, July 15). Senate panel wrangles with "A Tale of Two Sonias." *The New York Times*, p. A17.

Subervi-Vélez, F. A. (2008). *The mass media and Latino politics: Studies of U.S. media content, campaign strategies and survey research: 1984–2004*. New York: Routledge.

Suro, R., & Escobar, G. (2006, July 13). *2006 national survey of Latinos*. Retrieved from http://pewhispanic.org/files/reports/68.pdf

USA Today. (2009, July 15). Beyond Sotomayor's "Latina" gaffe, consider her record. *USA Today*, p. 10A.

VanDijk, T. A. (1991). *Racism and the press*. London: Routledge.

Winter, N. J. (2008). *Dangerous frames: How ideas about race and gender shape public opinion*. Chicago, IL: University of Chicago Press.

Chapter 5

The New Role of Bilingual Newspapers in Establishing and Maintaining Social Group Identities among Latinos

Arthur D. Santana

> For a people who cannot entirely identify with either standard Spanish nor standard English, what recourse is left to them but to create their own language? A language which they can connect their identity to, one capable of communicating the realities and values true to themselves—a language with terms that are neither *español ni inglés*, but both. (Gloria Anzaldúa, Borderlands/*La Frontera*, 1987)

Latino media outlets, which have traditionally served immigrant populations with Spanish-language media, are increasingly adjusting to the challenge of serving both the native and immigrant populations through bilingual publications. And it appears a trend is afoot: The number of bilingual newspapers has more than doubled since 2000, and every few weeks, another Spanish newspaper makes the conversion from Spanish-only to bilingual (Feldherr, 2009). According to Kirk Whisler with Latino Print Network, there were 179 bilingual newspapers in 2009 in the United States with a circulation of 3.9 million and another 95 bilingual magazines with a combined circulation of 7.6 million.

This chapter will focus on the Latino identity-building role of bilingual newspapers as they attract members of the country's largest and fastest-growing minority group. Bilingual newspapers have already secured the loyalty of many Spanish-speaking Latinos. Acknowledging that most of the growth of their target audience is now from American-born Latinos who are more likely to speak and read mainly in English, they are switching to a new format in order to cast a wider net.

In providing a contextual framework for the sociological effects of the bilingual newspaper, this chapter will examine the relevant literature, addressing three overarching areas of Latino life: language, identity, and acculturation. After a brief overview of the history of the U.S. Latino press, this chapter, which is intended as a call for further research, will conclude with an assessment of the modern Latino bilingual press and explore the ways it is both adapting to and engaging the blurred identity of the later-generation Latino. Border theory scholars have explored the cultural hybridity of these later-generation Latinos and the extent to which they possess an ambivalent cultural identity, existing on a psychological and sociological "border." Their identity is rooted in what has been described as "hybrid" (García Canclini, 1995; Hall, 1993) or a "cultural blend" (Keefe & Padilla, 1987), a term adopted to denote a person who draws from American and Latino cultures.

The bilingual newspaper, itself a product of cultural contradictions, hopes to capitalize on the "neither-nor" cultural identity of the later-generation Latino by creating a product, which, it hopes, speaks uniquely to them in a language they understand and about issues about which they care. The bilingual newspaper, essentially facilitating the cultural shift already taking place among many Latinos, hopes to speak uniquely to acculturated Latinos since it is like them, a hybrid.

Language

Most second-generation Latino adults born in the United States say they are fluent in English. In comparison, only a few of their parents describe themselves as skilled English speakers (Hakimzadeh & Cohn, 2007). Overall, 41% were found to be primarily Spanish speakers while 15% were primarily English speakers. But outnumbering both of those categories were the 44% of Latinos who indicated they were bilingual (Hakimzadeh & Cohn, 2007). Simply put, the later the generation for Latinos, the more likely they are to speak and read English proficiently. Bilingualism, however, has been significantly present across three generations; 34% of immigrants, 22% of third-generation, and 68% of second-generation Latinos indicated they were proficient in both languages (Hakimzadeh & Cohn, 2007).

The term *code-switching* (Anzaldúa, 1987; Auer, 1998; Cashman, 2008; Gumperz, 1982) has been used to describe a linguistic phenomenon whereby speakers, fully versed in two (or more) closed, fixed languages, switch from language to language during a conversation. Anzaldúa (1987), herself a sixth-generation Tejana, wrote that such a form of bilingualism could be considered its own language. Similarly, instead of describing "Spanglish" as a hybrid language, combining both Spanish and English, Morales (2002) described it instead as a state of mind of the cross-cultural Latino, "of belonging to at least two identities at the same time" (p. 8).

Different conditions, including the effects of individual, family, social, and demographic characteristics, can have an effect on the maintenance of Spanish among English-speaking Latino youth (Lutz, 2006). The literature reflects that no one single factor determines a person's ability to speak two languages; rather, a host of factors are at play, including parental income and single parent status. Generational, racial, family, and community contexts are also key in predicting the maintenance of Spanish (Lutz, 2006). Gender, too, is a predictor as is a Latino's desire for socioeconomic mobility. Proficiency in English is well established by the second generation and "completed" by the third among Latinos (Rumbaut, 2008, p. 233). Among Latinos in California, members of the "1.5" generation (those with one foreign-born parent) were found to be twice as likely to drop out of high school than to graduate from college, but the second generation reverses that pattern (Rumbaut, 2008).

Still other conditions, such as age at the time of immigration, can facilitate the process of loss or retention of Spanish. Foreign-born Latinos who arrived at ages 10 and younger were most likely to be most comfortable speaking both Spanish and English; 77% of those in this group indicated they were bilingual (Hakimzadeh & Cohn, 2007). Still, other research has found that even if children immigrate at an early age, if parents do not reinforce the home culture, they are apt to experience a loss of some or all of the native language (Perez & Padilla, 2000). The extent to which families reinforce home culture is, of course, not uniform across the Latino population. Purposefully placing children in an environment where Spanish is regularly spoken increases their bilingual abilities. People are more likely to speak both Spanish and English when others around them are doing the same (Linton, 2004). Linton's work contributes to a small but growing body of sociological research that looks at bilingualism, rather than English monolingualism, as an endpoint to linguistic assimilation.

Overall, the rates of speaking only English suggests that Anglicization is occurring at roughly the same pace for Asians as it did for Europeans but is slower among Spanish speakers (Alba, Logan, Lutz, & Stults, 2002).

Identity

Anzaldúa (1987) wrote that being Mexican American "is a state of soul—not of mind, not of citizenship" and that a Latino need not live on the physical border of Mexico and the United States to live on a metaphorical border (p. 84). Generally speaking, later-generation Latinos face this bicultural reality: their Anglo friends see them foremost as Latinos, nevermind how acculturated; they affix their cultural blinders and impose on Latinos their Latinoness—their names, appearance, mannerisms, and choices are perceived to be exotic. At the same time, Latinos' immigrant friends see them in the opposite way; they affix their cultural blinders and impose on them their Angloness—their names, appearance, mannerisms, and choices are perceived to be Anglicized. Latinos are what Keefe and Padilla (1987) labeled a "Cultural Blend":

These individuals participate selectively in both orientations, but they are not equally proficient in both cultures. They recognize that they are not Mexicans, and they do not identify as Mexicans, noting, for example, their lack of fluency in Spanish or their non-acceptance of some Mexican cultural practices. At the same time, Cultural Blends draw a clear distinction between themselves and Anglos, and although they appear comfortable in many aspects of American life, they have many ethnically based preferences that keep them separated from Anglos. (p. 96)

Both perceptions, as subtle forms of rejection, construe a type of marginality (Bennett, 1993) since neither culture can fully claim Latinos. They are "the products of several interlocking histories and cultures, belonging at the same time to several 'homes'—and thus to no one particular home" (Hall, 1993, p. 362). Our Latinos are thus locked in a bicultural world where antipathy is a natural reaction; Latinos either adopt a culturally ambivalent identity or, as Anzaldúa suggested, reject their rejection and create their own identity by embracing that which makes them outsiders.

These multicultural men and women (Sparrow, 2000) thus experience a constant struggle to be recognized. In the absence of discovering validation in either culture, they seek to position themselves in a group most like themselves; indeed the search for group affiliation is key to their self-identity. Personal identity can only be developed via a three-dimensional recognition diagram: primary relationships (love and friendship), legal relations (rights), and communities of value (solidarity) (Heidegren, 2002). This schema is a "precondition for human self-realization" (Heidegren, 2002, p. 436).

Racial, cultural, and ethnic identities also contribute significantly to one's overall identity, and those characteristics are apt to change with the development at a personal and social level in conjunction with transnational migration, settlement choices, and acculturation (Bhugra & Becker, 2005). In essence, Latino identity is governed by two overall factors: place (settlement choices, voluntary or compulsory) and time (generation). All of the other chief markers of cultural and ethnic identity—including transnational attachments, religion, language preference, media usage, social engagement, home ownership, politics, education, and so forth—are generally dependent on one or both of these factors.

Latinos' socioeconomic status has been seen as having the strongest effect on self-identity. Latinos have been predicted to climb the socioeconomic ladder over time, beginning with the first generation and moving up in later generations. Middle-class Latinos, for example, tend to identify themselves as American or some hyphenated version thereof whereas

Latinos with lower socioeconomic status tend to identify themselves by national origin (Portes & MacLeod, 1996; Rumbaut, 1994).

About 48% of Latino adults describe themselves first by their country of origin; 26% use "Latino" or "Hispanic" first; and 24% call themselves "American" on first reference. Overall, 36% prefer the term *Hispanic*, 21% prefer the term *Latino*, and the rest have no preference (Passel & Taylor, 2009).

The totality of one's identity is not just tied to how one self-identifies but also how others perceive one. Indeed, how Latinos elect to classify themselves racially or ethnically is often at odds with how they are perceived and treated by others (C. E. Rodriguez, 2000). In her research on the extent to which the lives of middle-class third-generation Latinos are both racialized and gendered, Vasquez (2010) found that the racialization continuum extends from being an "insider" to being subject to negative stereotypes. She uses the term *flexible ethnicity* to describe the ability of many third-generation Latinos to navigate two different social worlds, a mainstream U.S. culture and a Latino-oriented community. The effectiveness of their "flexible ethnicity" was limited, however, by how others perceive, treat, and racially mark them, which was largely dependent on their gender. Third-generation Latinas were generally afforded more "flexible ethnicity" than men in that they had the ability to be considered an "insider" in different racial/ethnic communities. Third-generation Latino men were perceived to be less "flexible." Men were racialized as threats to safety while women were racialized through exoticization (J. M. Vasquez, 2010).

Other research sheds light on the social position of the people who possess "plural personalities" (Anzaldúa, 1987) as they navigate their hybrid personality in California, the state with the largest Latino population (Rumbaut, 2008). Vasquez's examination (2010) of the complexities of borderland identities is otherwise rarely addressed in the literature, she points out, due to the widespread assumption that third- and later-generation Latinos are sufficiently acculturated so as not to merit scrutiny. She argues that although many third-generation Latinos exhibit "flexible ethnicity," racialization hampers their efforts to define the terms of their own race/ethnicity (2010). Many third-generation Latinos, aware of their own acculturation, suffer from a kind of cultural bereavement for want of an ancestral root restoration; as such, their Latino identity is fraught with questions of belonging (J. Vasquez, 2005). They are aware of their "neither-nor" position. Third-generation Latinos, for example, are more likely to attend college than their parents (Rumbaut, 2008), and once there, tend to find ethnic validation in college courses that focus on Latino-authored literature (J. Vasquez, 2005).

One 28-year-old third-generation Latino college student put it this way: "My whole lifestyle is pretty American. But I do feel, at times...

when I read history books or see the horrible things that this country has done, I'm like, 'Oh, man, I'm so glad I'm not 100 percent American.' I don't feel like I fit in anywhere. I'm right in between—and it's okay" (J. M. Vasquez, 2010, p. 59). A 25-year-old third-generation Latina college student echoed the sentiment: "I see myself as Mexican, but a little more whitewashed. I'm part of the generation that is a little lost. Some people consider me not Mexican enough but I'm not American enough. So I'm really stuck in the middle" (J. Vasquez, 2005, p. 60).

Acculturation

The acculturation process is a common trope of the immigrant experience, albeit complex and varied across nationalities and genders. Still, researchers have pointed to some predictable patterns. Early assimilation theorists assumed all immigrants will eventually assimilate into the host Anglo-Saxon core (Gordon, 1964). Classic assimilation theory predicts the steady loss of ethnic identification over time, beginning with the immigrant and continuing into later generations. As Golash-Boza points out (2006), "dropping the hyphen could be seen as the ultimate act of assimilation" (p. 30).

Other scholars point to myriad factors that can accelerate or stunt the assimilation process. They can include family structure, cultural and economic obstacles, the perceived race of immigrants, the human and financial capital of the immigrant parents, and the community and family resources available to the immigrants and their children in the United States (Rumbaut & Portes, 2001). This segmented assimilation identifies three paths into U.S. society: *upward assimilation*, which occurs when social and financial capital allow the immigrant to experience a favorable reception in the U.S.; *downward assimilation*, which occurs when immigrants have few resources and are unable to find suitable wages, resulting in their confinement to poor areas; and *selective acculturation* where immigrant parents encourage their children to assimilate while also reinforcing traditional cultural values (Rumbaut & Portes, 2001).

Contemporary scholars focus on four primary benchmarks of assimilation: *socioeconomic status* (defined as educational attainment, occupational specialization, and parity in earnings); *spatial concentration* (dissimilarities in spatial distribution and of suburbanization); *language assimilation* (English language ability and loss of mother tongue); and *intermarriage* (defined by race and only occasionally by ethnicity and generation). The literature shows that today's immigrants are assimilating into American society along each of these dimensions (Waters & Jiménez, 2005).

Most Latino immigrants maintain some kind of connection to their native countries. Those connections can take the form of sending remittances, traveling back, or making telephone calls. But the extent to which they engage in transnational activities varies (Flores, 2009). In line with assimilation theory, those Latino immigrants who have been in the United States for decades as well as those who arrived as children appear less committed to transnational attachments than those who migrated as adults or arrived more recently. The best way to characterize the recent immigrants' "here-there" connection, it has been suggested, is to describe them as "in between" (Waldinger, 2007).

Unlike European American immigrants, there are no signs of "complete" assimilation among Latinos even by the fourth generation, though the loss of Spanish is a predominant marker (Telles & Ortiz, 2008). Indeed, increasing evidence suggests that while Latinos selectively adapt to and create a positive relationship with mainstream American culture, they also remain strongly rooted in a shared ethnic identity (Korzenny & Korzenny, 2005). Studying three generations of adolescents, researchers found that Latino cultural orientation decreases while American orientation increases in linear trends across the first three generations of Latinos. Despite the predictable patterns, adolescent Latinos still retained allegiance to their Latino cultural values. While home and cultural orientation diminished across generations, it did not disappear completely (Perez & Padilla, 2000).

Their racialization by the dominant society may help explain some of that cultural allegiance. Researchers have found that Latinos who have experienced discrimination are less likely to self-identify as "Americans" and more likely to self-identify with pan-ethnic or hyphenated American labels (Golash-Boza, 2006). Golash-Boza contends that this is because experiences of discrimination teach some Latinos that other U.S. citizens do not view them as "un-hyphenated Americans" (p. 29).

Latinos and the Media

Golash-Boza (2006) also asserts that Latino discrimination is driven by how they are portrayed in the mass media. Indeed, the way racial minorities are framed usually influences the way audience members evaluate and consider issues surrounding minorities. These portrayals influence public opinion by activating certain stereotypes already in the minds of the audience, including issues of welfare, crime, and immigration (Larson, 2006).

The National Association of Hispanic Journalists (NAHJ) has studied the portrayal of Latinos on general-market television news. According to the NAHJ's 2005 report, out of an estimated 12,600 stories aired by ABC, CBS, and NBC in 2005, only 105 (.83%) were found to be exclusively about Latinos or Latino-related issues (Montalvo & Torres, 2006). More recently, of 34,452 news stories across media platforms studied, 645 (1.87%) contained substantial references to Latinos, and only 57 (.16%) of those stories focused directly on the lives of Latinos in the United States (Pew Hispanic Center, 2009).

Overall, the literature concludes that Latinos are rarely sought out as expert sources; they are oftentimes seen in terms of stereotypes; and issues of interest and importance to them are not generally covered (Rivas-Rodriguez, 2003). And Latinos have noticed; fully 44% of all Latinos believe that the English-language media contribute to a negative image of the U.S. Latino population (Suro, 2004). Even the best attempts at writing about diversity often founder. Analyzing the narrative strategies of 34 feature stories in the American Society of Newspaper Editors' diversity writing competition, I. Rodriguez (2009) found that news reporters from general-market newspapers tended to focus on an "American dream" narrative that reinforces a model of national integration.

Overall, the literature regarding Latinos in the newsroom has reached several conclusions, including: a shortage of Latino journalists; a lack of knowledge about the Latino community; a reliance on old stereotypes about Latinos; and newsroom values that are at odds with covering Latinos (Rivas-Rodriguez, 2003). Because Latinos are underrepresented and often negatively stereotyped in the news media, concern is frequently expressed that repeated exposure to these distorted portrayals may reflect poorly on Latino adolescents' self-esteem (Rivadeneyra, Ward, & Gordon, 2007). How Latinos see themselves in the media informs their self-perception. Some Latinos, for example, see themselves portrayed as a threat, and younger generations feel a cultural contradiction of citizenship and belonging (Chávez, 2008).

The dearth of Latino sources, Latino issues covered, and the way they are portrayed may be among the reasons for the choices Latinos make when choosing a news source. Many factors, including language preference, identity, and acculturation are among the chief driving forces governing that choice. For example, evidence suggests that the more acculturated Latinos are, the less likely they are to read publications that are in Spanish only (Shoemaker, Reese, & Danielson, 1985). Research has also suggested that ethnic identity may affect Latinos' preference for media consumption. One of the challenges for Latino newspapers is the research that shows that Latinos were, overall, the group least likely to read a newspaper. Surveys show that in 2008, about 29% of Latinos read a daily newspaper, compared to 47% of Whites; Black and Asian readership habits hovered just above 40% (Edmonds, 2009). Latinos value Spanish-language television news the highest of all Spanish-language television programming (DeSipio & Hofer, 1998), and Spanish-language media preference may be predicted by one's degree of ethnic identity (Ruggiero & Yang, 2005). The underlying idea is that media choice is not solely based on the language in which the news is delivered;

acculturated Latinos may be drawn to a bilingual publication because of news content and story placement priorities. They may wish to partake in the cultural experience of perusing the newspaper since the act of reading a Latino newspaper, if it is seen as a "cultural product" (Anderson, 1991, p. 33), is a cultural statement.

For the past 10 years, the Spanish-language press has been the only sector in the newspaper market that was seeing growth. But in 2008, the three biggest Spanish-language daily newspapers all had declines in circulation of varying degrees (Feldherr, 2009). Still, posting only small declines was seen as an achievement as compared to the overall drop in general-market daily print circulation. Some point to a couple of reasons for why the Latino press has fared well: Spanish-language newspapers offer news differently from the general-market media, and many have shown a willingness to adapt to a culturally and linguistically diversifying population (Feldherr, 2009).

But beyond embracing a bilingual format to reach a broader section of the population, the Latino press has had a long history in the United States of serving a dual role (Subervi-Velez, 1986): both integrating its people to the larger society while at the same time preserving their cultural ties. Across history, these ethnic newspapers have been characterized as typically run by people who earn little to no salary (Riggins, 1992) and who understand it as their journalistic responsibility to fill the void left by the mainstream media—namely to write stories about members of their own people that are of specific interest to them. As A. Rodriguez (1997) points out, "U.S. Latino media are audience centered: the distinct and particular interests and needs of the presumptive audience of U.S. Latinos (or Hispanics) motivate their production" (p. 184).

Latino Press

Throughout the history of the United States, the Spanish-language press has largely followed a different journalistic paradigm than its English-language counterparts, one that has embraced an activist and advocacy position. In the 1850s and 1860s, for example, as English-language U.S. newspapers around the country were embracing a more objective form of journalism, Spanish-language newspapers across the Southwest were in the throes of what could be considered their own muckraking era. Most of the Spanish-language newspapers of the time were busy exposing atrocities, demanding public services, and urging readers to fight back against their European American oppressors. Acting as a sort of consciousness for Latinos, the Spanish-language press of the era could be seen as being unconcerned with the journalistic paradigm shift taking place in the English-language press at the time, one of nonpartisanship, detachment, and objectivity (Mindich, 1998).

Despite their variety, Spanish-language newspapers have shared a few overarching characteristics: Gutiérrez (1977) outlined three major roles that Spanish-language newspapers have historically played as: instruments of social control, instruments of social activism, and reflections of Chicano life. Cortés (1987) added three more roles: preservers and transmitters of Chicano history and culture, maintainers and reinforcers of language, and strengtheners of Chicano pride. Other common threads include a resistance to the dominant culture and the regeneration of Latin American cultural forms in the United States (América Rodriguez, 1999). The ethnic press has been characterized as fulfilling other functions, including serving as a message-exchange system and protesting and counterbalancing distortions otherwise seen in the mainstream media (Rubin, 1980).

Instead of using *ethnic* or *immigrant* as an all-inclusive term, some have suggested that—considering the 1848 territorial transfer that left the Mexicans living in the northern territories instant foreigners in their native land (Weber, 1973)—"exile press" would be more appropriate to describe the Latino press (Kanellos, 1998). Latinos were subjected to more than a century of racial oppression through such doctrines as Manifest Destiny. Migration and immigration of Mexicans *to* the United States were directly related to the domination of their homelands *by* the United States: Thus, "their immigration and subsequent cultural perspective on life in the United States have been substantially different from that of the 'classic' immigrant groups" (Kanellos & Martell, 2000, p. 76).

As the belief in Manifest Destiny took hold, many Spanish-language newspapers of the mid- to late-19th century were keenly aware of the threat of being assimilated and losing a piece of their culture, especially their language. The Spanish-speaking people of the Southwest and California, because of their unique position as displaced native-born inhabitants rather than immigrants, created and supported newspapers calling for strong cultural identity rather than Americanization (Kessler, 1984). Indeed, references to the dangers of assimilation are found throughout the history of the Spanish-language press.

Today, while Spanish-language newspapers have largely adopted the objective journalistic principles of their English-language counterparts in order to gain what they perceive to be a measure of credibility, they nevertheless still possess the power to facilitate a Latino political agenda (A. Rodriguez, 2007). A. Rodriguez (1999) has argued that some portions of the partiality of the Spanish-language press to the objectivity model is a "professional and political declaration" of freedom from the Mexican government's authoritarian control of its antecedents (p. 86). The objectivity model of the Spanish-language press is nevertheless constantly being tested. As one journalist for the Los Angeles-based *La Opinión* put it: "Journalists are not supposed to be activists. But at times, some of us walk a very thin line, particularly when we engage in our craft with some measure of civic and social responsibility" (Marrero, 2001, p. 26).

These ideas provide further insight into why some Latinos tend to favor Spanish-language media. The tendency to prefer media products from one's own culture has been described as "cultural proximity" (Ksiazek & Webster, 2007). It has emerged as a central theoretical hypothesis for explaining Latino audience behavior. Language offers a powerful explanation for the media choices of Spanish-speaking Latinos but is far less important for English-speaking Latinos. Such behavior suggests that English-speaking Latinos have a "multicultural fluency," making them receptive to media from different cultures. Conversely, monolingual audiences seem to have a more limited range of media they perceive as culturally proximate (Ksiazek & Webster, 2007).

Spanish-language newspapers have also been found to be far more effective than English-language newspapers as a communication resource that Latinos could use to meet their crucial needs, such as health care (Vargas & Pyssler, 1999). An overwhelming majority of all Latinos (78%) say that Spanish-language media are very important to the economic and political development of the Latino population (Suro, 2004). This view of Spanish media as a valuable ethnic institution is even shared by a majority (61%) of Latinos who get all their news in English (Suro, 2004). In other words, later generation Latinos who never pick up a Spanish-language newspaper nevertheless still think it is a valuable resource to the Latino community as a whole. This suggests that the Spanish-language media play an esteemed role as representative for the Latino population and that, as social and cultural institutions, they have a significant influence in the formation of Latino identities (Suro, 2004).

Bilingual Press

Sampan, a Boston Chinatown community newspaper founded in 1972, is the oldest existing bilingual newspaper in the United States. A print forum that brings together both Chinese-language readers and English-language audiences, *Sampan* offers articles in both languages, which often differ in their content, expressions, style, and approaches. Research has shown that its embrace of bilingualism has enabled it to serve as a bridge, representing its readers, serving as a source of information, negotiating with the mainstream culture, and promoting a better cultural understanding (Da, 2009).

Today, modern Latino publications are addressing the new realities of a growing biracial, bilingual audience. Bilingual newspapers are acknowledging their acculturated brethren—ethnic members who may have lost the language but not an affinity to the culture. In doing so, these newspapers have signaled that they are willing to break the traditional role of their predecessors, though not abandon it altogether. Bilingual newspapers are still committed to preserving Latino cultures by covering issues or emphasizing topics not seen in general-market publications. Eastern Group Publications, founded in 1979, boasts the largest chain of bilingual newspapers in the United States. Focusing on community news in East Los Angeles, the 11 newspapers, which share many stories, have a combined weekly circulation of 104,000, a noteworthy figure since they share the same coverage area of *La Opinión*, the country's largest Spanish-language newspaper with a daily circulation of 116,000 (Alliance for Audited Media, 2012).

Bilingual consumers tend to rely on Spanish-language media for certain things, and English-language media for others (Feldherr, 2009). Two primary streams of cross-cultural transformations are at work: as Latino immigrants, who are most comfortable with Spanish, spend more time in the United States, they tend to become more bicultural, which includes the implementation of more English-language media. At the same time, many native-born predominantly English-speaking Latinos also seek to become more bicultural, perhaps via the emblem embodied in a bilingual newspaper. For some later-generation Latinos, reading a publication that contains a language they don't fully understand transcends mere information consumption; it is an acknowledgment of an alternate reality of the people with whom she or he identifies. In this way, Latino media preference is no longer based solely on language but on content that reflects Latino culture (Feldherr, 2009).

While it is generally true that the longer Latinos are in the United States, the more likely they are to stop using Spanish media, Latinos' preference for both English and Spanish news media crosses the generational spectrum (Suro, 2004). Fully 50% of foreign-born Latinos get all their news in Spanish and English; by the second generation, that number dips to 43%; preference for media in both languages persists among 25% of third- and higher-generation Latinos. By 2050, when the Latino population is expected to be 128 million, or 29% of the U.S. population, the generational ratio of Latinos will be evenly split three ways: 33% first generation, 34% second generation, and 33% third generation (Passel & Cohn, 2008). Suro (2004) notes that the "single most extensive cross-cultural experience for the Hispanic population" (p. 1) could be the tendency for U.S. Latinos to get their news in two languages.

The bilingual newspaper is a unique publication since its content has the potential to cover the journalistic models of both the Latino press and the U.S. general-market press—namely an advocacy position (however strained) and, with notable exceptions, an objectivity one. Readers of the November 4, 2009, *Vida en el Valle*, Fresno's weekly newspaper, found a banner story in Spanish calling for Latinos to enroll in college and also a centerpiece in English about the debut of *López Tonight* with host George López, the first Latino (who often code-switched in his on-air dialogue) to host his own television talk show in English. Under this model of journalism for the Latino press, the dynamic social processes that transform "immigrants" into "ethnics" (A. Rodriguez, 1997, p. 184) takes on a new elements when "ethnics" become "mixed." Rather than being a step in the road toward cultural assimilation, the bilingual newspaper's hybridity becomes a site of transformation, a sort of denunciation of assimilation since bilingual newspapers seek to attract an acculturated demographic while exposing them to the mother tongue. The inclusion of English is not just an acknowledgment of their acculturated brethren but also a gesture of welcome.

The San Diego Union Tribune ran an Associated Press story on July 6, 2010, about the federal government's lawsuit against Arizona's controversial immigration law. The first person quoted is Arizona Gov. Jan Brewer. *La Prensa San Diego*, San Diego's bilingual newspaper, carried a story on the same topic in English, and the first person quoted in the story is an undocumented Latino worker. By writing this kind of counternarrative in English, the newspaper is appealing to a cross-section of Latinos previously assumed to be too assimilated to care; they are perhaps instead too Americanized to read Spanish but Latinized enough to appreciate the frame. This hybrid reader can be seen to be aligned with what *The New York Times Magazine* called the "post-Hispanic" in describing Julián Castro, San Antonio's mayor who, as a third-generation Latino, is not fluent in Spanish but who nevertheless insists on the accented ("HOO-lee-un) pronunciation of his name. These cultural blends see the expression of language in news media as an emblematic expression of their dual-ethnic self. Many Latinos build on the concept that the consumption of Spanish-language media "is an activity of ethnic U.S. Latino expression, a declaration and reproduction of a distinct ethnic identity" (A. Rodriguez, 1997, p. 189). Thus, they might be inclined to reject a Spanish-only *and* English-only newspaper since neither fully and accurately reproduces their distinct dual-ethnic identity. Johnson put it this way in her research of Latina magazines, "Latinos in the United States are forming an identity that is based on Spanish and embellished by Spanish, but not dependent on Spanish" (Johnson, 2000, p. 243). Brought up with English in a Spanish-speaking culture, they are most comfortable on the metaphorical border, and via bilingual media—either from Los Angeles or Miami or Chicago or Phoenix—they affiliate themselves and one another as sharing common group interests. A collective identity is established, "constructed out of a synchronic web of affiliations and sentiments" (Maier, 2007, p. 67) via the institutional construct of the press. Readers consciously or unconsciously align themselves alongside each other, thus constructing a boundary condition, "a cultivated awareness of qualities that separate 'us' from 'them'"

(Maier, 2007, p. 67). The newspaper contributes to this sense of community consciousness in the creation of an "imagined community" among a specific assemblage of fellow readers (Anderson, 1991, p. 62).

From a business-model perspective, the goal for a newspaper of maintaining social group identities for a hybrid Latino identity might seem daunting. Bilingual newspapers, in trying to carve out a new audience, have cast themselves as competitors with not just the Spanish-language press but also the bilingual niche products of many general-market newspapers, such as *Conexión* the weekly bilingual tabloid connected to Hearst's *San Antonio Express-News*. The realistic expectation that the ethnic identity of an immigrant Latino will be vastly different from that of the third- or later-generation Latino is at the heart of what bilingual newspapers must regularly confront when considering story content, length, and placement. The bilingual newspaper, by its very nature must be constantly negotiating what it perceives to be its readers' dual ethnic identity. Newsroom managers must decide which stories appear in English, which appear in Spanish, and which appear in both based on their assumptions of the identity of their presumptive audience, always mindful that Latinos are not a monolithic group. Further, they must be proactive in this process, not trying to merely attract all generations of Latinos with news and entertainment but also trying to retain them.

Spanish-only newspapers that switch to a bilingual format are thus broadcasting several messages: they are willing to reinvent themselves, willing to break from the traditional role of Latino newspapers in order to capture a new audience; they, like many members of the ethnicity they hope to cover, are a hybrid with a bicultural identity; they acknowledge that their new audience of later-generation Latinos will be neither interested in all-English nor all-Spanish news, but both; they also acknowledge the acculturation taking place among the people they serve; and that in doing so, they are not only addressing but rather advocating a hybrid Latino identity. Much the way Chicano musicians use a bifocal approach to enter the mainstream by linking up with an oppositional, dominant culture (Lipsitz, 1987), so too have bilingual newspapers found their primary weapons in their struggle to survive to include bifocality.

Bilingual newspaper readers also broadcast several messages: that their social status and structural assimilation allows them the leisure to read a newspaper in the first place; that the experience of reading the news in a bilingual newspaper acknowledges a parallel reality; and that this alternate reality speaks to their identity and their place within a group; that, as a site of transformation, the consumption of the bilingual newspaper—especially if they do not speak or read Spanish—is to pull back on the reigns of the inevitable march of assimilation, a receding of the "progress" toward Americanization; that their hybridity does not need to be viewed as part of their cultural assimilation but rather their transformation.

Conclusion

Building on landmark studies that demonstrated how the immigrant press serves an assimilating function (Park, 1922) while also encouraging the distinctive identity of the ethnic community (Subervi-Velez, 1986), this chapter highlights the idea of the importance of recognizing the role of a press which is neither "immigrant" nor "ethnic." These media, which have been around in some form for nearly two centuries, deserve a more suitable name than *bilingual* in order to better reflect the reader they hope to serve, a reader who may not actually be bilingual. When reconceptualized, Subervi-Velez's model (1986) holds true; the press still encourages a distinctive identity but of a new community, in this case a "neither/nor" Latino.

These later-generation Latinos exhibit "flexible ethnicity," able to move freely in both cultures, though their racialization by others hampers their efforts to define the terms of their own ethnicity (Vasquez, 2010). The now-outdated assimilation theory predicts that an immigrant will eventually "progress" toward Americanization, reaching a point when his or her assimilation is "complete." But despite the myriad factors that affect their assimilation, research has suggested that there are no signs of "complete" assimilation among Latinos even by the fourth generation (Telles & Ortiz, 2008) and that Latinos, throughout the process of their identity construction, remain rooted in a shared ethnic identity (Korzenny & Korzenny, 2005).

Thus, when Latinos—the majority of whom are bilingual (Hakimzadeh & Cohn, 2007)—turn to news media, they are faced with few choices that support their unique interests. General-market media generally have been shown to carry few Latino stories; they rely on old stereotypes; and general-market journalists, relatively few of whom are Latinos, generally lack a basic knowledge about the Latino community (Rivas-Rodriguez, 2003). By comparison, the Spanish-language press has historically followed a different journalistic model, one that has embraced activism and advocacy (Santana, 2010a) and, like all ethnic press in general, served as "a connecting force" (Johnson, 2000, p. 243). Editors of such newspapers have been dubbed "ambassadors of culture" for the role they have played in arbitrating the linguistic and cultural gap between Anglo and Spanish cultures (Gruesz, 2002, p. 100).

Bilingual newspapers recognize the historical underpinnings of their past while adapting to the changing demographics of their target audience. In doing so, they take on a new identity, one that reflects the hybridity of their readers. The full extent to which that identity has been embraced, however, remains to be seen. Despite the promising potential to carve out a new audience—attracting readers from both English-only and Spanish-only publications—the success of the bilingual newspaper is largely unproven. The most recent figures available indicate that, while growing, the sector remains comparatively small. While this chapter has argued that such growth can be attributed to both demographic factors and the way in which such a newspaper functions as a site for group identity, any attempt to quantify the growth of bilingual newspapers at a time when other traditional papers are in decline requires reliable, consistent data. What follows is an urgent need for future research on Latino bilingual newspapers.

Their promising potential should be ample catalyst for new inquiries to fill the paucity of extant research. An examination of the content and coverage of bilingual media and the ways they act as a cohesive, definable press is crucial to understanding how they compare with both the traditional model of Spanish-language newspapers and the general-market press. Qualitative analysis on the motivations for starting a new bilingual newspaper or moving from an all-Spanish format to a bilingual one, including their marketability, would give a fuller picture of who publishers hope to reach, including, as some have suggested (Santana, 2010b), non-Latinos. In addition to insights from publishers about publishing economics, research should include coverage decisions from editors and framing decisions from reporters. What are the factors deliberated upon in deciding which stories appear in Spanish, which appear in English, and which appear in both? To gauge effectively the effect that bilingual newspapers have on their reading public would move this discussion from beyond the speculative and also require survey research of Latinos across the generational spectrum, especially the highly coveted "youth market," a demographic often invoked in discussions about bilingualism.

Finally, future researchers should examine the extent to which changes in the media landscape are affecting bilingual newspapers as more and more general-market newspapers embrace a new participatory form of online journalism. Implications include the financial feasibility of regional and even national bilingual online newspapers, which, through the global reach of the Internet, can serve the 77% of bilingual Latinos 16 years and older who go online (Livingston, 2010). Such transformations in communication technology have the potential to reinforce bilingual newspapers' role as site for group identity by reaching a bigger audience via individualized media.

References

Alba, R., Logan, J., Lutz, A., & Stults, B. (2002). Only English by the third generation? Loss and preservation of the mother tongue among the grandchildren of contemporary immigrants. *Demography, 39*(3), 467–484.

Alliance for Audited Media. (2012). *Newspapers, research and data*. Retrieved from http://www.auditedmedia.com/free-reports.aspx

Anderson, B. R. O'G. (1991). *Imagined communities: Reflections on the origin and spread of nationalism*. New York: Verso.

Anzaldúa, G. (1987). *Borderlands/La frontera: The new mestiza*. San Francisco, CA: Spinsters/Aunt Lute.

Auer, P. (1998). *Code-switching in conversation: Language, interaction and identity*. New York: Routledge.

Bennett, J. M. (1993). Cultural marginality: Identity issues in intercultural training. In R. M. Paige (Ed.), *Education for the intercultural experience* (pp. 109–135). Yarmouth, ME: Intercultural Press.

Bhugra, D., & Becker, M. (2005). Migration, cultural bereavement and cultural identity. *World Psychiatry, 4*(1), 18–24.

Cashman, H. R. (2008). *Accomplishing identity in bilingual interaction*. Berlin, Germany: Mouton de Gruyter.

Chávez, L. R. (2008). *The Latino threat: Constructing immigrants, citizens, and the nation*. Stanford, CA: Stanford University Press.

Cortés, C. E. (1987). The Mexican-American press. In S. M. Miller (Ed.), *The ethnic press in the United States: A historical analysis and handbook* (pp. 247–260). New York: Greenwood Press.

Da, Z. (2009). Sampan, a bilingual bridge: An exploration of socio-political functions of bilingualism and ethnic press. *Chinese Journal of Communication, 2*(2), 227–246.

DeSipio, L., & Hofer, J. (1998). *Talking back to television: Latinos discuss how television portrays them and the quality of programming options*. Claremont, CA: TRPI.

Edmonds, R. (2009). *(Newspaper) audience*. Pew Project for excellence in journalism. The state of the news media 2009. Retrieved from http://www.stateofthemedia.org/2009/index.htm

Feldherr, E. (2009). *Growth in bilingual media*. Pew project for excellence in journalism. The state of the news media 2009. Retrieved from http://www.stateofthemedia.org/2009/index.htm

Flores, J. (2009). *The diaspora strikes back: Caribeño tales of learning and turning*. New York: Routledge.

García Canclini, N. (1995). *Hybrid cultures: Strategies for entering and leaving modernity* (C. L. Chiappari & S. L. López, Trans.). Minneapolis, MN: University of Minnesota Press.

Golash-Boza, T. (2006). Dropping the hyphen? Becoming Latino(a)-American through racialized assimilation. *Social Forces, 85*(1), 1.

Gordon, M. M. (1964). *Assimilation in American life: The role of race, religion, and national origins*. New York: Oxford University Press.

Gruesz, K. S. (2002). *Ambassadors of culture: The transamerican origins of Latino writing*. Princeton, NJ: Princeton University Press.

Gumperz, J. J. (1982). *Discourse strategies*. New York: Cambridge University Press.

Gutiérrez, F. (1977). Spanish-language media in America: Background, resources, history. *Journalism History, 4*(2), 34–68.

Hakimzadeh, S., & Cohn, D. (2007, November 29). *English usage among Hispanics in the United States*. Pew Hispanic Center. Retrieved from http://pewhispanic.org/reports/report.php?ReportID=82

Hall, S. (1993). Culture, community, nation. *Cultural Studies, 7*(3), 349–363.

Heidegren, C. G. (2002). Anthropology, social theory, and politics: Axel Honneth's theory of recognition. *Inquiry, 45*, 433–446.

Johnson, M. A. (2000). How ethnic are U.S. ethnic media: The case of Latina magazines. *Mass Communication & Society, 3*(2/3), 229–248.

Kanellos, N. (1998). A historical perspective on the development of an ethnic minority consciousness in the Spanish-language press of the southwest. *Ethnic Studies Review, 21*, 27–50.

Kanellos, N., & Martell, H. (2000). *Hispanic periodicals in the United States, origins to 1960: A brief history and comprehensive bibliography.* Houston, TX: Arte Publico Press.

Keefe, S. E., & Padilla, A. M. (1987). *Chicano ethnicity.* Albuquerque, NM: University of New Mexico Press.

Kessler, L. (1984). *The dissident press: Alternative journalism in American history.* Beverly Hills, CA: Sage.

Korzenny, F., & Korzenny, B. A. (2005). *Hispanic marketing: A cultural perspective.* Burlington, MA: Elsevier Butterworth-Heinemann.

Ksiazek, T., & Webster, J. (2007, November). *The role of cultural proximity in audience behavior: Media choices among Hispanic Americans.* Paper presented at the National Communication Association 93rd Annual Convention, Chicago, IL.

Larson, S. G. (2006). *Media and minorities: The politics of race in news and entertainment.* Lanham, MD: Rowman & Littlefield.

Linton, A. (2004). A critical mass model of bilingualism among U.S.-born Hispanics. *Social Forces, 83*(1), 279–314.

Lipsitz, G. (1987). Cruising around the historical Bloc: Postmodernism and popular music in East Los Angeles. *Cultural Critique, 5*, 157–177.

Livingston, G. (2010, July 28). *The Latino digital divide: The native born versus the foreign born.* Pew Hispanic Center. Retrieved from http://pewhispanic.org/reports/report.php?ReportID=123

Lutz, A. (2006). Spanish maintenance among English-speaking Latino youth: The role of individual and social characteristics. *Social Forces, 84*(3), 1417–1433.

Maier, C. S. (2007). "Being there": Place, territory, and identity. In S. Benhabib, I. Shapiro, & D. Petranovic (Eds.), *Identities, affiliations, and allegiances* (pp. 67–84). Cambridge, MA: Cambridge University Press.

Marrero, P. (2001). A journalist struggles with objectivity vs. obligation. *Nieman Reports, 55*(2), 26.

Mindich, D. T. Z. (1998). *Just the facts: How "objectivity" came to define American journalism.* New York: New York University Press.

Montalvo, D., & Torres, J. (2006, Oct.). *Network brownout report: The portrayal of Latinos and Latino issues on network television news, 2005.* National Association of Hispanic Journalists. Retrieved from http://www.nahj.org/2006/09/2006-network-brownout-report/

Morales, E. (2002). *Living in Spanglish: The search for Latino identity in America*. New York: St. Martin's Press.

Park, R. E. (1922). *The immigrant press and its control*. New York: Harper & Bros.

Passel, J. S., & Cohn, D. V. (2008, February 11). *U.S. population projections: 2005–2050*. Pew Hispanic Center. Retrieved from http://pewhispanic.org/reports/report.php?ReportID=85

Passel, J. S., & Taylor, P. (2009, May 28). *Who's Hispanic?* Pew Hispanic Center. Retrieved from http://pewhispanic.org/reports/report.php?ReportID=111

Perez, W., & Padilla, A. M. (2000). Cultural orientation across three generations of Hispanic adolescents. *Hispanic Journal of Behavioral Sciences, 22*(3), 390–398.

Pew Hispanic Center. (2009, December 7). Hispanics in the news: An event-driven narrative. Retrieved from http://www.journalism.org/analysis_report/hispanics_news

Portes, A., & MacLeod, D. (1996). What shall I call myself? Hispanic identity formation in the second generation. *Ethnic and racial studies, 19*(3), 523.

Riggins, S. H. (1992). *Ethnic minority media: An international perspective*. Newbury Park, CA: Sage.

Rivadeneyra, R., Ward, L. M., & Gordon, M. (2007). Distorted reflections: Media exposure and Latino adolescents' conceptions of self. *Media Psychology, 9*(2), 261–290.

Rivas-Rodriguez, M. (2003). *Brown eyes on the web: Unique perspectives of an alternative U.S. Latino online newspaper*. New York: Routledge.

Rodriguez, A. (1997). Cultural agendas: The case of Latino-oriented U.S. media. In M. E. McCombs, D. L. Shaw, & D. H. Weaver (Eds.), *Communication and democracy: Exploring the intellectual frontiers in agenda-setting theory* (pp. 183–194). Mahwah, NJ: Erlbaum.

Rodriguez, A. (1999). *Making Latino news: Race, language, class*. Thousand Oaks, CA: Sage.

Rodriguez, A. (2007, March). *The role of the Spanish language news media in Chicago Latino political and grassroots organizing*. Paper presented at the Western Political Science Association, Las Vegas, NV.

Rodriguez, C. E. (2000). *Changing race: Latinos, the census, and the history of ethnicity in the United States*. New York: New York University Press.

Rodriguez, I. (2009). "Diversity writing" and the liberal discourse on multiculturalism in mainstream newspapers. *Howard Journal of Communications, 20*(2), 167–188.

Rubin, B. (1980). *Small voices and great trumpets: Minorities and the media*. New York: Praeger.

Ruggiero, T. E., & Yang, K. C. C. (2005, May). *Latino identity, linguistic acculturation, and Spanish language media preference*. Paper presented at the International Communication Association, New York.

Rumbaut, R. G. (1994). The crucible within: Ethnic identity, self-esteem, and segmented assimilation among children of immigrants. *International Migration Review, 28*(4), 748–794.

Rumbaut, R. G. (2008). The coming of the second generation: Immigration and ethnic mobility in southern California. *The Annals of the American Academy of Political and Social Science, 620*(1), 196–236.

Rumbaut, R. G., & Portes, A. (2001). *Ethnicities: Children of immigrants in America.* Berkeley, CA: University of California Press; New York: Russell Sage Foundation.

Santana, A. D. (2010a, March). *Speaking for La Raza: A historiography of the U.S. Spanish-language press: 1808–1958.* Paper presented at the Association for Education in Journalism and Mass Communication, Midwinter Conference, Norman, OK.

Santana, A. D. (2010b, Aug.). *Experiment and adapt: The mantra of survival for one startup Latino newspaper.* Paper presented at the Association for Education in Journalism and Mass Communication, Denver, CO.

Shoemaker, P. J., Reese, S. D., & Danielson, W. A. (1985). Spanish-language print media use as an indicator of acculturation. *Journalism Quarterly, 62*(4), 734–762.

Sparrow, L. M. (2000). Beyond multicultural man: Complexities of identity. *International Journal of Intercultural Relations, 24,* 173–202.

Subervi-Velez, F. A. (1986). The mass media and ethnic assimilation and pluralism: A review and research proposal with special focus on Hispanics. *Communication Research: An International Quarterly, 13*(1), 71–96.

Suro, R. (2004, April 19). *Changing channels and crisscrossing cultures.* Pew Hispanic Center. Retrieved from http://pewhispanic.org/reports/report.php?ReportID=27

Telles, E. E., & Ortiz, V. (2008). *Generations of exclusion: Mexican Americans, assimilation, and race.* New York: Russell Sage Foundation.

Vargas, L. C., & Pyssler, B. J. D. (1999). U.S. Latino newspapers as health communication resources: A content analysis. *Howard Journal of Communications, 10*(3), 189–205.

Vasquez, J. (2005). Ethnic identity and Chicano literature: How ethnicity affects reading and reading affects ethnic consciousness. *Ethnic and Racial Studies, 28*(5), 903–924.

Vasquez, J. M. (2010). Blurred borders for some but not "others": Racialization, "flexible ethnicity," gender, and third-generation Mexican American identity. *Sociological Perspectives, 53*(1), 45–72.

Waldinger, R. (2007, October 25). *Between here and there: How attached are Latino immigrants to their native country.* Pew Hispanic Center. Retrieved from http://pewhispanic.org/reports/report.php?ReportID=80

Waters, M. C., & Jiménez, T. R. (2005). Assessing immigration assimilation: New empirical and theoretical challenges. *Annual Review of Sociology, 31*(1), 105–125.

Weber, D. J. (1973). *Foreigners in their native land: Historical roots of the Mexican Americans.* Albuquerque, NM: University of New Mexico Press.

Chapter 6

Prehistory of a Stereotype
Mass Media Othering of Mexicans in the Era of Manifest Destiny

Michael J. Fuhlhage[1]

Scholars such as Charles Ramírez Berg and Arthur G. Pettit have traced media stereotypes about Latinos to the turn of the twentieth century,[2] but a look at what Whites in the American Southwest wrote and said about Mexicans in the nineteenth-century mass media reveals a much earlier origin for stereotyping. By the time the first kinetoscopes brought moving pictures to the masses in the 1890s, negative representations of Mexicans had been congealing into conventional wisdom for a half-century. In the conclusion of his groundbreaking *Latino Images in Film*, Berg challenged readers, asking, "How can we utilize our experience to lessen the stereotyping of Others who remain at society's fringes?" To do this, we must understand the conditions under which stereotypes brewed in the nation's media. Contemporary media scholars have examined the representation of Latinos as well as subgroups defined by national heritage and geographic origin, such as Mexicans, Puerto Ricans, and Cubans. Stereotypes about Latinos developed over decades from seeds of Anglo-Iberian hostility before the American Revolution that sprouted in a climate of increased U.S.–Mexican interaction that followed Mexico's overthrow of Spain in 1821.

Initially, Americans regarded the people of Spain's colonies in present-day Mexico and the Southwest as brave, decent, hardworking, devout people whose nation could grow into a thriving democracy alongside the United States.[3] They were perceived as different, but not necessarily inferior. Elites of both nationalities found common ground, forming partnerships to preserve wealthy Mexicans' power, help American capitalists prosper, and dampen poor Mexicans' resistance to American colonization. In this context, Mexican elites were conferred honorary Whiteness and referred to as "Spanish" gentlemen and ladies, while the poor were labeled "Mexican" peons, cutthroats, and harlots. The subjugation of lower-class Mexicans promoted the American mission of empire by dampening political resistance and maintaining an inexpensive and compliant labor force for mining, ranching, and agriculture.

A variety of scholars have contributed to our knowledge of the development of the Mexican image in the American mind. Berg has provided groundwork in the field of cinema. Literary scholars, most notably Pettit and Shelley Streeby, have examined the ways popular literature set in the Southwest reflected the zeitgeist of the United States in the era of Manifest Destiny.[4] Social historians such as Robert W. Johannsen have elaborated on the U.S.–Mexico War's place in the American imagination in the late 1840s.[5] Yet we still lack an understanding of the *processes* that first brought Mexicans into the American consciousness—the work of newspaper and magazine journalists who reported the details of Mexican life and culture to readers in the East. This chapter combines cultural studies with communication history to illuminate the ways American correspondents' identities informed and were implicated in the construction of Mexican identity in the English-language press.

This chapter proposes that U.S. correspondents on the trail of Anglo-American empire-building in the midnineteenth century reflected the norms of Easterners who coveted the West's resources—many under the control of Mexicans who nominally became U.S. citizens after the U.S.–Mexico War of 1846–1848. The process and product of marginalizing Mexicans mirrored Western European representations of the Orient. As Edward Said detailed in *Orientalism,* European experts on the Middle East portrayed the native society, economy, government, religion, and sexuality of their colonies as inefficient, backward, despotic, irrational, evil, morally degenerate—in short, inferior in every way to the image of European progress and values.[6] In North America, journalists played a significant role in this process of Othering, regardless of whether they were catalysts of change or merely mirrors of their communities. Correspondents for the penny papers of the 1840s and '50s provided not just the facts, but detailed interpretation of the context of events in California and the Southwest. While just-the-facts reporters were anonymous contributors to the newspaper, the editor was a persona in his own right. So was the correspondent, a personage whose status and creative freedom were loftier than those of newsworkers who were paid by the column inch and received no byline.[7]

Media and Latinos in the Nineteenth-Century Press: An Overview

Given that stereotypes of Hispanics did not always exist as they are today, it is instructive to consider research on nineteenth-century representations of Latinos in the Borderlands, most of whom were Mexicans. Raymund A. Paredes systematically analyzed nineteenth-century American writers' descriptions of the Mexican character. Writers in his 1977 study included travelers, trappers, government agents, soldiers, and journalists. Paredes noted that American writers characterized Mexicans in Texas and New Mexico as treacherous, cruel, cowardly, and indolent and strongly influenced American attitudes about Mexicans at the exact historical moment when the United States sought justification to invade Mexico.[8] California Mexicans were described as indolent, fond of dance parties, and governed by Catholic priests. Anglos felt compelled to justify destruction of Mexican life in the West by portraying Mexicans as "villainous and decadent."[9] Paredes focused on the writers' messages as products but not on how the messages were produced. David J. Langum proposed that the similarity between European and American judgments about Mexicans was due to the influence of the Industrial Revolution.[10] David J. Weber responded, "Langum has based his argument on a faulty assumption. The commonality of viewpoints regarding the supposed laziness of Californios does not necessarily indicate that Protestantism, racism, and a commonality of the broad impulses of 'religion, racism, and nationalism,' which took the particular American form of Protestantism, Anglo-Saxon racism, and Manifest Destiny, influenced Europeans as well as Americans."[11] Hispanophobia festered for centuries in Northern Europe, driven by the "Black Legend," the belief that the Spanish were uniquely depraved, cruel, treacherous, proud, fanatical, cowardly, corrupt, decadent, authoritarian, and indolent.[12] Weber suggested the Spanish missions' mismanagement of land and labor might have diminished individual initiative and industry. But he wrote that this did not explain the image of indolence. Nor did it explain why some writers accused all Mexicans of laziness while others contradicted themselves by writing that Californios were indolent but also lived well.[13]

Contemporary mainstream journalists' tendency to represent Latinos in stereotypical ways grew out of ideologies that were reified in early film and late nineteenth-century literature. But the mechanisms, culture, and historical conditions that influenced the ways those ideologies developed are little studied. This chapter proposes that the intellectual raw material for stereotypes about Latinos grew out of prejudice against Mexicans. Journalistic accounts of Mexican life and culture provided the basis for prejudice to develop in the English-language press. Correspondents learned about Mexicans through experience, government sources, and the thriving print culture of their age. Journalists were also influenced by the culture in which they lived. Their gaze was influenced by whether they were Northern or Southern, aristocrat or yeoman, Quaker or Congregationalist, Whig or Democrat. Each of these facets of social identity and culture refracted the image of the Mexicans whom Anglo correspondents perceived. These facets of identity-produced stereotypical portrayals of Mexicans were fashioned from the 1840s onward. Ethnohistorians Russell J. Barber and Frances F. Berdan have proposed a "reality-mediation model" for interpreting evidence of cultural interaction in the past. Their approach emphasizes that sources must be interpreted for authorial presence and intent and examined to see whether those sources reflect external reality.[14] But the method of analysis presented in this chapter, cultural contrapuntal reading, goes a step further by elaborating in depth on the influence of social identity on authors' creation of texts about the Mexican Other as well as authorial presence and intent. This framework is new in the study of journalism and communication history.

Theory and Methodology: Cultural Contrapuntal Reading

To understand how a journalist's social identity influences his or her portrayal of members of an out-group, three elements must be examined. The first is contemporaneous American media portrayals of Mexican life and culture in the form of articles, editorials, and books. The second is evidence about the mentality of the writer. This may be revealed in letters to family and trusted colleagues, diaries that contain the writer's private thoughts about Mexicans that may not be evident in his or her publicly available writing, and library records that reveal the books he or she read about Mexico. The third is an understanding of the dominant cultural influences of the writer's time and place, including the creed and disciplines of the writer's religious denomination, an examination of the teachings of his or her spiritual and political leaders, and so on. By comparing written artifacts and epistemologies, one may discern whether the writer's mental map of Mexicans before he or she reached the Borderlands matched the cultural territory encountered. This method, cultural contrapuntal reading, draws from the content assessment work of Marion Marzolf and Said's method of contrapuntal reading. Said's interpretation of Orientalism resulted in a picture of a monolithic, dominant European culture. Applied to the representation of Mexico in the American press, research would logically result in a picture of a monolithic, dominant American culture, a racialized hegemonic power called Anglos matched up with a racialized, dominated group called Latinos. But just as not all Latinos, let alone all Mexicans, are alike, neither are all Anglos alike. American identity is assumed to be monolithic in studies of American Othering, too. One example is John M. Coward's excellent examination of the construction of Native American identity in the nineteenth-century press, *The Newspaper Indian*. But that study concentrates mainly on the representation of the Other and not the identity of the journalists who observed Indians.[15] The present chapter is concerned with not just representation of the Other, but the interaction between the author's social identity and the author's perception and representation of the Other.

Marzolf proposed that journalism historians draw from American studies and employ "content assessment" to understand journalism in cultural context. This method relies on "reading, sifting, weighing, comparing and analyzing the evidence in order to tell the story."[16] Marzolf detailed three prongs in this approach: assessment of content for the ways media convey values, attitudes, and social norms and embrace or exclude groups; examination of the backgrounds and social systems of the producers of media content; and the significance of journalism's presentation of information, values, and opinions. This significance includes impact on society, including whether people acted on what they saw in media.[17] John Nerone argued that a cultural history of communication is not possible unless it takes into account Robert Darnton's concept of the communication circuit; that is, taking into account the process of production, the content of messages, and the ways audiences used those messages.[18] So in examining the ways that culture shaped correspondents' perceptions and representations of Mexicans, it is crucial to remember that writers are also readers and that mass media encompass more than periodicals. Writers' work resonated far beyond their initial audiences, flowing from newspaper and magazine presses into lyceum lectures and best-selling books. So the correspondents' interaction with texts and other writers also must be considered.

"Social identity lies in difference, and difference is asserted against that which is closest, which represents the greatest threat," Pierre Bourdieu wrote.[19] Dominant groups distinguish themselves as superior to other groups in order to continue those groups' subordination. Said's *Orientalism* illustrates this. Said found that Europeans ascribed the attributes of backwardness, degeneracy, and inferiority to the people of the Orient. Europeans adapted Darwinism to their race thinking in order to find "scientific" validity in their understanding that humanity consisted of two classes: advanced, ruling races and backward, subservient ones.[20] Just as the end of Orientalism was the accumulation, consolidation, and extension of European imperial power, an American form of Orientalism served to do the same things for Anglos in the Southwest. Orientalism responded more to the culture that produced it than to the culture it portrayed.[21] Its American equivalent in the Mexican Borderlands—perhaps best termed *Mexicanism* since it represents an Eastern American view of the Western lands in the Manifest Destiny-fueled zone of colonization and empire-building— also responded more to the cultures that produced its representations of the Mexican. The elements of Othering portrayal lurk in "style, figures of speech, setting, narrative devices, historical and social circumstances, not the correctness of the representation nor its fidelity to some great original."[22] To identify these elements, one must examine two factors: *strategic location* and *strategic formation*. Strategic location was defined by Said as "a way of describing the author's position in a text with regard to the Oriental material." Strategic formation is "a way of analyzing the relationship between texts and the way in which groups of texts, types of texts, even textual genres, acquire mass density, and referential power among themselves and thereafter in the culture at large."[23] Said made his means of detecting the Orientalists' Othering more explicit in *Culture and Imperialism*, in which he called his method "contrapuntal reading." While this combination provides potent means for understanding Othering in a general sense, it represents colonizers as if they were identical and relies largely on discursive products to understand discursive production.

But it would be a mistake to assume all Americans were alike; to do so would be to essentialize the American just as Said essentialized the European even as he argued that the European essentialized the Oriental. Anthropologists and ethnohistorians have questioned this tendency and written about the need to deconstruct Othering representations.[24] To understand the center of an empire, one cannot assume that every powerful group within the empire is the same. Therefore, to fully understand representations of the Mexican Other requires a finer-grained analysis that takes into account the pluralism within the center of the empire. Adding this dimension, examining Othering messages in the context of the cultural cleavages of the colonizing power with an understanding that such powers consist of a variety of cultures and an understanding that each individual's identity consists of multiple social identities that shift according to context, yields a new method heretofore unused in the study of mass communication history: cultural contrapuntal reading.

The complexity of mass communication production poses the greatest limitation on the method proposed here. As journalistic enterprises matured, they added layers of personnel to the editorial process. Each person in the communication chain introduces a facet in the prism of message production. Cultural contrapuntal reading would be extraordinarily difficult if used to examine messages produced by fully matured mainstream media. A typical contemporary news reporter's articles, for example, are subject to revision by a half-dozen or more editors, each of whose social identities must be taken into account to reliably establish a connection between the message producers' backgrounds and the content of the message. It would be less difficult to apply the method to early-stage new media writers, such as self-editing bloggers and editors-in-chief who have the power to protect their writing from interference from assigning editors, copy editors, news editors, managing editors, or producers. Thus, cultural contrapuntal reading is best employed in the study of the early stages of communication forms before their complexity increases. The remainder of this chapter applies cultural contrapuntal reading to mass media in just such a time: the mid-nineteenth century, the heyday of the partisan press at the cusp of the professionalization of journalism. The press represented a variety of viewpoints—every county seat in the country typically had one newspaper for each political party, the Whigs were strongest in the North and Democrats strongest in the South, the North was more industrial and the South more agrarian. Media outlets consistently promoted the aims of the party with which they were allied and hired partisans whose social identities were aligned with those of their bosses.

Mexico through Northern and Southern Eyes

Because New Englanders and Southerners had distinctly different worldviews, they portrayed the Borderlands from Texas to California in different ways. The Mexican image in the New England mind was refracted through the prism of Puritan values and Whig, Free Soil, and Republican ideologies. Southern correspondents saw Mexicans through the lens of White Anglo-Saxonism, martial tradition, and the taboo of miscegenation that economic dependence on slavery promoted. Manifest Destiny, the belief that Americans had a divine calling to spread democracy, influenced correspondents' representation of Mexicans regardless of their sectional origin.

This chapter focuses on correspondents from two generational cohorts of journalists who roved the West on behalf of Eastern publications. The first consists of travel writers who journeyed to California, Texas, and New Mexico when the region was virtually unknown from the 1820s to the 1840s. The latter cohort consists of correspondents who covered the Borderlands from the 1850s to 1870. Their roles in the print culture can be understood through two lines of inquiry. The content of their newspaper articles, magazine serializations, books, and lectures were read closely to understand how they represented Mexican people and culture in the Borderlands from Texas to California. Their private and personal writings in letters, journals, and other manuscripts were scrutinized to ascertain what and who influenced their ways of seeing Mexicans.

Northern Observers in the Borderlands

Richard Henry Dana Jr. played a major role in drawing American attention to California.[25] What distinguished Dana's view from the Southern outlook on Mexicans was the absence of judgment based on race. Instead, he focused on environmental and social impacts: bad government, hence poor education and lawlessness; forgiving climate, hence laziness resulting from a lack of want; corrupt religion, hence faithlessness. Dana's depiction of the Californio character was an inverse of the Puritanical ideal. A line from an 1835 letter to his brother and sister-in-law, sent from San Diego, distilled the view of Mexicans that he scattered across the pages of *Two Years Before the Mast*: "This is a beautiful country, a perfect climate, and every natural advantage; but the people are lazy, ignorant, irreligious, priest ridden, lawless, vicious, and not more than half civilized."[26] In his book, he declared, "In the hands of an enterprising people, what a country this might be!"[27] But his antipathy for California was plain to see. He cautioned that balmy weather and abundant food could wither American initiative to the level of the Californios.[28] Dana described the Californios who bought New England products as "an idle, thriftless people, and can make nothing for themselves."[29]

What most jarred Dana about California Catholicism was that Spain required any American or Englishman who intended to live there to become Catholic.[30] This was particularly bothersome because of the depth of his exposure to Protestant thought and his careful consideration of his own faith. Though raised a Congregationalist, he was confirmed in the Episcopal Church on his return to Boston.[31] Catholicism, to Dana, was associated with not just idleness, but moral bankruptcy and intemperance. When the Spanish took control of California from the Indians, they put the Indians under control of the priesthood, who avoided labor by enslaving their charges.[32]

William Watts Hart Davis provided the first extended look at New Mexico with his book *El Gringo, Or, New Mexico and Her People*.[33] Experience in Mexico, knowledge of Spanish, prolonged contact with New Mexicans of all walks of life, official positions that gave him access to the old Spanish archives, editorship of a Santa Fe newspaper, and a curious mind prepared him to observe and write the work. Its subtitle alluded to the dual purpose of introducing people to the alien landscape and the Mexicans who lived there. Davis had multiple objectives when he wrote *El Gringo*. His deal with Harper & Brothers gave him royalties of 10 percent beyond the first thousand copies sold.[34] Davis intended his treatise on New Mexicans to serve as a demonstration of his frontier expertise, understanding of the people's deficiencies, and the rightness of his thinking about how to guide the territory's development. He was frantic that his father and other political allies put it in the hands of President James Buchanan in the hope that it showed he was the right man to be appointed governor of the territory.[35]

El Gringo has been categorized as travel literature.[36] But the book was something more: It was a political prospectus. Davis arrived in Santa Fe in 1853. In his book and newspaper dispatches, he portrayed the territory as a land of opportunity and a chance to spread American democracy. But he revealed in private that he thought New Mexico was a desolate backwater whose main virtues were that he might extract mineral wealth or political capital from it.[37] Frequent references to the passage of Mexican customs as "superior" American ways took root make it clear that while sympathetic to Mexicans, Davis believed they must embrace American ways. In contrast to the modernity that Anglos represented, Davis made Mexicans seem more exotic by describing the poor not as farmers and laborers, but as "the peasantry," a term that cast them as vassals in a feudal, primitive land.[38] Again and again, he cited examples of Mexican agriculture and technology that were inferior to that of the United States. Mexicans had "made no effort to improve" their methods and machinery for plowing, animal husbandry, timber harvesting, carpentry, transportation, and manufacturing since the Spanish conquest.[39] Davis found corruption throughout the culture of New Mexico.[40] Although he admired Catholics' faith and works, Davis condemned the church, blaming Mexicans' character faults on their Catholic leaders.[41]

Davis traced the vices and deficiencies he saw in Mexicans to their Spanish lineage, which he said gave them the "imaginative temperament and fiery impulses" of the Moors, the "politeness and spirit of revenge," and the "cruelty, bigotry, and superstition" of the Spanish.[42] In the New World, intermarriage with the Indians meant that "The Spaniard, Moor, and the aboriginal were united in one and made a new race, the Mexicans."[43] Davis made explicit his belief in White superiority: "The intermixture between the peasantry and the native tribes of Indians is yet carried on, and there is no present hope of the people *improving in color* [emphasis added]."[44] Racial mixing amalgamated the national character of Moors and Spaniards with those of the Indians, whom Davis said possessed "cunning and deceit."[45] Despite these differences, Davis concluded Mexicans had their virtues. He declared that Mexicans could be modernized.[46]

Dana and Davis's work influenced and inspired subsequent generations of Anglos who wrote about the Borderlands. The most prominent ones of the next generation wrote for the *New York Tribune*. Bayard Taylor and Albert Deane Richardson disagreed on whether Mexicans annexed by the United States could be elevated to the point that they could join in self-governance. Taylor believed Californios could learn American ways as long as they were of European and not mixed descent. Richardson made no such distinctions. In his eyes, all were demoralized, backward, half-breed, and priest-ridden, and the only way to make New Mexico worthy of statehood was to bring more Americans into it. What best explains this divergence of opinion is the difference in their faiths, their life experiences, and the conditions under which they first came to encounter Mexicans.

Taylor, a Quaker eight years older than Richardson, was sent off by Horace Greeley to cover the California Gold Rush of 1849 at the age of 24. By that time, he had already tramped around Europe and become fluent in German, French, and Spanish. Taylor's relative degree of tolerance for Mexicans came from the tolerance taught by Quaker belief and the cosmopolitanism he developed during his European adventures. Both men enjoyed similar educational opportunities, attending school and feeding their minds with lyceum lectures and library books. But Richardson had been exposed to people and ideas different from those that influenced Taylor: the anti-Catholicism of Congregationalism and the anti-Mexicanism of Texas. Richardson was less cosmopolitan, having come of age on the ever-expanding American frontier. Before he rode off to Texas at age 26 in 1859, he served as adjutant general of the Kansas Territorial Militia. Congregationalist in upbringing, he covered the battle over popular sovereignty in Kansas and was friends with Henry Ward Beecher, the minister who armed Free State settlers for their guerrilla war against border ruffians who tried to bring slaves into the territory from Missouri.

Quakers followed a tradition of tolerance, egalitarianism, and respect for fundamental human rights.[47] Pennsylvania's pluralism sprouted amid this tradition of tolerance.[48] The religious tenets of the Society of Friends permeated life in Taylor's hometown of Kennett Square, the most fundamental of them that each human being had a personal and unique connection with God and had a responsibility to discover for him- or herself the nature of that person's relationship with the Creator.[49] The meeting house fed Taylor's soul, but the library and the lecture hall fed his mind. Taylor owned 670 books by theologians, scientists, phrenologists, philosophers, explorers, poets, and men of letters.[50] Among them were John Ross Browne's report *Mineral Resources of the West*, *History of the Jesuits*, *The Bible in Spain*, and *Types of Mankind*, by George Gliddon and Josiah Nott. These books and lectures prepared Taylor for a life of wandering the nations of the world and writing about them. He parlayed a series of letters he sent the *New York Tribune* about his travels in Europe into a job as an editor at the paper in 1848.

Horace Greeley sent Taylor to California to cover the Gold Rush and the state constitutional convention. Like Davis before him, Taylor believed that the Mexicans were inferior, uneducable, and resigned to the advance of the Americans. "They acknowledged our greater power and intelligence as a nation, without jealousy, and with an anticipation rather than a fear, that our rule will one day be extended over them," he wrote in March 1850.[51] Taylor told readers that Americans tolerated

Mexicans as long as they made a profit off Mexican labor.[52] "They work steadily and faithfully," Taylor wrote, "and are considered honest, if well watched."[53] Taylor could not ignore the class differences he found in the newborn state of California. He pitied Hispanic laborers but admired wealthy Californios, to whom he offered a measure of respect because they were socially refined and educated.[54] Any superiority that Taylor found in Californios he attributed to their Spanish heritage. By his account, the Catholic fathers who established the California missions were wise and thrifty benefactors of the Indian population they enslaved.[55] Those who were not European were not civilized, according to this logic.

While gentility shaped Taylor's view of Californios, his fellow *Tribune* correspondent Albert Deane Richardson's depictions of Mexicans in Texas and New Mexico were influenced by his Congregationalist faith and the things he heard from Southerners on the trail. Born October 6, 1833, in Franklin, Massachusetts, Richardson grew up in an area where his family had farmed for nearly 200 years.[56] The family was not well off, but his parents valued education and saw to it that he got one. Christian faith, Congregationalist teachings about the perils of slavery and Catholicism, and participation in print culture shaped Richardson's way of seeing the world. Richardson was brought up a strict Orthodox Congregationalist in a stronghold of Calvinist belief.[57] Congregationalism emphasized the notion that the governed choose who will govern them.[58] Catholics were painted by the most dominant Congregationalist thinkers as a horde beholden to the papal throne of Rome and not to American democracy.[59] The Congregationalist structure of governance and tenets of worship were thus at odds with those of the Catholic Church. Richardson believed Mexicans subscribed to a tainted faith. The church, with its hierarchical system of governance, was bad enough in the eyes of a Puritan. But Mexican Catholics' blend of folk belief with Catholic ritual appalled Richardson beyond belief. Richardson approved of Hispanos' piety and devotion to Christ.[60] But he had only scorn for the Holy Week ceremonies of the *Penitentes,* a lay Catholic secret society that came to be vilified and driven underground by rumor and prejudice sown by Anglos in the late nineteenth and early twentieth centuries. Richardson saw their rites as a throwback to the pagan days that predated the Conquest.[61]

Allusions to Anglo-Saxon superiority were frequent in Richardson's journalism. He cast Anglo settlers as heroic figures pushing the edges of civilization into the frontier, while Indians were portrayed as generally an obstacle but still redeemable through the civilizing influence of "the Anglo Saxon race." Mexicans, in Richardson's eyes, were beyond redemption not only because of their mixed blood but also because of their Iberian Catholic heritage. Their legacy, he believed, had to be washed away by a tide of Americans bearing democratic government and progress.[62]

Richardson owed his second-hand knowledge of Mexicans to the Southerners he encountered on the trail into the Southwest. Richardson made numerous references to things he had overheard from Texans who still had an ax to grind with Mexicans. His first extended contact with Mexicans only came in the fall of 1859, when he journeyed to El Paso and then north through New Mexico to Colorado. He only found more Anglo animosity toward Mexican men when he crossed the Rio Grande into New Mexico. A pioneer told him Mexican women were the kindest in the world. When Richardson asked if the men were treacherous the stranger responded, "*I never had any trouble with them; but stranger, I always watch a Greaser, and at night I never let one travel behind me. It's the safe way, if you don't want to get stabbed or shot in the back.*"[63]

Richardson explained that peon labor was cheaper than slave labor in West Texas and was common because "the Mexican, with the thriftlessness of his race, is always ready to contract a debt, and afterwards to bind himself in writing to work it out.... This arrangement once made, he is wholly dependent upon his master, constantly keeping up or increasing the indebtedness, by purchasing necessities of him at exorbitant prices."[64] Peonism was particularly problematic to Richardson because as a Republican he believed paid labor was superior to both Southern slavery, which he saw as little different from the Mexican peon labor system. The normal cycle of the Northern man's working life was to hire himself out early for wages, save enough of the proceeds to establish a business, and then hire other men who would then perpetuate the cycle. This cycle, the logic went, would create a prosperous free society in which all men were capable of being their own masters, and to live forever dependent on wages was to be little more than a slave.[65]

Taylor and Richardson built on the notions of the Mexican Other that had been built by Dana and Davis. Dana planted the seeds for the idea of Mexican indolence that flowered into Taylor's belief that Mexicans stood in the way of vigorous Anglo-Saxons who came to extend democracy into the Golden State. Davis, along with Southerner Josiah Gregg, pushed the idea of Mexican backwardness, Catholic wickedness, and priestly corruption that Richardson detailed in his *Boston Journal* articles and *Beyond the Mississippi: From the Great River to the Great Ocean,* which sold 100,000 copies. What made Richardson and Taylor different from these earlier writers was their exposure to Southern ideas, the emergence of class as a category of difference between Yankees and Mexicans, and a decade and a half in which anti-Mexican prejudices bloomed in the American mind. Both Taylor's and Richardson's writing asserted Mexican inferiority. And the way Texan hatred of Mexicans primed Richardson to do the same also explains why he saw Mexicans so differently from Taylor. But the prejudice of Albert Deane Richardson and Bayard Taylor could scarcely compare with that of their Southern counterparts of the same period.

Southern Views of Mexicans

By virtue of timing and circulation, Josiah Gregg and George Wilkins Kendall's best-selling books and newspaper correspondence constituted the foundation for most Americans' understanding of Mexican life and culture in the 1840s. These adventurer-correspondents made sense of the Southwest in light of their political and religious beliefs, the things they learned in their formative years, and what they read in adulthood about Mexico by adventurers, traders, and diplomats such as Zebulon Pike and John Poinsett. Gregg, a Santa Fe trader from Missouri, based his *Commerce of the Prairies* on four round-trip trading expeditions between the United States and Mexico. Kendall, the roving editor-correspondent of the *New Orleans Picayune*, based his *Narrative of the Texan Santa Fe Expedition* on a series of stories that he published in the *Picayune* about his journey with a band of armed Texans who tried to annex eastern New Mexico in 1841. Both books were published in 1844.

Issues of race, labor, class, and politics are evident throughout their books, just as they were in other Southern works on Mexico. William H. Prescott's *History of the Conquest of Mexico* and Frances Calderón de la Barca's *Life in Mexico* were popular among U.S. soldiers, who used them to learn what to expect in Mexico.[66] The U.S. Navy ordered one copy of the Prescott book for each ship's library during the war.[67] These books influenced Josiah Gregg, one of the first Southern correspondents to ply the Santa Fe Trail, whose *Commerce of the Prairies* served as a guidebook for American troops in Mexico.[68]

To do things the Mexican way was to do things the inferior way, Gregg implied. *Commerce of the Prairies* tells the story of Gregg's experience of Northern Mexico chronologically. A close reading of the book reveals how his attitudes about Mexico developed over time. Initially, Gregg displayed a sense of wonder and discovery, characterizing Mexicans at first in terms of their difference from Americans. As his experience of their culture deepened, recognition of difference turned to declarations of Mexican inferiority. "In architecture, the people do not seem to have arrived at any great perfection, but rather to have conformed themselves to the clumsy style which prevailed among the aborigines, than to waste their time in studying modern masonry and the use of lime," he wrote of Santa Fe's adobe buildings, in a typical comparison to American ways.[69]

Mexican Catholic rituals drew Gregg's fiercest criticism. "In the variety and grossness of popular superstitions, Northern Mexico can probably compete with any civilized country in the world," he wrote.

"Others may have their extravagant traditions, their fanatical prejudices, their priestly impostures, but here the popular creed seems to be the embodiment of as much that is fantastic and improbable in idolatrous worship, as it is possible to clothe in the garb of a religious faith."[70] Gregg scoffed at Mexican reverence for the Virgin of Guadalupe, Mexico's patron saint, and he ridiculed the faithful's practice of praying to saints for intercession in times of sickness and distress.[71] Gregg called the practice of kneeling and genuflecting in the presence of the Communion Host "abject idolatry"[72] and thought Catholic Masses were so filled with ritual that they left no room for real faith, declaring that "these religious exercises, however, partake but seldom of the character of true devotion."[73]

Viewed through the lens of his Quaker upbringing, it is apparent why Gregg reserved his greatest criticism for Mexican Catholics' use of rituals and sacramental objects. Quakers in the early nineteenth century believed that Christ's power of salvation should not be tied too closely to physical or "outward" forms, such as the Bible, ordained ministry, liturgies, or sacraments.[74] Divine light was revealed to every person, not just religious ministers.[75] It was only natural that Gregg viewed priests with suspicion. To him, the padres were drawing people away from the light. Gregg detested the Catholic hierarchy for its alignment with the Mexican government, which he saw as a parasite that thrived by overtaxing American traders like himself, and for mirroring the government's corruption by overcharging the faithful for weddings and other sacraments.[76]

In Mexico, George Wilkins Kendall found a land of cruel men, kind women, and corrupt priests. The stories he wrote about his imprisonment in Mexico were widely circulated after he published them in the *Picayune*. He offered "thanks to the many journals throughout the country which have copied these sketches and kindly commended them to notice."[77] Eleven editions of his *Personal Narrative of the Texan Santa Fe Expedition* were published through 1851.[78] In the New Mexico that Kendall saw, Mexican women continually threw themselves at the manly Anglo-Saxons, bringing them gifts of food, water, and liquor.[79] In contrast, Mexican men were "brutal, piratical-visaged" scoundrels.[80] Kendall considered Mexican men to be "a semi-civilized enemy—cruel, relentless, and treacherous—who looked upon us as heretics and the common enemies of their religion and race."[81]

Before he experienced Mexico, Kendall wrote that the country's Catholic priests preached with "intolerant zeal" against Protestants. But by the time he returned to New Orleans, Kendall found that "the Protestant stranger will seldom find other than a hospitality the most munificent within the gates of the padres," whom he termed to be "men of liberal and enlightened views, well-educated and entertaining companions, tolerant and charitable."[82] Nonetheless, Kendall wrote that the church held dangerous political power over the "ignorant and superstitious population."[83] To maintain this power, Kendall claimed they kept their flocks from learning about other faiths.[84] Kendall was Presbyterian, a denomination that generally supported the war.[85] But anti-Catholicism does not entirely explain his vicious portrayal of Mexicans. Kendall married a French Catholic, though he kept the marriage secret.[86] Suspicion of hybridity could explain Kendall's disdain for Mexicans and their religion. He described Mexican worship as "the strange mingling of Indian customs with the rites of the established Catholic Church" that occurred because early Spanish missionaries "were never able to entirely eradicate the superstitious ceremonies of the original inhabitants, but by allowing them to ingraft [sic] some of their own rites upon Catholicism, they partially brought them over to their faith."[87]

The following generation of Southern writers in the Borderlands extended the association Kendall made between non-Whiteness and inferiority, but class identity complicated the picture and forced Anglos to accept some non-Whites by conferring honorary Whiteness on wealthy and well-connected Mexicans, whom the Anglo newcomers referred to as "Spaniards," to capitalize on their wealth and political power. George Douglas Brewerton sailed to California with the First New York Volunteers during the U.S.-Mexico War, a post secured for him by his father, the superintendent of the U.S. Military Academy. Brewerton accompanied frontiersman Kit Carson from California to New Mexico in the late 1840s, an adventure that resulted in a series of articles for *Harper's New Monthly Magazine* and a subsequent book, *Overland with Kit Carson: A Narrative of the Old Spanish Trail in '48*. The *Harper's* articles provided a detailed picture of class relations and popularized the classification of wealthy Californios as "Spanish" and laboring Californios as "Mexican." His Baptist faith and nativism gave him a vicious view of the Roman Catholic Church. Hatred of church and distrust of common Mexicans were the most prominent aspects of his work.

Born in 1827, Brewerton spent the first nine years of his life in Charleston, South Carolina, where his father worked with the U.S. Army Corps of Engineers to prepare Fort Sumter's defenses.[88] Brewerton's identification with the Baptist denomination, nativism, and proslavery politics shed light on his portrayals of Mexican Catholics. At the age of 30, he became a minister in the Baptist church.[89] Among the tenets of Baptist faith in Brewerton's time were belief in a regenerate church membership by baptism; the priesthood of every believer; the primary power and authority of the local congregation and no provision for bishops or other central authority, such as a pope; and that church and state must be separate to protect religious freedom.[90] None of his sermons remain, but one copy of a nativist publication he edited survives. The July 1854 edition of *Young America, or, The Child of the Order* provides the clearest available clues to his political beliefs in the years when Mexicans most drew his attention. *Young America* billed itself as a "Native American Anti-Jesuit Monthly Magazine" and presented this statement of values: "It advocates American principles and American men, and is opposed to foreign and Roman Catholic influence under any form."[91]

Judgments about the proper place of women, people of color, and the working class are scattered throughout Brewerton's articles for *Harper's*. Vices were trivial if the right people indulged in them. For example, when upper-class Californians of Spanish descent smoked and sauntered, Brewerton hinted that he saw a certain charm in it. But by the time he reached New Mexico and saw the same activities in the village of Taos, he was appalled. "Its inhabitants exhibit all the indolent, lounging characteristics of the lower order of Mexicans, the utter want both of moral and mental culture making itself everywhere apparent," he wrote.[92] When he spoke of Mexican women who had intermarried with respectable American men, Brewerton conferred honorary Whiteness on the women by referring to them as "Spanish" and not Mexican. Brewerton called Kit Carson's spouse "his amiable wife, a Spanish lady, and a relative, I believe, of some former Governor of New Mexico."[93] The emphasis of Hispanic women's European heritage was typical. Texas historian Neil Foley noted, "When Anglo Texans married Mexicans, they often juggled the nomenclature to whiten their spouses by calling them Spanish Americans or simply Spanish. Mexican men, however, were only rarely accorded status as white persons, such as when they were owners of large ranches with marriageable daughters."[94]

In contrast, Brewerton pronounced, lower-class Mexican men were dishonest, thieving, exaggerating, ugly, and difficult to keep in line.[95] Brewerton did admire Mexicans' abilities as horsemen and mule drivers, but he warned readers that they were untrustworthy.[96] The boundaries of the binary, white–black racial system of the South constrained Brewerton's view of Mexicans. In his eyes, Mexican peons were similar to Negro slaves but more difficult to keep in line. That is, he believed they were fine laborers who required constant supervision. They drove mules, cooked, and looked after affairs in camp well but would steal if given the opportunity.[97] Brewerton equated Mexican servants with slaves, "for they are little better."[98]

If Brewerton's vision of American conquest was military and ecclesiastical, then John Ross Browne's vision of conquest was largely commercial. Browne seemingly modeled his life after those of Richard Henry Dana Jr. and Bayard Taylor. Life as an adventure correspondent provided him with the opportunity for material gain—first by mining his own experiences and refining them into stories for *Harper's New Monthly Magazine,* then into books and lectures. The knowledge of prospecting that he gained along the way led him into lucrative work documenting mining practices and holdings for Eastern capitalists. Over time, entanglements with industry led him from recognition of the Mexican as Other to vicious denunciations of mixed-race Mexicans. Like Brewerton's works, Browne's articles and books privileged wealthy and fair-skinned Mexicans.

Browne alternated between journalism and government service throughout his career.[99] But his service to the mining industry proved the most lucrative. Browne's credibility flowed from his expertise as well as the perception that he was an unbiased and neutral observer. However, as Browne's career progressed, he became entangled in the industry to the point that its interests became his. Between his articles, industrial reports, and services as a land broker, mineral industries in Western lands wrested from Mexicans made Browne a wealthy man.[100]

In his articles for *Harper's,* Browne vacillated between embracing Latinos as a necessary labor force and rejecting them as an obstacle to Anglo-Saxon progress. By Browne's logic, neither the Spanish nor the Mexicans did enough to relieve the earth of its valuable commodities and must therefore get out of the way of American progress or take part as its disciples. Browne concluded that Californios made better miners than any other nationality, including Americans. Mexicans and Californians were model workers. They were unsurpassed as prospectors because they were "willing to run any amount of risk," and he concluded, "Under a rigid supervision they are accounted among the most useful men in the employ of the Company."[101] Browne claimed the Mexicans who would not work deserved to be displaced. Arguing that "avarice is a sign of civilization," Browne claimed California Mexicans were primitive because they did "many things from hatred and malice, but seldom do any thing for money."[102] By this logic, greed was a virtue because it brought about capitalistic progress. Avarice, after all, was the key to prying land from the natives. "The only practical way of acquiring real estate in Lower California is to settle among the people and lend them money at usurious interest, secured by mortgage," Browne recommended. "They are never able to pay it back; and their property falls a sacrifice to their indolence or want of forethought."[103] Browne believed that poverty, laziness, and lack of vigor resulted from intermarriage. "When these mixed races are compelled to work they sicken and die," Browne pronounced, commenting that they barely farmed enough to sustain themselves.[104]

Miscegenation was also implicated in Browne's depiction of Mexican women. Those who behaved like Anglos met his approval, but those who looked too Indian or African were singled out as malevolent and carnal.[105] The women came in two categories: beautiful young Spanish señoritas and half-breed criminals, all fine dancers with a taste for flashy jewelry and brightly colored dresses "in which flowers, lace, and glittering tinsel combined to set off their dusky charms."[106] The roles Browne assigned Mexican men and women reinforced an emerging image of males subordinated to employers and females relegated to the status of objects of sexual desire. On payday, Browne, wrote, "The Spaniards are flush, and like sailors, spend their money on the fair sex with a prodigal hand. Señoritas from San Jose know where their charms can be appreciated."[107]

These correspondents' writing constituted a two-pronged approach to eliminate Mexican competition from lands newly occupied by Americans. The first wave challenged the Catholic Church, largely on grounds that it corrupted government and established a precedent of hybridization with Indian religion that challenged American homogeneity. The mission that American portrayal of Mexican life and culture fulfilled discounted Mexican religion as superstition that could be ignored and established American ways as superior. The second wave of correspondents asserted Mexican inferiority to justify the American takeover of land and resources in the Southwest. They rationalized American men's intermarriage with the wealthy daughters of Californios and Tejanos and the establishment of alliances between American and Mexican elites by delineating which Mexicans were acceptable (the wealthy, or "Spaniards") and which were inferior (the poor, or "Mexicans"). From these beginnings thus grew the stereotype that the Mexican is only worthy of laboring for capitalists.

Conclusion

Reports about Mexicans represented an empire-building gaze upon an Occidental Other that constrained conceptions of Mexicans' abilities, the value of their culture and products, their suitability for intermarriage, their worthiness to continue occupying their land, the appropriateness of their religious and political institutions as compared to American institutions, and their potential for advancement in a modernizing world. The consequences were not merely symbolic or psychological. Hispanics in the Borderlands suffered consequences that were material and legal. New Mexicans' right of statehood, guaranteed at the end of the U.S.–Mexico War under the Treaty of Guadalupe Hidalgo, was denied fifteen times from 1850 to 1910. Albert Deane Richardson, as if in answer to debates over the territory's fitness for statehood, wrote:

> (They) are entitled, under the treaty, to exercise the elective franchise. They are almost universally ignorant and priest-governed, and have no just idea of the duties and responsibilities of citizenship.

An old Kentuckian—a pro slavery man—who has long resided here, expresses the opinion that the negroes of his native State are better qualified to become voters than they, and it seems to be a correct one.[108]

Harper's correspondent and government agent John Ross Browne concurred. Writing about the mixed-race people of New Mexico and Arizona in 1869, he commented, "I ... do not believe a good citizen of sound morals ever resulted from such an abominable mixture."[109] The *New York Times* picked up on such sentiments in 1872, emphasizing the mixed-race ancestry of New Mexico's political leaders, calling Santa Fe "a decayed, decaying town, hostile to progress," and declaring in an editorial that statehood should be denied because "the population of New-Mexico ... is too mixed, and on the whole too inferior, in habits and intelligence, to be entrusted with the dignity and powers of Statehood."[110]

Media accounts filtered up to Congress, where they were employed as evidence that New Mexico was unfit for admission. Quoting George F. Ruxton's book *Adventures in Mexico and the Rocky Mountains,* Congressman Truman Smith of Connecticut told the House of Representatives that its people were "liars by nature ... treacherous and faithless to their friends, cowardly and cringing to their enemies; cruel as all cowards are, they unite savage ferocity with their want of animal courage.... Is it at all surprising that the Mexican people should have found themselves incapable of self-government?"[111]

It was no coincidence that suspicion of Catholicism played so dominant a role in the correspondents' work. American culture grew out of British culture, which had viewed the Roman Catholic Church as an enemy for centuries. Papal involvement in politics was anathema, and Americans inherited disdain for the church. Because of the church's wealth and political power in Mexico, it was seen as an obstacle in the way of American progress. Because American Protestant denominations emphasized local autonomy and disdained ritual as a spiritual contaminant, American correspondents, who were largely Protestant, had grown up believing Catholicism was a threat to man's closeness to God. Thus, the Roman Catholic Church constituted both a political and religious threat to cherished American institutions. That Catholicism was practiced by people who were phenotypically different from Anglo-Saxon Americans provided cultural fuel for the fires of anti-Catholic animosity.

By 1876, the nativism and anti-Catholicism of Brewerton and Richardson were taken as gospel in Congress. A House report recommending denial of New Mexico statehood claimed the population was ignorant and undereducated, tainted by miscegenation, lazy, and beholden to the pope.[112] Perhaps the most damning points employed in the report came from *Beyond the Mississippi,* in which Richardson wrote that the territory was beyond redemption as a state:

> Twice or thrice New Mexico has suffered from the frontier epidemic of constitution-making, but until new gold discoveries bring in thousands of immigrants to develop its wide and varied mineral resources, and revolutionize its industries and social life, it will not and should not be admitted to the Union as a sovereign state.[113]

The report also quoted *El Gringo* and *Commerce of the Prairies,* both decades out of date. These examples illustrate the power of othering in the media. Media constructions of Mexican identity, thus, provided Anglos with a rationale for denying Mexican Americans' rights as citizens, which cleared Anglo commercial interests to seize Mexican property in the "new" territories. The symbolic capital of media portrayals was transformed into political capital through introduction in Congress, then transformed into economic capital through legislative means.

Cultural contrapuntal reading may be used to examine the construction of other marginalized groups' social identities in the media and the political, legal, and economic consequences described herein. The case of Mormon marginalization in Utah and Indian marginalization in other Western states in the late nineteenth and early twentieth centuries pose ripe possibilities for future research. The place to begin is this question: How did the Othering reflect the identity of the author? Which of a single author's multiple identities (ideological, sectional, religious, class, occupational) serves to refract his or her perception of the Other? In asking these questions, we must consider that Othering is not unidirectional. After all, the colonized as well as the colonizers possessed the power of the printing press. Kirsten Silva Gruesz, Tom Reilly, and Nicholas Kanellos have detailed the Spanish-language press's resistance to the English-language press's construction of Mexican identity.[114] But this has not been examined using the methods of cultural contrapuntal reading. Future research could show how the social identity of the editors of the Spanish-language press represented Anglos and judged their writing about Mexicans.

Religious difference's strong role in Anglo assertions that Mexicans were unworthy of their possessions, incapable of self-governance and self-control, and dangerous to American institutions bears a strong resemblance to anti-Muslim rhetoric during the current "war on terror." Fox News, to take one example, has constructed Islam as an exotic, different, and dangerous institution bent on undermining American governance and substituting religious for secular law.[115] Fred Vultee, informed by Said's Orientalism, found that Fox News created discourse with its audience that helped establish a foundation for polarized commentary and legitimized support for a limitless war against the unknown.[116] While these studies have relied on close reading of media messages in the context of the corporation that produced them, a cultural contrapuntal reading could examine the construction of these images in the context of both corporate culture and the social identity of Fox News commentators—personages in their own right with considerable control over the messages they create—or in the context of the social identity of executives who oversee the creation of Fox's media messages. Cultural contrapuntal reading has potential for a variety of uses in the study of social identity and communication, both historical and contemporary, as long as one keeps in mind the complexity of communication processes, isolates each influence on the creation of messages, and selects appropriate research subjects.

Notes

1. The author wishes to thank Frank E. Fee Jr., Lucila Vargas, and Barbara Friedman for their help with this chapter. The chapter was funded with the assistance of the Triad Foundation and the Margaret Blanchard Dissertation Support Fund.
2. Charles Ramírez Berg, *Latino Images in Film: Stereotypes, Subversion, and Resistance* (Austin: University of Texas Press, 2002); Arthur G. Pettit, *Images of the Mexican-American in Fiction and Film* (College Station: Texas A&M University Press, 1980); Gary D. Keller, "The First Decades: Film Types," *Bilingual Review* 18, no. 2/3 (May–December 1993): 70–111; Charles Ramírez Berg, "Colonialism and Movies in Southern California, 1910–1934," *Aztlán* (Spring 2003): 75–96.
3. These characterizations are found in the most extensive descriptions of early Anglo encounters with the people of New Spain and Mexico: Zebulon Pike, *The Expeditions of Zebulon Montgomery Pike, to Headwaters of the Mississippi River, Through Louisiana Territory, and in New Spain, During the Years 1805–67*, ed. Elliott Coues (New York: F. P. Harper, 1895) and James Ohio Pattie, *The Personal Narrative of James O. Pattie of Kentucky* (Cincinnati: John H. Wood, 1831).
4. Arthur Pettit, *Images of the Mexican-American in Fiction and Film*; Shelley Streeby, *American Sensations: Class, Empire, and the Production of Popular Culture* (Berkeley: University of California Press, 2002).
5. Robert W. Johannsen, *To the Halls of the Montezumas: The Mexican War in the American Imagination* (New York: Oxford University Press, 1985).
6. Edward Said, *Orientalism: Western Conceptions of the Orient* (New York: Vintage Books, 1978).
7. John Nerone and Kevin G. Barnhurst, "US Newspaper Types, the Newsroom, and the Division of Labor, 1750–2000," *Journalism Studies* 4, no. 4 (2003): 444.
8. Raymund A. Paredes, "The Mexican Image in American Travel Literature, 1831–1869," *New Mexico Historical Review* (January 1977): 12.
9. Ibid., 25.

10. David J. Langum, "Californios and the Image of Indolence," *The Western Historical Quarterly* 9, no. 2 (April 1978): 181–96.
11. David J. Weber, "Here Rests Juan Espinosa: Toward a Clearer Look at the Image of the 'Indolent' Californios," *The Western Historical Quarterly* 10, no. 1 (January 1979): 61–69.
12. Ibid., 62.
13. Ibid., 68.
14. Russell J. Barber and Frances F. Berdan, *The Emperor's Mirror: Understanding Culture through Primary Sources* (Tucson: University of Arizona Press, 1998).
15. John M. Coward, *The Newspaper Indian: Native American Identity in the Press, 1820–90* (Chicago: University of Illinois Press, 1999).
16. Marion Marzolf, "American Studies—Ideas for Communication Historians?" *Journalism History* 5, no. 1 (Spring 1978): 16.
17. Ibid, 15.
18. John Nerone, "The Future of Communication History," *Critical Studies in Media Communication* 23, no. 3 (August 2006): 258.
19. Pierre Bourdieu, *Distinction: A Social Critique of the Judgement of Taste* (London: Routledge and Kegan, 1984), 479.
20. Edward Said, "Latent and Manifest Orientalism," in *Race and Racialization: Essential Readings*, eds. Tania Das Gupta, Carle E. James, Roger C. A. Maaka, Grace-Edward Galabuzi, and Chris Andersen (Toronto: Canadian Scholars' Press, 2007), 45–47.
21. Ibid., 22.
22. Ibid., 21.
23. Ibid., 20.
24. Barber and Berdan, *The Emperor's Mirror*, 44–45.
25. Franklin Walker, *A Literary History of Southern California: The American Period* (Berkeley: University of California Press, 1950), 25; Justin Smith, *The War with Mexico*. 2 vols. (New York: Macmillan, 1919; reprinted Gloucester, MA: Peter Smith, 1963), 1:323; Robert Glass Cleland, *A History of California: The American Period* (New York: Macmillan, 1922), 96; Tony Stanley Cook, "Richard Henry Dana and American Immigration to California, 1840–1850," *Southern California Quarterly* 68, no. 2 (1968): 97–118.
26. Richard Henry Dana Jr. to Charlotte Dana and Edward Trowbridge Dana, March 20, 1835. Dana Family Papers, Massachusetts Historical Society.
27. Richard Henry Dana Jr., *Two Years Before the Mast. A Personal Narrative of Life at Sea*, ed. John Haskell Kemble, 2 vols. (Los Angeles: The Ward Ritchie Press, 1964), 1:172.
28. Ibid., 1:172.
29. Ibid., 1:82.
30. Dana, 1:87.
31. Charles Francis Adams, *Richard Henry Dana, A Biography* (Boston: Houghton Mifflin, 1891), 21.
32. Dana, *Two Years Before the Mast*, 1:171.
33. Mabel Major, *Southwest Heritage—A Literary History with Bibliography* (Albuquerque: University of New Mexico Press, 1948), 70. According to Major, *El Gringo* and a later Davis work, *The Spanish Conquest of New Mexico* (1869) "made accessible in a clear, pleasant style, the materials of the early Spanish narratives."
34. Contract between W. W. H. Davis and Harper & Brothers for the writing

and publication of *El Gringo; or, New Mexico and Her People*, August 5, 1856. Davis Papers, Beinecke Library, Yale University.
35. W. W. H. Davis to John Davis, February 27, 1857; February 28, 1857; March 26, 1857; March 28, 1857; April 29, 1857.
36. Raymund A. Paredes, "The Mexican Image in American Travel Literature, 1831–1869," *New Mexico Historical Review* 52, no. 1 (1977): 5–13.
37. W. W. H. Davis to Elizabeth Davis, March 26, 1855. Davis Papers, Yale.
83. W. W. H. Davis, *El Gringo: Or, New Mexico and Her People* (Boston: Harper Bros., 1856), 179.
39. Ibid., 173.
40. Ibid., 184.
41. Ibid., 217.
42. Ibid.
43. Ibid., 216.
44. Ibid.
45. Ibid., 217.
46. Ibid., 388.
47. Melvin B. Endy Jr., "The Society of Friends," in *Encyclopedia of the American Religious Experience*, eds. Charles H. Lippy and Peter W. Williams (New York: Charles Scribner's Sons, 1988), 612.
48. Ibid., 611.
49. Richard Croom Beatty, *Bayard Taylor: Laureate of the Gilded Age* (Norman: University of Oklahoma Press, 1936), 16.
50. *Executor's Sale Catalogue of the Library of the Late Mr. Bayard Taylor* (New York: Bangs, 1879).
51. Bayard Taylor, "Mexico. Bayard Taylor's Letters No. XXXVIII," *New-York Tribune*, March 7, 1850, 5.
52. Bayard Taylor, "Bayard Taylor's Letters No. XVIII," *New-York Tribune*, November 15, 1849, 1.
53. Ibid.
54. Bayard Taylor, "Bayard Taylor's Letters No. XXVIII," *New-York Tribune*, December 28, 1849, 1.
55. Bayard Taylor, "Bayard Taylor's Letters No. XXIX. Missions of California," *New-York Tribune*, January 7, 1850, 1.
56. Junius Browne, "Albert D. Richardson," *Phrenological Journal and Packard's Monthly* (July 1870), 45.
57. "Albert D. Richardson. Obituary," *New-York Tribune*, December 2, 1869.
58. Mary K. Cayton, "Congregationalism," in *Encyclopedia of the American Religious Experience*, eds. Charles H. Lippy and Peter W. Williams (New York: Charles Scribner's Sons, 1988), 357–73.
59. "Lyman Beecher," in *Encyclopedia of American Religious History Vol. 1*, eds. Edward L. Queen II, Stephen R. Prothero, and Gardiner H. Shattuck Jr. (New York: Infobase, 2009), 299.
60. "Hispano" is a term commonly used in northern New Mexico and southern Colorado to refer to Latinos who descended from the region's original Spanish colonists. This ethnic subgroup and its roots are discussed by Richard L. Nostrand, *The Hispano Homeland* (Norman: University of Oklahoma Press, 1992).
61. Albert Deane Richardson, *Beyond the Mississippi: From the Great River to the Great Ocean* (Hartford, CT: American Publishing Co., 1869), 263.
62. Richardson, *Beyond the Mississippi*, 268.
63. Ibid., 247.

64. Richardson, "Jottings from the Far West—No. XXII," *Boston Daily Journal*, November 26, 1859, 4.
65. Eric Foner, *Free Soil, Free Labor, Free Men: The Ideology of the Republican Party Before the Civil War* (New York: Oxford University Press, 1970), 15–17.
66. Robert W. Johannsen, *To the Halls of the Montezumas* (New York: Oxford University Press, 1985), 150.
67. Ibid.
68. Ibid.
69. Gregg, *Commerce of the Prairies*, 144.
70. Ibid., 173.
71. Ibid., 173–77.
72. Ibid., 178.
73. Ibid., 179.
74. Melvin B. Endy Jr., "The Society of Friends," in *Encyclopedia of the American Religious Experience*, eds. Charles H. Lippy and Peter W. Williams (New York: Charles Scribner's Sons, 1988), 596.
75. Ibid., 604.
76. Gregg, *Commerce of the Prairies*, 182–83.
77. Fayette Copeland, *Kendall of the Picayune* (Norman: University of Oklahoma Press, 1943), 113.
78. *National Union Catalog Pre-1956 Imprints, Vol. 293* (London: Mansell, 1973), 127–28.
79. George Wilkins Kendall, *Personal Narrative of the Texan Santa Fé Expedition* (New York: Harper & Brothers, 1850), 288–89.
80. Ibid., 293.
81. Ibid., 292.
82. Ibid., 341.
83. Ibid., 343.
84. Ibid., 343–44.
85. Ted C. Hinckley, "American Anti-Catholicism during the Mexican War," *Pacific Historical Review* 31, no. 2 (May 1962): 132.
86. Georgina Kendall Fellowes to Fayette Copeland, July 11, 1941. Fayette Copeland Papers, Western Historical Collection, University of Oklahoma.
87. Kendall, *Narrative of the Texan Santa Fe Expedition* II, 182.
88. Jourdan Moore Houston and Alan Fraser Houston, "California on His Mind: The Easel and Pen of Pioneer George Douglas Brewerton," *California History* 81, no. 1 (2002): 5.
89. "Soldier Turned Preacher," *New York Observer and Chronicle*, April 28, 1859, 131.
90. Eldon G. Ernst, "The Baptists," *Encyclopedia of American Religious Experience: Studies of Traditions and Movements* eds. Charles H. Lippy and Peter W. Williams (New York: Charles Scribner's Sons, 1988), 555.
91. "The Infant of the Monthlies," advertisement, *New York Daily Times*, June 15, 1854, 5.
92. Brewerton, "Incidents of Travel in New Mexico," *Harper's New Monthly Magazine* (April 1854): 577.
93. Brewerton, "A Ride with Kit Carson through the Great American Desert and the Rocky Mountains," *Harper's New Monthly Magazine* (August 1853): 334.
94. Neil Foley, *The White Scourge: Mexicans, Blacks, and Poor Whites in Texas Cotton Culture* (Berkeley: University of California Press, 1997), 24.

95. Brewerton, "Ride with Kit Carson," 309.
96. Ibid.
97. Brewerton, "Ride with Kit Carson," 309–310.
98. Ibid., 313.
99. Lina Ferguson Browne, *J. Ross Browne: His Letters, Journals, and Writings* (Albuquerque: University of New Mexico Press, 1969), xvi.
100. John Ross Browne to Lucy Browne, September 27, 1864, and May 28, 1865, and John Ross Browne to R. B. Harris, March 13, 1865, in *J. Ross Browne*, 312.
101. J. Ross Browne, "Down in the Cinnabar Mines," *Harper's New Monthly Magazine* (October 1865): 553.
102. J. Ross Browne, "Explorations in Lower California, 1st Paper," *Harper's New Monthly Magazine* (October 1868): 582.
103. Ibid., 583.
104. J. Ross Browne, "A Tour Through Arizona, Fourth Paper," *Harper's New Monthly Magazine* (January 1865): 140.
105. J. Ross Browne, "A Dangerous Journey. In Two Parts—Part 2," *Harper's New Monthly Magazine* (June 1862).
106. Ibid, 16.
107. Ibid.
108. Albert Deane Richardson, "Jottings from the Far West—No. XXIV," *Boston Daily Journal* (Nov. 23, 1859), 6.
109. John Ross Browne, *Resources of the Pacific Slope* (San Francisco: H. H. Bancroft & Co., 1869), 141.
110. "Our Next Two States," p. 1, and "Minor Topics," p. 5, *New York Times*, January 27, 1871.
111. "Speech of Mr. Truman Smith of Connecticut, Delivered in the House of Representatives of the United States, March 2, 1848." (Washington, DC: J. & G. S. Gideon, Printers, 1848), 29.
112. U.S. Congress, House, Committee on the Territories, *New Mexico*, 44th Cong., 1st sess., House rep. 503, 1875, 6.
113. Ibid.
114. Kirsten Silva Gruesz, *Ambassadors of Culture: The Transamerican Origins of Latino Writing* (Princeton, NJ: Princeton University Press, 2002); Tom Reilly, "A Spanish-Language Voice of Dissent in Antebellum New Orleans," *Louisiana History* 23, no. 4 (1982): 325–29; Nicolás Kanellos with Helvetia Martell, *Hispanic Periodicals in the United States, Origins to 1960: A Brief History and Comprehensive Bibliography* (Houston, TX: Arte Público, 2000).
115. Fred Vultee, "'Fatwa on the Bunny': News Language and the Creation of Meaning about the Middle East," *Journal of Communication Inquiry* 30, no. 4 (2006): 319–36.
116. Fred Vultee, "Jump Back, Jack: Mohammed's Here: Fox News and the Construction of Islamic Peril," *Journalism Studies* 10, no. 5 (2009): 623–38.

Chapter 7

Overview of Research on Media-Constructed Muslim Identity
1999–2009

Ammina Kothari

Mass media messages have been an important tool for creating public perceptions about social groups. After the 9/11 terrorist attacks, Islam and Muslims began to be featured regularly in news, politics, and conversations in the United States and across the globe. While the general population may be aware of the existence of Islam and Muslims, their knowledge is rudimentary and tends to be associated with 9/11, increasing chances of misrepresentations and stereotypes, resulting in hate crimes against Muslims and the stigmatization of the religion of Islam (Ibrahim, 2010). Furthermore, perceptions of Islam and Muslims tend to be tied to stereotypes based on medieval Europe, connecting Islam to violence and bloodshed (Abdallah, 2005).

The negative stereotypes about Islam and Muslims perpetuated through media messages are continuously transmitted and reinforced globally via advanced communication technologies (Samad, 1998). As a result, certain symbols and values have become associated with Islam and Muslim identities globally. For example, stereotypes in the United States about Islam are often closely tied to the *hijab* (head scarf worn by some Muslim women), which is interpreted as a conservative and oppressive practice of Islam (Kumar, 2010). For Muslim women, however, the *hijab* is an important part of their public identity (Shirazi & Mishra, 2010). Similarly, actions of certain individuals who commit acts of terrors in the name of *jihad* (struggle) have resulted in a perception of Islam as being "a deadly disease and its followers as carriers about to infect the rest of the world" (Abdallah, 2005, p. 125).

In order to understand the impact of media representations of a social group, it is useful to trace related changes in communicative media studies. Effects of media representations manifest themselves differently in minority social groups, compared to majority ones. Mass communication has been one area where these differences are clearly visible. The many interpretations of group identity include those of scholars who consider group identity a largely socially constructed phenomenon; Korostelina (2007) explains that it is beneficial to understand the formation of group identity as a process grounded in shared "history and practice through the collective work of evoking, confirming or declining participation in collective practices" (p. 28). Mass media through their content tend to provide key information that enables people to identify with certain groups while alienating groups that are considered to be the Other. Because media-constructed identities are so closely tied to public self-identification and understanding of others, it is important to investigate how communication scholars envision or contextualize Muslim identity. Social stereotypes are also produced and repeated through the media (Korostelina, 2007), making it important to chart and analyze how scholars are trying to understand the social construction of Muslim identity based on media discourses. Furthermore, as Edeani (1988) explains, tracing research patterns is an important and necessary endeavor because it is a means of "evaluating progress, detecting problems, and describing future directions" (p. 151).

This overview of research conducted on the media-constructed identity of Islam and Muslims explores how researchers have conceptualized Muslim communities and their resultant identities in the media over a 10-year period from 1999 to 2009. The analysis summarizes which media, methodologies, and theories were used to conduct the analyses and offers suggestions for future research agendas. In order to conduct a comprehensive and current analysis, scholarship included in this study was retrieved from peer-reviewed journals because most empirical research is usually first published in academic journals. This analysis encompasses all communication research on Islam and Muslims, rather than a single communication medium or topic. The articles were gathered by searching *Communication and Mass Media Complete*, *Communication Abstracts*, EBSCO, and Google Scholar, using the keywords *Muslims, Islam, Arabs, identity,* and *media*.

The search identified 31 articles that focus on how media have constructed Islam and Muslim identity. Each publication was read carefully and was coded for the name of the journal, year of publication, location of the author, location of the study, focus or subject of analysis (for example, a particular Muslim group or Islam in general), type of mass media, research methodology, and communication theories. Extensive notes were taken to identify key findings of the studies and opportunities for future research.

The first section of this chapter describes the current status of communication research on the media-constructed identities of Muslims and Islam. Key research findings are summarized in the second section. The third section explores the implications of scarcity of research on representations of Muslims and Islam in the media, prioritizes certain topics and countries for research, and offers suggestions for future research agendas. The analysis indicates that American scholars dominate research in this area, followed by Australian and British scholars, with research focusing largely on general construction of Muslim identities. In addition, the research on Muslim identities in the media is largely limited to text-based analyses of traditional mainstream media and predominantly uses the Orientalism framework as its theoretical context. The conclusion argues that lack of diversity in the location of research, scarcity of scholarship, and exclusion of multiple Muslim voices, all limit understanding of how media-constructed identity of Muslims and Islam influences audiences and Muslim groups themselves.

Current Research Agendas

The analysis of 31 articles obtained from peer-reviewed journals during the period from 1999 to 2009 highlights themes and variations in research during this decade. The articles were published in 23 journals, with the *Journal of Communication Inquiry* publishing the highest number of articles (5). Four other journals each published more than one article: *Global Media Journal, International Communication Gazette, Journal of Ethnic and Migration Studies,* and *Journal of Muslim Minority Affairs*. The rest of the articles were published in 18 other journals, which reflect the wide spectrum of journals interested in publishing scholarship on Islam and Muslims, including the *Australian Journal of Social Issues, Journal of Arab and Muslim Media Research, Journalism Studies,* and *The Radio Journal—International Studies in Broadcast and Audio Media*. (See appendix A for a complete list of the 23 journals.)

While research focusing on media-constructed identity of Islam and Muslims is published in a variety of journals, the focus of these publications is primarily religion, Arabs and Muslims, thereby limiting the scholarship's exposure to communication scholars who either specialize in religions, Islamic or Middle Eastern studies. Furthermore, the limited number of articles published on this subject confirms the observation of Pollock, Piccillo, Leopardi, Gratale, and Cabot (2005) that, despite ample media coverage about Islam, "communication studies of media and Islam are scarce" (p. 16).

Nationalities of Studied Muslims

British Muslims and Arabs made up the most prevalent group used for the analysis of media-constructed identity, followed by Canadian and Australian Muslims. This is partly a result of most analyses being conducted by scholars based in Western countries, with American scholars leading in publications, followed by Australians, British, and Canadians.

The remaining studies focused on Arab Americans, Arabs in Israel, and Chechens. My analysis showed that there has been a clear increase in research since 2006. In that year, eight articles were published, in 2008 seven were published, and in 2009 six were published, meaning that 21 of the 31 articles were published in the last 3 years of the decade. This trend illustrates that research exploring how media construct the identity of Muslims and Islam and their effects on Western audiences and Muslim communities is receiving increased attention globally. Perhaps the increase in research is a result of heightening awareness of Muslim communities in various Western countries, resulting in an increase in media coverage of Muslims and Islam following the terrorist attacks on September 11, 2001 in the United States and on July 7, 2005 in London.

Types of Content Analyzed

Four types of content were used in the 31 journal articles to analyze how media-constructed identity of Islam and Muslims: (a) traditional mainstream Western newspapers and television, (b) alternative and diaspora ethnic Muslim media, (c) documentaries, and (d) audience responses. Newspapers (n = 9) and audience responses (n = 9) were most commonly used for analysis. The rest of the studies focused either on documentaries or Muslim-oriented media. Several studies included analyses of online news message boards and forums to complement their studies of traditional forms of media. Inclusion of the Internet as a medium of mass communication validates its utility because minority groups particularly need an accessible medium that allows them to communicate across national and communal boundaries and maintain their identities.

Methodologies Used in Research

In the 31 journal articles, qualitative methods were used considerably more frequently than quantitative methods, partly because most of the studies focused on text-based analyses with discourse and textual analysis methods. That accounted for 64% of all articles, followed by interviews at 19%. Only one study employed a mixed-methodology approach, combining textual analysis with interviews. Quantitative methods were employed in only 9.6% of the articles, with content analysis being the most popular method, followed by surveys and experiments. The dominance of qualitative methods in these journal articles is partly a result of the subject itself, which requires close reading of data to understand ideological constructions presented by the media, as well as communication scholars' interest in understanding audiences' responses to media-constructed identities.

Communication Theories Guiding the Research

The tendency in communication research to conduct atheoretical research as identified recently by Ogan et al. (2009) in their meta-analysis of development communication and Kim and Weaver's (2002) thematic meta-analysis of communication research on the Internet, is also evident in this research on how media construct social identities. Fifty-one percent of the studies in the sample did not employ any theoretical framework to support their arguments. In 49% of the articles which mentioned or tested a theory, Orientalism was used most frequently at 25% followed by framing, circuit of culture, theories of diaspora and media, and third-person effect. While the recurring use of the Orientalism framework to contextualize analyses about Islam and Muslims validates the importance of Edward Said's (1995) work and its relevance to this subject, it also limits our understanding of evolving construction and resistance to media-constructed identities. When scholars employ Orientalism to ground their work, the analysis is more likely to focus on identification of dominant stereotypes and Othering examples of Muslims and Islam in the Western media. This approach does not allow room for exploration of alternative representations of Muslims and Islam in the general-market media. For instance, it does not illuminate variations in Muslim representations in Western media, which may explore topics unrelated to terrorism or Islamic fundamentalism. A more pervasive use of framing theory, critical discourse analysis, or grounded theory with inductive coding may provide a richer view of evolving Muslim identity in the media.

Media-Constructed Identity of Islam and Muslims

This section provides a review of key findings on how general market media construct identities of Islam and Muslims. The summaries are broken down into four sections: traditional media, Muslim-oriented news media, documentaries, and audience responses to media-constructed identity.

Traditional General-Market News Media and Muslim/Islamic Identity

Studies of representations of Muslims and Islam in the media usually begin with text-based analysis of media samples. Martin and Phela (2002) conducted a lexical analysis of *CNN News* and its message boards to study how Islam was constructed in the news and message boards after 9/11. They found that while the news itself was moderate in its coverage, the message boards were predominantly constructing Islam as a terrorist and fundamentalist religion. Interestingly, however, some of the message board responses did separate the identity of American Muslims from the rest of the world in their construction of a fundamentalist identity of Islam. Muscati (2002) conducted an overview of how media portray Arabs and Muslims to justify the war in Iraq and found that Arabs and Muslims were constructed as inferior, threatening, immoral, and dehistoricized people practicing a religion that threatened the West. The analysis shows how constant negative portrayal and lack of context about a group of people can change the context in which media audiences understand war in the Middle East.

While scholars have generally found Muslim identity to be associated with negative connotations in the media, there are exceptions to this norm. For example, Weston (2003) examined how Muslims were portrayed before and after 9/11 in U.S. newspapers and the *Detroit News* website using a textual analysis approach. She found that before 9/11 the coverage was sparse but generally negative about all Muslims; however, after 9/11, American Muslims were presented as loyal victims of persecution in the United States, while their counterparts in the Middle East were tied to a fundamentalist Islamic identity. Weston's (2003) analysis highlights the nuances of media-constructed identity of Muslims in America and separation of American Muslim identity from foreign counterparts.

The influence of U.S. media and its representations of Muslims and Islam is not restricted to America: it has global repercussions. Erjavec and Volcic (2006) textually analyzed how Slovakian and Croatian newspapers construct discourses around Muslims and Croatians/Bosnians. They found that all Muslims were portrayed as terrorists, both the rebels and the victims. This analysis is useful if we are to understand how global (U.S.) terrorism rhetoric is employed at local and other national levels around the world to construct Muslim identity. Kabir (2006) conducted a similar analysis of Australian news media, where he employed a mixed-methodology approach, conducting both a textual analysis of media coverage and interviews with Australian Muslims. His analysis found that Muslims were portrayed as extremists and Islam as a violent religion. In-depth interviews with Muslims also showed that they were aware of media biases against them and did not approve of their stereotyped portrayal. However, their status as a minority in Australia meant that they lacked the ability to challenge the media coverage; as a result, even when they became targets of hate crime, perhaps because of negative representations in the media, there was little to no coverage of their plight.

Consequences of media-constructed identity of Muslims are also apparent in the United Kingdom. A discourse analysis was employed to understand how British print-media journalists in their discourse about political rights present and construct Muslim identity in Britain (Meer, 2006). Most news media took a secular liberal and conservative nationalist position against Muslims, who were presented as the Other, demanding equal rights in the national discourse. Meer showed how media-constructed identity of a group can impact its influence on social and political agendas. Another study examining how political and national agendas can be tied to media-constructed identities of Muslims and Islam found that Iranian Muslim identity was tied to religious discourse about the threat of nuclear weapons (Izadi & Saghaye-Biria, 2007). Specifically, editorials in U.S. newspapers tied the identity of Iran with Islam and constructed the threat of nuclear weapons in Iran using religious discourse, thereby defining Islam as a threat.

Posetti (2008) explored the gendered nuances of media-constructed Muslim identity using content and textual analysis of Australian talk radio programs. The results showed that the coverage of Muslim women in the radio programs was generally constructed in terms of oppressed, exotic, or deviant individuals, or those prone to terrorist tendencies, especially when coverage focused on foreign countries. Furthermore, Muslim women's identity was tied to their *hijab* (head scarves) and limited to their religious beliefs. In certain cases, Muslim identities are also understood as a national identity, as illustrated by the work of Ali and Khaled (2008), who conducted a content analysis of *Newsweek* and *Time* magazine from 1991 to 2001. Their results show that Muslims are not presented as individuals or groups, but rather as citizens of particular countries and the tone and context of the coverage is influenced by America's relationship with the particular country; American allies were covered positively, compared to nations perceived as hostile. Mishra (2008) observed a similar trend when she examined how U.S. newspapers reported on democratization in Muslim countries (Iran, Iraq, and Turkey). Islam was portrayed as being incompatible with democracy, while Muslims were constructed to be either Westernized or premodern, depending on the U.S. relationship with the country. This study highlights how news media's support for U.S. foreign policy and bias against the Muslim world can influence the coverage of democratic processes in the Middle East.

Coverage of Islam and Muslims is not limited to stereotypes and the rhetoric of terrorism/fundamentalism; some media construct Muslims as animalistic to justify their extinction. Steuter and Wills (2009) employed a symbolic lexicon and metaphoric analysis to examine how Canadian newspapers constructed identity of people in Iraq and Afghanistan in the context of war. Most of the newspaper headlines constructed Muslims using animal and disease metaphors, reducing them to dehumanized beings that deserved to be eradicated. Although Steuter and Wills found many instances of dehumanizing discourse associated with Muslims in the Canadian media, newspapers published by *CanWest*, which owns a large media market share globally, used animal metaphors most frequently in their headlines. "Animal, prey and disease-related metaphor simultaneously identifies, marks, symbolizes and profoundly devalues the Other," Steuter and Wills (2009, pp. 19–20) said, thereby allowing media consumers to respond to Muslims by reenacting linguistic representations in real-life experiences, such as the production of and responses to prisoner abuse at Abu Ghraib.

When Western media cover issues that impact the whole nation it is easier to stereotype or marginalize one group of Muslims, but when the topic is related to Islam and involves multiple Muslim groups then the coverage becomes more complicated. Sharify-Funk (2009) examined how Canadian media reported on the Ontario Shari'ah debate, which was fueled by legislation that allowed religious groups (including Jewish, Catholic, Muslim, and Aboriginal communities) to convene their own independent arbitration tribunals for settling civil disputes. As a result, there was a conflict among Canadian Muslims, with some supporting the initiative and others opposing it, citing concerns about whether the Shari'ah arbitration would be able to protect Muslim women's rights. Since two prominent Muslim nonprofit organizations fueled the debate, Sharify-Funk found that dominating the coverage was a dichotomous (regressive vs. modern) stereotyped image of Islam and Muslims in Canada. Sharify-Funk's analysis illustrates that, when selected voices dominate a discourse (even if these voices represent Muslims), there is a risk of constructing a limited view of the identity of a community based on a few groups' vested interests being reported in the media.

Muslim Identity in Muslim-Oriented Media

Empirical analyses exploring how Muslim media construct identities are useful for expanding knowledge about Muslim communities and the multiple identities constructed and resisted within these diverse groups. Mandaville (2001) reviewed multiple forms of media available to Muslim youth of the Western diaspora and how they construct, debate, and reimagine their identities as liberal and progressive Muslims. He argued that the expansion of technological innovations and new media allows the youth to bypass traditional sources of religious information and instead engage in rereading of religious texts and interactive discussions on websites. Kosnick's (2004) study of Alevi migrant television programs broadcast through Berlin's open-access television channel Offener Kanal Berlin in Germany exemplifies the trend of minority Muslim groups taking an initiative to establish their own media to construct and communicate their identities. Kosnick found that the Alevies (who are usually described as a Shia minority with roots in Turkish mystical Islam and

Anatolian folk culture) employed multiple strategies, including vilification and stereotyping of other Muslim communities, especially Sunnis, to construct a unique identity for their group as a Shia-Sufi progressive sect and engage their German audiences who were not familiar with their culture. Kosnick's analysis makes an important contribution to communication and scholarship using the Orientalism framework, with her observations on how Orientalists can operate within and between various Muslim communities.

Siapera (2006) studied how British Muslims navigate multiculturalism in new media and found that individuals using self-representations on Muslim websites constructed multiple self-identities. British Muslim citizens were able to access and contribute information which empowered them to participate in civil discourse and speak up against injustices without being perceived as advocating radical outlooks or being labeled jihadists. Likewise Hirji's (2006) study of the *Montreal Muslim News Online Service* showed how Canadian Muslims construct their own identities online in terms of their roles as citizens during the challenging and potentially polarizing period of the Iraq War. Media outlets originating in the Muslim diaspora allow Muslim youth to challenge mainstream media representations and offer antiwar activism opportunities. However, in some instances, the result of exposure to media of diasporic origin can lead to a conflict of feelings in Muslims as they attempt to show their allegiance to their motherland and nation of citizenship, while expressing support for other Muslim nations. Kaufer and Al-Malik's (2009) analysis represents one of the first to examine how Arab Americans construct their own identity in the media. It employed rhetorical analysis to explore how Arab American media responded to attacks on and profiling of their communities after 9/11. Arab Americans portrayed themselves as victims of American foreign policies and presented a hybrid identity, which allowed them to maintain their Pan-Arab and mainstream American identity, while distancing themselves from the extremists.

Alternative media venues are also opening in the Middle East to meet the needs of their Muslim audiences who are starting to prefer a "modern" reconciliatory and flexible version of Islam, which allows them to enjoy material pleasures while adhering to Islamic principles. Alternative Muslim media in the Middle East provide content that mimics Western media formats and accommodates voices and perspectives that challenge conservative Muslims. Echchaibi (2008) analyzed how the new religious media are constructing the image of modern Muslims and their religious identities based on material consumption that is transmitted via an Islamic television channel, Iqra', a 24-hour Saudi religious channel reputed to be the first Islamic entertainment television station. He found that Islam was presented as a progressive religion by a new generation of business- and media-savvy revivalist Muslim speakers, who are beginning to attract an increasing audience of young Muslims to their shows. These revivalist Muslim speakers encourage use of Islam as a success formula for spiritual self-fulfillment and material achievement.

Scholars studying Muslim media have also looked at how Muslim television shows construct identities about Islam and Muslims in the diaspora. Canas (2008) examined the TV comedy show *The Little Mosque on the Prairie*, which attempts to dispel myths about Islam and Muslims and present an alternative cohesive identity. She found that the show's attempt to challenge Orientalist discourse of the "Muslim Other" in the general-market media by focusing on a generalized, unified view of Islam and its followers, created its own silence through its omission of differences between Sunnis, Sufis, and Shias. This study highlights the challenges associated with the construction of an accurate, diverse, and positive identity through media.

Documentaries

Struckman (2006) analyzed gender representations of Muslim Chechen rebel fighters in the documentary *Terror in Moscow*, which included original footage recorded during the 2002 Chechen siege in a Moscow theater. This documentary provides an opportunity to study how objective and constructed realities can be juxtaposed to create an identity about a group. Struckman found that Chechen men were lumped together into a group of gunmen and constructed as "naturally" violent, while Chechen women were represented as passive individuals, dependent on their men. The documentary also failed to provide information about the lives of the rebels prior to their involvement with the struggle, hence limiting their identities to the stereotyped constructions of violent Muslim men and passive Muslim women.

The Return to Kandahar, a documentary about the journey of Nelofer Pazira, an Afghan-Canadian girl, to search for her friend in Afghanistan, portrays Afghan women as passive and oppressed beings trapped in a conflict-ridden, backward Muslim country. Ansari (2008) employed a discourse analysis to deconstruct how Pazira becomes an "Orientalized insider" as she constructed the identity of Afghan women as the Others. This analysis highlights the ability of "insiders" to create group identity by acting simultaneously as a Westernized outsider as well as a native.

Using content and textual analysis, Khoury-Machool (2009) conducted a discursive analysis of *The Power of Nightmares* documentary films. He found that while the premise of these films was to dispel ethno-religious stereotypes of Arabs and Muslims that a recurring use of Orientalist discourse and misinformation led instead to reinforcement of misconceptions. Adam Curtis, the producer of these documentaries, included more perspectives expressed by Western representatives than by Arab-Islamic countries' representatives, thereby marginalizing Muslim voices and denying them opportunities to reconstruct or correct the media-constructed identities. As a result, Khoury-Machool (2009, p. 44) concluded, Islamists were reduced to "passive participants in the 'War on Terror,'" and their identities remained tied to the violent activities of "militant groups." These three aforementioned studies analyzing documentaries demonstrate how manipulation of images, editing of facts and silencing of voices can enable biased construction of group identities, which are then presented as "facts."

Audience Responses to Media-Constructed Identity

Even though most of the studies reviewed in this chapter focus their analyses on media texts, a few other studies focus on audiences and their responses to Islam and Muslims as reported in the news media. Bard (2004) interviewed Muslim women in Houston to learn how they constructed their identities based on media coverage and self-perceptions after 9/11. She found that immigrant Muslim women were more likely to hide their Muslim identity by not wearing the *hijab* compared to American born Muslim women who publicly embraced the *hijab* as part of their identity after 9/11. This analysis shows how the media-constructed identity of Muslims forces Muslims to rethink their identities and adapt based on their understandings of how others perceive them in the United States. Wicks (2006) used a quasi-experiment to test the effects of media-constructed identity of Muslims. He exposed peer group members of the Presbyterian, Jewish, and Muslim faiths to six identical video clips that featured Middle Eastern and African Muslims as violent and extremist individuals. The media stimulus produced a range of responses including hostility, anger, and outrage. However, the responses were influenced by individuals' relationships with Islam. When exposed to stereotyped negative representations of Islam and Muslims, Muslim participants frequently displayed outrage, while Jewish and Presbyterian participants displayed anger and fear.

Orientalist behavior toward Muslims by the West has been well documented, yet not many studies have examined similar instances in Muslim communities. Harb and Bessaiso (2006) interviewed British Muslim Arabs in order to understand how they construct their identity based on media coverage of Islam and wars post-9/11. In this study, British Muslim Arabs displayed instances of ethnocentrism in response to the construction of Muslims as violent, isolationist, and led by fanatics. These Muslims asserted their agency by actively engaging with and resisting stereotyped representations in the media by either boycotting Western media or with displays of ethnocentric behavior, whereby they consider Muslim-oriented media such as Al-Jazeera to be more accurate than Western media.

Aly (2007) observed a similar trend while conducting focus groups with Australian Muslims to study their attitudes and responses to the media discourse on terrorism. She found that while Muslims internalized media stereotyping of their religion and communities as being antisecular, they also reconstructed their identity using victimization and a sense of persecution as bonding factors against media-constructed identity. Tsfati (2007) identified similar phenomena caused by the third-person effect while surveying Arabs in Israel about their identity in the media. The third-person effect is an indirect media effect, caused by an individual's perception that while he or she is immune to media influence that others (third persons) are not and that they thereby come to accept, approve, or support the media message. The analysis showed that the Arabs in Israel were more likely to be influenced by hostile coverage in the media, which resulted in self-alienation among some participants, as they internalized what they perceived to be a negative identity tied to their community.

In order to justify their actions toward Muslims, other countries around the world also have adopted the negative media discourse about Muslims in the United States. Erjavec and Volcic (2007) interviewed Serbian intellectuals to understand how they would explain tension with Muslims in Serbia. Many of their interviewees defined Bosnian Muslims as aggressors, criminals, hordes, extremists, mujahideen (Muslim freedom fighters), and Islamic fanatics, and Islam as a terrorist's religion. The discourse of "the war on terrorism" was appropriated by Serbians to characterize themselves as victims of violence and Muslims as terrorists.

Hopkins (2008) criticized scholars' tendency to lump all Muslims as Arabs, reinforcing some of the very problems that the research aims to elucidate, such as general stereotyping of Muslims and Islam. Hopkins supported her argument with an analysis she conducted in Australia with the Turkish Muslim population. She examined how Turkish Muslims viewed themselves in the larger Muslim discourse in Australia. Her respondents explained that they did not agree with Australian media representations of Muslims in general; their Islamic identity was not defined by Arabic Muslim identity. In fact, many Australian Turks preferred to align themselves with a more moderate Mediterranean culture, instead of conservative Middle Eastern culture. This analysis provides insights into how various Muslim communities construct their identities and highlights the diversity of Muslim people around the globe. Likewise, Croucher, Oommen, and Steele (2009) observed a similar distancing in their second-generation French Muslim interviewees, who expressed resistance to assimilation into the mainstream French society, similar to that of their parents. Young French Muslims demonstrated their agency by distancing themselves from a culture that they perceived to be against them, and instead chose to align their values and views with those expressed in ethnic media.

Even portrayals in action and adventure films can have an effect on Muslims and how non-Muslims respond to Muslims. Wilkins (2009) held focus groups with Arab Americans and other U.S.-based communities to study how they contextualized representations of the places and people in the action films with their real life experiences or understanding of the world. She found that non-Arab Americans were more likely than Arab Americans to associate danger with Middle Eastern nations and to fear people from the Middle East.

Future Research Agendas

The goal of this chapter was to provide an overview of how communication scholars have studied the media-constructed identity of Islam and Muslims and to categorize and summarize the results of these studies. Although the extent of coverage on Islam and Muslims is limited, the analyses have enriched scholarship on Islam and Muslim representations in the media. There is still an urgent need to diversify research on how the media construct identities of various Muslim groups and Islam. This overview has shown that currently scholars from the West, particularly North Americans, dominate research. Analyses tend to focus on text-based studies of Arab Americans or generalized Muslim groups' representations in the general-market mainstream news media. Few scholars have taken the initiative to include Muslim-oriented media or news discourse on the Internet in their analyses, partly because of language barriers, a hurdle that can be overcome with collaborative research projects. Muslim scholars can contribute their language expertise and cultural insights together with their communication research experience while working with their Western counterparts. Lack of funding and resources also limits scholars from examining media effects from audiences' perspective.

This current research trend has three key limitations: One, the lack of diversity of scholars limits mass communication scholarship's access to how the rest of the world examines media coverage of Islam and Muslims and their findings. Correcting this could help contextualize work and expand research agendas. Two, when Western scholars focus their analysis on Muslims living in the West then they are privileging the experiences of those who live in developed countries and marginalizing similar groups living in developing countries who are also affected by media-constructed identities of their communities as being associated with terrorism. Three, when media scholars design their studies to capture how the media cover Muslims and Islam generally, they are guilty of the same error they critique media of committing; namely, they conflate Islam and Muslims' various sects and groups. Many of the studies included in this overview have contextualized their research using this conflating approach, and while their analyses do contribute to communication research, they are reinforcing misconceptions propagated by the Western media about Muslims being a single entity, tied to one religion of Islam. In reality, more than 1.5 billion Muslims live around the world, of whom about 90% are Sunni and 10% are Shia, and Islam is practiced differently in each country depending on the customs and traditions of its people (Kumar, 2010).

In other words, while media bias influences an incorrect representation of Islam and its followers, scholars need to make extra efforts to correct these misconceptions and design their studies to highlight the nuances and richness of these diverse communities. Furthermore, scholars need to expand the location of their studies to African and Asian countries, which have also been dealing with terrorism issues and have large Muslim populations, both indigenous and migrant. Since the West often sets the research agenda, which is then adapted by the rest of the world, greater care should be taken to test and formulate theories that will capture media effects accurately. Many of the studies in this sample employed the Orientalism framework, which is grounded in the concept of "us" versus "them." When scholars ground their research within this framework, their analysis will be limited to identifying instances of Orientalist assertions. Alternative and new theoretical frameworks need to be proposed and applied to study media representations of Muslim and Islam and to parse out the nuances of media-constructed identities. Do Muslim-oriented media in the West present Muslims and Islam more positively compared to general-market Western media? Does the representation differ based on the topic—war and terrorism versus cultural events and holidays?

I concur with Ibrahim (2009), who recommends that future research should incorporate more in-depth interviews of the news media producers, journalists, and editors, to understand how misconceptions about media are continuously recycled. The studies in this sample which either conducted audience analysis or supported their text-based analyses with interviews were able to provide critical insights into how Muslim communities and other audiences view and contest media-constructed identities. The differences between older generations of migrant Muslims and younger generations are also important to study, as technological advances and changing dynamics in the era of globalization are forcing new generations to rethink their religious and national identities, and how they interact with media texts.

In order for communication scholarship on Islam and Muslims to become comprehensive and representative there needs to be more collaborative work between scholars in the West and the East. This would allow for more in-depth analyses and provide opportunities for Muslim voices to contribute to scholarship about their own communities and increase understanding of Islam as a religion and its followers. Future studies could focus on the following four areas, which are currently understudied: (a) comparative analyses of media coverage of international issues; (b) role of new media in defining Muslim identities, as it allows for communities in the diaspora to connect with their homelands and build shared identities in the cyberspace; (c) use of ethnic media in migrant Muslim communities; (d) audience responses to media-constructed identities of Islam and Muslims and its effects on Muslims.

Historically, it has been difficult to conduct comparative analyses of media coverage internationally, especially in Muslim countries. However, with the spread of the Internet, most of the dominant media globally have established an online presence, which eases access to their content and potentially allows for insightful comparative analyses. For example, analyses of Muslim-oriented media in the West could be compared with ethnic or general-market media in Muslim countries to understand the similarities and differences in how they construct identities of Muslim communities.

As Muslim communities in the West become more established, they are increasingly likely to invest in establishing their own ethnic media, which would serve their information needs and provide an alternative venue for reaffirming their identities and alliances to their motherland. This subject deserves further analysis, as it is not only an alternative to the Orientalist perspective of Muslims but also provides opportunities for scholars to understand how migrants from different nations reconcile their values and adapt to new countries, while at the same time remaining connected with their community of origin.

Today, many people around the world are able to access and respond to media coverage through e-mailed letters to the editor, online message boards, and other social media. Since the general media do report on Muslims and Islam consistently, it is important to analyze how audiences respond to this coverage. Do audiences separate American Muslims' identities from those of Muslim immigrants? Are audience responses more critical of media coverage of wars in the Middle East compared to terrorism-related issues at home?

Lastly, future studies should focus on individual Muslim groups in the West and how the perceived perceptions of these communities in the media shape how they practice and present their Muslim identities. Binary portrayals of Muslims as being Westernized or premodern have long-term effects on how future generations of Muslims in the West will construct and express their identities, as the ongoing globalization of the media in the West will continue to shape how the rest of the world views and understands Islam and Muslim identities.

Appendix A: Journals Including Communication Research on Islam and Muslims, 1999–2009 (Number of articles in parentheses)

1. Australian Journal of Communication (1)
2. Australian Journal of Social Issue (1)
3. Critical Studies in Media Communication (1)
4. Cultural Dynamics (1)
5. Culture and Religion (1)
6. Discourse and Society (1)
7. European Journal of Scientific Research (1)
8. Global Media and Communication (1)
9. Global Media Journal (2)
10. International Communication Gazette (2)
11. International Journal of Media and Cultural Politics (1)
12. Journal of Arab and Muslim Media Research (1)
13. Journal of Communication (1)
14. Journal of Communication Inquiry (5)
15. Journal of Ethnic and Migration Studies (2)
16. Journal of Intercultural Communication Research (1)
17. Journal of Media and Religion (1)
18. Journal of Muslim Minority Affairs (2)
19. Journalism Studies (1)
20. Newspaper Research Journal (1)
21. Prometheus (1)
22. Rhetoric Review (1)
23. The Radio Journal—International Studies in Broadcast and Audio Media (1)

References

Abdallah, A. (2005). View from the news desk: Post-9/11 media and Muslim identity in American media. In C. H. Badaracco (Ed.), *Quoting God: How media shape ideas about religion and culture* (pp. 12–128). Waco, TX: Baylor University Press.

Ali, S., & Khalid (2008). US mass media and the Muslim world: Portrayal of Muslims by "News Week" and "Time" (1991–2001). *European Journal of Scientific Research, 21*(4), 554–580.

Aly, A. (2007). Australian Muslim responses to the discourse on terrorism in the Australian popular media. *Australian Journal of Social Issues, 42*(1), 27–40.

Ansari, U. (2008). "Should I go and pull her burqa off?" Feminist compulsions, insider consent, and a return to Kandahar. *Critical Studies in Media Communication, 25*(1), 48–67.

Bard, H. (2004). Islamic identity re-covered: Muslim women after September 11th. *Culture & Religion, 5*(3), 321–338.

Canas, S. (2008). The Little Mosque on the Prairie: Examining (Multi) cultural spaces of nation and religion. *Cultural Dynamics, 20*(3), 195–211.

Croucher, S. M., Oommen, D., & Steele, E. L. (2009). An examination of media usage among French-Muslims. *Journal of Intercultural Communication Research, 38*(1), 41–57.

Echchaibi, N. (2008). Hyper-Islamism? Mediating Islam from the halal website to the Islamic talk show. *Journal of Arab and Muslim Media Research, 1*(3), 199–214.

Edeani, D. (1988). West African mass communication research at major turning point. *International Communication Gazette, 41*, 151–183.

Erjavec, K., & Volcic, Z. (2006). Mapping the notion of "terrorism" in Serbian and Croatian newspapers. *Journal of Communication Inquiry, 30*(4), 298–318.

Erjavec, K., & Volcic, Z. (2007). "War on terrorism" as a discursive battleground: Serbian recontextualization of G.W. Bush's discourse. *Discourse and Society, 18*(2), 123–137.

Harb, Z., & Bessaiso, E. (2006). British Arab Muslim audiences and television after September 11. *Journal of Ethnic & Migration Studies, 32*(6), 1063–1076.

Hirji, F. (2006). Common concerns and constructed communities: Muslim Canadians, the Internet, and the war in Iraq. *Journal of Communication Inquiry, 30*(2), 125–141.

Hopkins, L. (2008). Muslim Turks and anti-Muslim discourse: The effects of media constructions of "Islamic" and "Arabic" in Australia. *Australian Journal of Communication, 35*(1), 41–55.

Ibrahim, D. (2009). The Middle East in American media: A 20th-century overview. *International Communication Gazette, 71*(6), 511–524.

Ibrahim, D. (2010). The framing of Islam on network news following the September 11th attacks. *International Communication Gazette, 72*, 111–125.

Izadi, F., & Saghaye-Biria, H. (2007). A discourse analysis of elite American newspaper editorials: The case of Iran's nuclear program. *Journal of Communication Inquiry, 31*(2), 140–165.

Kabir, N. (2006). Representation of Islam and Muslims in the Australian media, 2001–2005. *Journal of Muslim Minority Affairs, 26*(3), 313–328.

Kaufer, D., & Al-Malki, A. M (2009). The war on terror through Arab-American eyes: The Arab-American press as a rhetorical counterpublic. *Rhetoric Review, 28*(1), 47–65.

Khoury-Machool, M. (2009). The re-mythologization of Islam and the Arab world in Adam Curtis's *The Power of Nightmares*. *Global Media & Communication, 5*(1), 35–55.

Kim, S. T., & Weaver, D. (2002). Communication research about the Internet: A thematic meta-analysis. *New Media Society, 4*(4), 518–538.

Korostelina, K. V. (2007). *Social identity and conflict: Structures, dynamics, and implications.* New York: Palgrave Macmillan.

Kumar, D. (2010). Framing Islam: The resurgence of Orientalism during the Bush II era. *Journal of Communication Inquiry, 34*(3), 254–277.

Kosnick, K. (2004). "Speaking in One's Own Voice": Representational strategies of Alevi Turkish migrants on open-access television in Berlin. *Journal of Ethnic & Migration Studies, 30*(5), 979–994.

Mandaville, P. (2001). Reimagining Islam in Diaspora: The politics of mediated community. *International Communication Gazette, 63*(2–3), 169–186.

Martin, P., & Phelan, S. (2002). Representing Islam in the wake of September 11: A comparison of US Television and CNN online message board discourses. *Prometheus, 20*(3), 263–269.

Meer, N. (2006). Get off your knees. *Journalism Studies, 7*(1), 35–59.

Mishra, S. (2008). Islam and democracy: Comparing post-9/11 representations in the U.S. prestige press in the Turkish, Iraqi, and Iranian contexts. *Journal of Communication Inquiry, 32*(2), 155–178.

Mostafa, G. M. M. (2007). Correcting the image of Islam and Muslims in the West: Challenges and opportunities for Islamic universities and organizations. *Journal of Muslim Minority Affairs, 27*(3), 371–386.

Muscati, S. A. (2002). Arab/Muslim "Otherness": The role of racial constructions in the Gulf War and the continuing crisis with Iraq. *Journal of Muslim Minority Affairs, 22*(1), 131.

Ogan, C. L., Bashir, M., Camaj, L., Luo, Y., Gaddie, B., Pennington, R., ... Salih, M. (2009). Development communication: The state of research in an era of ICTs and globalization. *International Communication Gazette, 71*(8), 655–670.

Pollock, J. C., Piccillo, C., Leopardi, D, Gratale, S., & Cabot, K. (2005). Nationwide newspaper coverage of Islam post September 11: A community structure approach. *Communication Research Reports, 22(1),* 15–27.

Posetti, J. (2008). Unveiling radio coverage of Muslim women. *The Radio Journal—International Studies in Broadcast and Audio Media, 6*(2&3), 161–177.

Said, E. W. (1995). *Orientalism.* Harmondsworth, England: Penguin.

Samad, Y. (1998). Media and Muslim identity: Intersections of generation and gender. *Innovation: The European Journal of Social Sciences, 11*(4), 425–438.

Sharify-Funk, M. (2009). Representing Canadian Muslims: Media, Muslim advocacy organizations, and gender in the Ontario Shari'ah Debate. *Global Media Journal—Canadian Edition, 2*(2), 73–89.

Shirazi, F., & Mishra, S. (2010). Young Muslim women on the face veil (niqab): A tool of resistance in Europe but rejected in the United States. *International Journal of Cultural Studies, 13*(1), 43–62.

Siapera, E. (2006). Multiculturalism, progressive politics and British Islam online. *International Journal of Media & Cultural Politics, 2*(3), 331–346.

Steuter, E., & Wills, D. (2009). Discourses of dehumanization: Enemy construction and Canadian media complicity in the framing of the war on terror. *Global Media Journal—Canadian Edition, 2*(2), 7–24.

Struckman, S. (2006). The veiled women and masked men of Chechnya: Documentaries, violent conflict, and gender. *Journal of Communication Inquiry, 30*(4), 337–353.

Tsfati, Y. (2007). Hostile media perceptions, presumed media influence, and minority alienation: The case of Arabs in Israel. *Journal of Communication, 57*, 632–651.

Weston, M. A. (2003). Post 9/11 Arab American coverage avoids stereotypes. *Newspaper Research Journal, 24*(1), 92–106.

Wicks, R. H. (2006). Emotional response to collective action media frames about Islam and terrorism. *Journal of Media & Religion, 5*(4), 245–263.

Wilkins, K. G. (2009). Mapping fear and danger in global space: Arab Americans' and others' engagement with action-adventure film. *International Communication Gazette, 71*(7), 561–576.

Chapter 8

Mass Media and African American Identities
Examining Black Self-Concept and Intersectionality

Meghan S. Sanders and Omotayo Banjo

It is no secret that the media are extremely powerful institutions, having an impact on users' social perceptions, attitudes, beliefs, behaviors, and how they conceive of themselves. For decades scholars in mass communication, communication studies, psychology, sociology, women's studies, and African American studies, have devoted theoretical and empirical research to understanding how media play a role in the development and preponderance of various social identities. Taking the differing findings as a whole, it is safe to say that media inform users of a group's position in society. Through images and other representations, media help to maintain the status quo (Harwood & Roy, 2005). These unintended consequences especially have an impact on marginalized groups, reinforcing subordinate identities and even influencing policy making that affects the well-being of these groups. Because television and other forms of media play a significant socializing role (Bandura, 2009; Gerbner, Morgan, Gross, Signorielli, & Shanahan, 2002), it is worth exploring the influence of media production and consumption on African Americans' lived experiences. In doing so, it is also important to recognize that the African American experience is not monolithic. There are a variety of social identities that one may possess and general-market and ethnic-oriented media both play roles in shaping these identities.

Many overviews examine the media's impact in regard to marginalized groups from the perspective of majority viewers and how media impact their attitudes toward and beliefs about minority groups. Less emphasis has been placed on how media impact in-group members. Even less scholarly attention has been given to the impact of contemporary Black-oriented programming. Additionally, research tends to examine media impact in regard to one dominant identity an individual possesses, such as ethnicity or gender, without recognizing the intersection of characteristics and traits that make up a person's complete identity.

The present chapter fills the aforementioned gap, paying particular attention to the influence media have on the construction and maintenance of African Americans' social identities. This chapter will discuss the role of general-market media, as well as ethnic-oriented media in the forms of news, entertainment, and advertising. Contemporary scholarship on ethnic media focuses primarily on groups with distinctive languages, namely, Hispanic (M. A. Johnson, David, & Huey, 2004) and Asian (Viswanath & Arora, 2000) groups. However, there exists a growing body of literature on Black-oriented media that gives insight into African Americans' identity creation and maintenance. Making a case for new agendas in studies of media and African American identities, we present current research and draw conclusions about the future of ethnic media research as it pertains to Black-oriented media and multicultural audiences.

Additionally, traditional scholarship has examined media's impact on group identities from a universal perspective, making generalizations derived from one aspect of identity. This chapter advances the discussion toward an examination of the relationship between media and multiple categories or the intersection of multiple social identities. This *intersectionality*, as women's studies scholars, psychologists, and sociologists refer to it, is an underresearched area that is an important puzzle piece for examining the complexity of media impact. Thus, it will be offered as an explanation that scholars should take into consideration as they move forward in examining the media's impact on African American identities.

African American Media Use

Generally, African Americans continue to be the ethnic group that watches television the most (Nielsen Media, 2005). While the group represents 12% of the U.S. population, it represents 13% of those in television-viewing households (Ward, 2004). African Americans also have a larger percentage of homes with multiple television sets than other groups, and are more likely to have extended cable services, premium channels, and a video game system. For children and teens, the story is similar. In 1995, African American teens accounted for 15.3% of the over 20 million 12- to 17-year-old television viewers in the country (Hodges, 1996). In 2004, African American viewers 2 to 17 years old viewed television an average of 4 hours, 6 minutes a day compared to the 3 hours, 1 minute average of all other groups (Nielsen, 2005). In 2010, viewing increased to 7 hours, 12 minutes a day (Nielsen, 2011). When it comes to what television content is viewed most often, African Americans are more likely to select television for entertainment purposes (Abrams, 2008), viewing primarily reality shows, dramas that feature ensemble casts with African American characters as secondary characters, and Black-oriented sitcoms (Nielsen, 2005, 2007).

While African Americans are the title holders in television-viewing, these same households are less likely to have personal computers with Internet access (Jackson, von Eye, Fitzgerald, Zhao, & Witt, 2010; Nielsen, 2005). However, this does not necessarily translate into a digital divide. According to the Pew Research Center (2010), African Americans are the fastest growing group and most active users of mobile Internet. Compared to 2007, Pew results showed a 141% increase in mobile Internet activity for the ethnic group. So, while there are low levels of broadband and other traditional Internet activity via a personal computer, this is offset by high levels of activity on mobile devices. When online, 48% of group members are searching for information, e-mailing, or instant messaging, and they have recently been identified as the most active users on Twitter (Edison Research/Arbitron, Inc., 2010).

When looking at other media outlets, African American usage varies considerably. In relationship to other media, African Americans are infrequent moviegoers: 93% report going to the movies only occasionally or not at all (Motion Picture Association of America, 2009). Readership of both general-market and African American newspapers has decreased among African American consumers (Project for Excellence in Journalism [PEW], 2009). This trend, however, is consistent with the growing decline of newspaper readership in general. On the other hand, radio has the highest penetration of all media among African Americans. Over 90% of African Americans over the age of 12 listen to the radio each week. This includes listening at home, at work, in the car, at restaurants, online, and via mobile devices (Arbitron, 2009). Historically, African Americans have also been high users of Black-oriented media, a trend that has increased steadily.

Understanding Ethnic Media

Ethnic media—either owned by, produced by, or targeted toward ethnic groups—have contributed to the growing and changing media landscape. Although Black-oriented media have long existed in the form of the black press and even early cinema, there has been an increase of ethnic media in recent years, primarily supported by younger users (Allen, 2001). These media aid in the creation of identities and therefore are worthy of scholarly attention. Demonstrating the profitability of targeting non-White markets, a 2005 New California Media poll found that ethnic media reach nearly 51 million ethnic adults, nearly one-fourth of the U.S. population (New California Media, 2005). In the same year, a New America Media poll found that nearly half of the 29 million ethnic adults they polled preferred ethnic media to their general-market counterparts (New California Media, 2005). Generally, these groups prefer ethnic programming because of their need for social support and identity reinforcement, and their disappointment with general-market portrayals (Renz, 2006). Despite the considerable growth of Black-oriented media, most of the research has examined groups with a distinctive language, such as media in Spanish and Chinese. The production and consumption of Black-oriented programming is just as noteworthy and should not be overlooked.

In regard to media ownership, progress has been slow but potent. Currently, BET and TV One are the two largest cable television networks that serve the African American community, reaching 87 million households and 45.3 million households, respectively (PEW, 2010). However, broadcast television representation in ownership and production remain lacking. African Americans own only eight of the nation's 1,379 broadcast stations (PEW, 2010). At the same time, a number of opportunities for production and distribution have increased for African American filmmakers because of advances in digital technology. Today, more African American actors and directors are producing direct-to-DVD films. In addition, many Black actors have formed independent production companies and partnered with independent distribution companies to produce more positive stories such as Laurence Fishbourne's *Akeelah and the Bee*, Tyler Perry's *Madea* series, or Will Smith's contribution to *The Pursuit of Happyness* (Squires, 2009). It is through these limited outlets that African American creative producers seek to serve the needs of the social group and to counter the cultural stereotypes presented in general market film and television (Squires, 2009). However, like general-market media, this content can sometimes result in negative effects on group identity, highlighting the complexity of identity creation and maintenance. The representations and effects of Black-oriented media are discussed throughout this chapter.

Intersectionality: Advancing the Study of Stereotypes and Identities

Scholarship on African Americans and the media reveals an imbalance in studying this ethnic group: most of the research emphasis is placed on television and the portrayals of women. Furthermore, discussions of media representations of African Americans and other ethnic groups seem to lump the differing aspects of social identity into one recognizable or dominant category. For example, the portrayals of African American women are usually examined in studies of African Americans as a group or studies of women as a group. This is problematic because the African American female experience is arguably different from that of African American males and White females. In this way, these groups' experiences and our understanding of them is not satisfactorily reflected (Warner, 2008). Gloria Wade-Gayles (1997, p. 6) explained that writing about African American womanhood is "like navigating between Scylla and Charybdis. When you think you have steered the analysis around the most difficult assumptions...you find yourself faced with new ones. They are many in number and they are problematic." Media also illustrate this difference. In this case, race and gender intersect, creating unique portrayals and identities. Social identity theoretical frameworks command that scholars consider the many layers of an individual's social identity. Feminist scholars, sociologists, and psychologists, among others, have argued for more than just surface-level assessments in which various social identities operate independently, or as additive models of gender, race, class, and other social categories. In reality, people belong to multiple social categories resulting in intersecting identities that cannot be explained by one social group membership alone (Warner, 2008).

Intersectionality arguments suggest that one category of identity is partially defined by its relationship with another category. This is not to say that intersectionality argues that race and gender, for example, operate jointly as two independent variables would operate in a factorial design or that each does not operate under its own autonomy to a certain degree (Warner, 2008). Rather, intersectional identities are "relationally defined and emergent" (Anthias & Yuval-Davis, 1983). In this way, the "identities in one category come to be seen as self-evident through the lens of another category" (Shields, 2008, p. 302). The individual actively engages in the formation and maintenance of the categories involved, even through media creation and usage.

Intersectionality allows a way for scholars to acknowledge and examine those who belong to what are known as *emergent groups* that have otherwise been left out or ignored (Nakano Glenn, 1999; Warner, 2008), and the complexity of society's structural framework. What may disadvantage a group may advantage the same group when compared to another intersected group. For example, Fuller (2004) identifies the conflict of attributing aggressive behavior as an acceptable male characteristic while the same characteristic would be detrimental to African American males. Similarly, while passivity is an accepted female attribute, African American females are often characterized as obnoxious. The difference in disadvantage comes as a result of where the categories intersect rather than an accumulation of disadvantages that come from being a member of two groups. In this way, some questions, including those related to the media, are more accurately examined through the lens of intersectionality. For African Americans, the issue of class is an acute indicator of one's perceived social standing in relation to the White numerical majority. The issue of class is pertinent to understanding television representations and television audiences specifically as cultural studies scholarship has noted a distinguishable relationship between the two. Cole and Omari (2003) maintained that, "The relationship between classes within the Black community can be understood only from a position of intersectionality" (p. 788). Therefore, in order to adequately understand the relationships between representations of African Americans and their impact on African American audiences, scholars should examine the intersections of class and racial identity.

Primarily, intersectionality has been examined from the perspective of individuals' lived experiences (i.e., experiences with sexism, racism, classism, homophobia, etc.), an avenue geared toward pinpointing a better and more accurate way of representing emergent social groups. So, an opportunity exists for media scholars in both intersectionality research and the mass communication discipline. For intersectionality, media scholars can bring the examination of message production, message content, and their impact to the discussion of intersectionality. The current state of research only allows a limited foray into such examinations. Through acknowledging and peeling back the layers of identities, we can also continue to discuss ways that media redefine social realities and better address social impartialities.

From a media perspective, an intersectionality approach provides a way to examine individual difference variables and characteristics in a more representative way. The goal is not for researchers to consider all components of an identity to the point of dissolving groups into individuals. The objective is now to expand how we theorize about and examine social groups in both qualitative and quantitative studies. Warner (2008) provides an overview of various issues to consider from both qualitative and quantitative perspectives. However, one area we want to highlight is the incorporation of intersectionality into the measures typically used to assess degree of group identity. Many quantitative measures that assess social group memberships and connectivity do so by referring to the participants' "social group" in the wording of the items; however, even those within the same dominant social group (i.e., race, gender) may be considering different emergent groups (i.e., African American female, African American male) when considering their answer to the question. In addition to the suggestions of Warner (i.e., use of grounded theory approach, use of factorial designs), we propose a revision in the way identities are assessed so that a conceptual fit exists that reflects intersected identities. In addition, how media content is analyzed needs to reflect the existing social structure and its role in producing intersected identities. The following sections apply intersectionality to both media content and media users.

News Media

Much scholarly attention has been paid to how African Americans are portrayed in the news. Because news represents fact/reality, many argue that it is one of the most influential types of content in shaping perceptions of the group. Consistently negative presentations make news-viewing one part of the process that contributes to individuals aligning African Americans with criminality. African Americans are more often presented as perpetrators of crimes, as nameless and threatening, and stories about them are more likely to be accompanied with prejudicial information (i.e., mug shots, information on prior arrests, etc.; Dixon & Linz, 2000a, 2000b). Heavier viewing of such content leads to increased ability and likelihood of accessing an African American criminal schema (Dixon, 2006, 2007). As a result, people tend to have harsher culpability judgments toward African Americans (Dixon, 2008a), underestimate African Americans' income levels, and perceive Blacks as intimidating (Dixon, 2008b). Increasingly, African Americans appear mostly in crime, sports, and entertainment stories; rarely are they shown making important contributions to the serious business of the nation (Entman & Rojecki, 2000).

Both representations have a thread of truth to them—African Americans are professionals and are perpetrators and victims of crime—however, the portrayals tend to exist independent of one another, and when examining these images and their effects, media scholars give little attention to how ethnicity and class work together to create resulting images and perceptions. From an intersectionality perspective, Iyengar's (1991,1999) ideas about thematic and episodic framing apply. Thematic framing of news and information provides a context for occurrences, incorporating the role of society's structure into that context. Episodic frames tend to focus only on the actual events, providing decontextualized information that promotes prejudiced beliefs about a marginalized group. Most media scholarship examines episodic framing as it is likely to exist in larger quantities. However, equal attention should be paid to the occurrences and impact of thematic framing as it, by definition, falls in line with the intersectionality approach: examining the societal factors and the multifaceted layers of identity. In doing so, scholars can begin to theorize better about messages of counterstereotypes and stereotype correction when it comes to news messages.

Entertainment: Film and Television

While studies have examined detrimental effects of stereotypical representations of African Americans in local and network news (Dixon, 2008a, 2008b), the results regarding portrayals in the entertainment realm have been mixed. Content and textual analyses that examine the portrayals of the group have yielded results showing both positive and negative portrayals, suggesting that representations are arguably improving, but maybe only in regards to numbers. Media content still promotes a narrow range of images, providing a limited and largely inaccurate depiction; as a result, media content helps create and maintain stereotypes held by both those inside and outside of this and other marginalized groups.

African Americans have moved from a state of near invisibility in the media to being represented in numbers similar to their occurrence in the population. From 1955 to 1986 only 6% of primetime television characters were African Americans (Lichter, Lichter, Rothman, & Amundson, 1987). Of those, nearly half came from a low economic status and lacked a high school diploma. By the early 1980s, more African American characters were featured as successful professionals and as authority figures (Mastro & Greenberg, 2000). During the 1990s and early 2000s, representations continued to improve, for a variety of reasons (see Mastro & Greenberg, 2000; Mastro & Behm-Morawitz, 2005), including more ethnic-oriented television channels and advertisers' desire to market to the group (Greenberg & Collette, 1997). According to a Children Now report, in the 2003–2004 season, African Americans made up 16% of all prime time characters. Many were shown in comedies and dramas (Children Now, 2004; Mastro & Greenberg, 2000) and lived and worked in middle-class America, exhibiting positive traits such as diligence and self-determination (Dates & Stroman, 2001). The Screen Actors Guild reported African Americans comprised 13.3% of all television and theatrical roles, with the majority of these being supporting roles (Children Now, 2004), and African Americans captured 14.7% of total screen time (UCLA Center for African American Studies, 2003).

However, the range of the African American experience is largely absent as, now, African American characters are primarily professionals (i.e., doctors, lawyers, students, etc.) and law enforcement officers (Children Now, 2004; UCLA Center for African American Studies, 2003). Negative images still exist in conjunction with the improvements. Mastro and Greenberg (2000) found that African American characters were more provocative and the least professional in their dress, and were portrayed as lazy and less respected than Latino and White television characters. Some of these negative portrayals remain visible in Black-oriented media. Gabbadon (2006) found that in Black sitcoms, specifically, all episodes contained sexual talk and the majority of episodes contained sexual behavior with very little talk of sexual risk or responsibility.

The study of African Americans in film has been largely examined from a critical cultural perspective and primarily using textual analyses of specific films or characters. Bogle's (1974) seminal analysis of representations of African Americans in early film suggested one of five recurring archetypes that essentially portray African Americans as hypersexual, violent, and submissive. Succeeding studies revealed more expansive portrayals, including overrepresentations of African

Americans as comical, poor, and uneducated, images consonant with Whites' perceptions of African Americans (Entman & Rojecki, 2000; Squires, 2009). Although some of these stereotypes are not as explicit today (Greenberg, Mastro, & Brand, 2002), visible trends still remain that resonate with old stereotypes.

For example, historically, African American women have been represented in films stereotypically, and in marginal roles. Even though more media exist that are produced by African Americans and star African Americans, there is still a tension that exists between shattering stereotypes in an effort to be socially conscious, yet maintaining some of their characteristics in an effort to be entertaining (see Harris, 2004). Harris found that while two iconic films featuring the African American female experience showed women professionally successful, strong, moral, and physically attractive, they also portrayed the women as sexually promiscuous, adulterous, overbearing, and emasculating. Sometimes the negative and positive traits existed in the same character. Today, there are still the images of the mammy, the matriarch, the welfare mother, and the Jezebel (see Collins, 1993). Part of the reason for this tension may be that these characters represent issues of race, class, and gender, as argued by intersectionality, and rather than looking at this experience as unique, the stereotypes of all three identities are conflated into one. Warner (2008) suggested looking at identity factors as categories rather than as levels of different factors. Content and textual analyses should do the same in moving forward the examination of entertainment media.

Advertising

African Americans possess the lowest household income of all racial groups (Project for Excellence in Journalism, 2010), yet this group has the largest buying power (Miller & Kemp, 2006). According to Miller and Kemp (2006), "the African American propensity for buying branded, high-ticket and high-margin items makes them more loyal and profitable customers than any other consumer segment" (p. 9). Further, African American culture has been found to be the leading inspiration for marketing trendy products (Miller & Kemp, 2006), so African Americas are seen as valuable demographic customers.

Despite being in the forefront of consumer spending, African Americans make up a small percentage of character roles in advertising in both television and magazines. African Americans make up 18% of character roles in commercials (see Mastro, 2009; Messineo, 2008) but unlike Whites, Hispanics, and Asians, African Americans are significantly overrepresented in minor roles; furthermore, they are underrepresented in major roles (Maher, Herbst, Childs, & Finn, 2008; Mastro, 2009). When it comes to local markets where advertisers are expected to tailor advertising messages to serve a given local market, Maher et al. (2008) found that compared to their actual numbers, African Americans were underrepresented in local advertisements in Philadelphia.

Although, African Americans are visible in general-market advertising, examining product category as a variable gives insight into how the advertising industry values the African American consumer. Scholarship in marketing and advertising research has long illustrated a trend of African American dominance in product categories related to unhealthy food and alcohol, and less so for areas like skin care and major health issues that are prevalent in the African American community (see Kean & Prividera, 2007; Mastin & Campo, 2006; Mastro, 2009; Tirodokar & Jain, 2003). In their study of portrayals of racial minorities in advertising on children's television, Maher et al. (2008), found African Americans were overrepresented in restaurant and food commercials, while their White counterparts were not attached to any particular product.

Regardless of numerical representation, research on portrayals in advertising has revealed distinct differences in representation in general-market media as compared to Black-oriented media. Black-oriented media are lacking in representing the African American family structure in advertising, depicting single-parent households; however, Black-oriented media more frequently feature ads that are multicultural and ethnically integrated (Hazel & Clark, 2007; Maher et al., 2008). Overall, African American women are portrayed as submissive and are less likely to be portrayed as an object of sexual desire in general-market media (Hazel & Clarke, 2007; Messineo, 2008). In comparing portrayals on African American versus general-market entertainment on broadcast and cable networks, African American women were more likely to be portrayed as sexually desirable on BET than on ABC, CBS, NBC, and Fox (Messineo, 2008) and as financially secure in African American magazines (Hazel & Clarke, 2007). Hazel and Clarke's study also found that representations of beauty were more consistent with African American standards of beauty (i.e., curly hair, shapely body).

While the results seem contradictory, the difference in depictions of African American women across media formats may be explained through the intersection of race and gender with class. Black-oriented media may be representing this three-way interaction, showing the upwardly mobile, financially secure professional in ads presented in journalistic content, and the opposite with entertainment content. Newer research examines more specifically the role advertisers play in constructing singular categories of identities by dismissing the intersections of race, gender, and sexuality (Barnum & Zajicek, 2008). In addition, advertising research can apply intersectionality approaches to understanding how to frame cultural messages to complex target audiences. For example, how might one clothing advertisement appeal to

African American women versus Latina women versus White women, given the differences in perceptions of body image and fashion.

Representations across the various media indicate that African Americans are numerically overrepresented in proportion to the population (Mastro, 2009). However, quantity and quality of portrayal still remain concerns. Among the concerns is the potential effect that overrepresentation of negative portrayals may have on the construction and maintenance of African American identity. There are a number of implications, including self-esteem, academic performance, and overall life satisfaction. What follows is a brief discussion of theories and concepts that help explain the moderating and mediating effects of media on African American self-concept.

Connecting African American Identities to Media

According to Shields (2008), identity refers to the social categories to which an individual belongs and the personal meanings the person assigns to those categories. However, identity also involves one's ability to express who one sees as being one's authentic self. This ability is related to an individual's levels of self-awareness, self-esteem, self-image, and ability to self-reflect. Identity, however, is not only formed as a function of the individual but it also reflects the power structure among groups that make up a particular identity category. When considering an intersectionality approach, it is important to remember that identities are not treated as ranked items, as many scholars tend to examine them, but rather comprise a complex process (Warner, 2008). Learning about and creating one's identity is a process influenced by a number of factors, including culture and society, personal experience, and internalization of images and messages at both the cultural and interpersonal levels (Townsend, 2008; Warner, 2008). Media are implicated in each of these factors, as argued by social cognitive theory (see Bandura, 2009), cultivation theory (see Morgan, Shanahan, & Signorielli, 2009), and others. For example, African American girls may learn what it is like to be an African American woman from society, their life experiences created by their social status, the women in their lives, film, and music videos. Based on these sources, for some, this identity may be one of sexual promiscuity, amorality, and risky sexual activity (Townsend, 2008). On the other hand, individuals may also avoid such media messages in favor of seeking out more positive ones that support healthier social identities (Abrams & Giles, 2007; Harwood & Roy, 2005). So, identities, while defining individuals and groups, also dictate attitudes and perceptions about the self, others, and one's behaviors.

Social Identity Theory

Group membership provides cognitive and behavioral norms. It is by categorizing the self and others that differences between groups are accentuated. According to social identity theory (SIT), the act of examining differences tends to result in in-group favoritism whereby in attempts to maintain positive views about one's own group identity, people compare the positive, favorable characteristics of their group to corresponding unfavorable characteristics of other groups (Mastro & Behm-Morawitz, 2005). In making this comparison, individuals protect and bolster their self-esteem and positive self-identity (Abrams & Hogg, 1990).

Media become important as a means of providing aid in forming social identity and information for the social comparison process for both Whites and ethnic minorities (Mastro, 2003). Additionally, the content provides information on and legitimizes a group's status (Trepte, 2006). Nonminority viewers may use mediated stereotypes of various ethnic and social groups as a way to make judgments about these groups, using the presented characteristics as unfavorable traits to which they can compare their positive ones. Likewise, members of marginalized groups may come to use the characterizations to do the same (Mastro & Behm-Morawitz, 2005). Some of the overall premises of such a social comparison process are to help one define one's place in society, to establish one's self-esteem, and to fulfill the need to know more about the self (for an overview, see Trepte, 2006). Thus, social identity also translates into the media selection process as many choose their media in accordance with group memberships (see Mastro, 2003; Trepte, 2004). However, media scholars have not applied SIT as a theoretical framework while simultaneously acknowledging the existence of intersected identities. The SIT comparison process is usually examined using the dominant category of ethnicity. The combined approach may shed light on seemingly contradictory findings.

Self-Categorization Theory

Although often used interchangeably, self-categorization theory is distinct from social identity theory because it assumes that an individual's social self-concept is multilayered. In this way, the theory incorporates an intersectionality approach. Further, self-categorization theory contends that social context significantly determines the category with which an individual self-identifies (Turner, 1985). This explains why minority viewers are more likely to be attracted to characters with whom they share group membership, and therefore report more favorable evaluations of those characters (Mastro, Tamborini, & Hullett, 2005).

Recent research has applied self-categorization theory to exploring the utility of ethnic media in the emerging media landscape (M. Johnson, 2010). Specifically, Johnson (2010) contends that the distinctive nature of ethnic media provides a context that illuminates the distinguishing characteristics of a given social group, offering contextual cues that prime various aspects of an individual identity. Therefore incorporating social identity theories into a model of studying ethnic media is crucial to identifying its role in the contemporary media landscape as well as understanding audience's self-concept. For example, as compared to general-market media, Black-oriented media induce greater identification because of "ethnic fit" or racial compatibility. Based on Johnson's (2010) model, Black-oriented programs are more likely to implement identifiable cultural norms associated with the group, and have more of a positive influence on African Americans. These variables must be considered when examining Black-oriented media content and African American audiences.

Media's Impact on Self-Concept

The relationship between African Americans and general-market media can be viewed as conflicted, since African American media consumers must continually accept favorable messages and reject unfavorable messages about their group (Carter & Allen, 2004). In doing so, ethnic minorities arguably work harder than most to negotiate a healthy self-concept. Byrne (1984) defines self-concept as an individual's "attitudes, feelings, and knowledge about abilities, skills, appearances, and social acceptability." Scholars have found that African American children and adolescents' self-concepts (Barnes, 1980; Stroman, 1986; Ward, 2004) can be both positively and negatively affected by media presentations and the absence or invisibility of their social group (Graves, 1999; Merskin, 2007; Stroman, 1986). For children, girls seem to be more positively influenced (Stroman, 1986), and children's positive self-concepts are impacted more by viewing Black-oriented media (McDermott & Greenberg, 1984). Media depictions, as well as media consumption habits, have the potential to shape these different aspects of self-concept, namely African Americans' self-esteem and self-efficacy or group vitality.

Self-Esteem

For African American viewers, the impact of stereotypes on their self-perceptions and perceptions of others has been examined less often, and with mixed results. Allen (2001) argued that images in general-market media have the potential to harm African Americans' self-esteem. While other studies have argued otherwise, Allen contends that stereotypical representations of African Americans are internalized and are directly correlated to poor academic performance as a result of stereotype threat (Carter & Allen, 2004). The impact of media content, generally, and of in-group stereotypes on African Americans has been found to depend on the dimension of self-esteem, the viewer's age, and the media genre (Ward, 2004). General-market entertainment content is related to lower self-esteem; however, content that is specifically produced with African American viewers in mind, has the opposite effect, being related to lower self-consciousness and a stronger "endorsement of positive stereotypical beliefs" (Ward, 2004, p. 285). Sports programs and music videos seem to have a negative impact on self-perceptions in regard to appearance, performance, and social aspects, while regular viewing of general-market and Black-oriented programs were found to have less impact on self-esteem (Ward, 2004).

Much of the recent research on the relationship between media consumption and exposure on African American self-concept has focused on body image among African American women, an area strongly related with one's self-esteem. Overall, studies have shown that African American women report higher self-esteem than their White counterparts (Allen, 2001), highlighting the intersection of race and gender and how responses differ based on the media source. For example, in her in-depth interviews of 60 African American teenagers, Milkie (1999) found that African American girls did not identify with or accept general-market standards of beauty as perpetuated by magazine images. Similarly, Fujioka, Ryan, Agle, Legapsi, and Toohey (2009) found that African American girls rated thinness as less important and desirable in African American culture as compared to White participants who rated thinness very important and more desirable in their culture.

Group Vitality

Group membership is an essential part of one's identity; the perceived importance of the group translates directly into how one perceives the self. A social group's position in regards to sociostructural features such as power, wealth, and influence is referred to as "group vitality" (Giles, Bourhis, & Taylor, 1977). A group is considered vital depending on its perceived status, demography, and institutional support in relationship to other social groups. For example, a group that has economic control, high collective self-esteem and pride in its history, a large number of members, and has gained representation in various institutions such as government, business, and mass media, is considered to have high vitality (Abrams, 2008; Abrams & Giles, 2007; Giles et al., 1977). Because television and other media are a strong socializing force, they are likely to play a part in constructing and impacting a group's vitality, particularly an emergent group, providing information on the "number and characteristics of a group, public support for a group, and the type of behaviors group members engage in" (Abrams, 2008, p. 3). In addition, media ownership and the ability and visibility of opposing or alternative representations of African Americans also factor into perceived group vitality (Harwood & Roy, 2005).

Abrams and Giles (2007) found that when African Americans select television content because it favors their ethnic identity, they also experience an increased sense of group vitality. However, the more they avoid content because they feel it is harmful, misrepresenting, or fails to meet ethnic identity needs, the less vital they feel their group to be. This avoidance is a stronger influencing factor than selection on group vitality. In other words, the more ethnic identity a person possesses, the more likely the person is to avoid television content, which results in lower group vitality perceptions. Media thus become a strong factor in how vital African Americans perceive their group to be. While representations have arguably improved, African Americans with stronger group identity continue to avoid media because they perceive that the media have not improved enough. The fact that they avoid what is there serves as an indication that the group views itself as having less status and power in various media institutions, consequently reducing overall feelings of group vitality. The picture still has yet to be painted in regard to groups with intersecting identities.

Adding to this lowered vitality is the fact that African Americans avoid media more often because of ethnic identity needs than they select media because of ethnic identity needs. In fact, African Americans are more likely to view television in order to learn, or to view television out of habit, or to avoid television because it is boring, than to view television as a means to fill or support their social identities (Abrams, 2008). However, when it comes to habitual television viewing, there is an increase in African Americans' perceptions of Whites' vitality. After wanting to be entertained and avoiding media to preserve self-concept (which decreases perceived vitality of the group), African Americans view media out of habit (which serves to increase perceptions of Whites' vitality). Combined together, this suggests that most media viewing by African Americans serves to decrease group vitality while reinforcing the idea of Whites having higher group vitality.

Racial Identity

Racial identity is only one part of an individual's self-identity, but it plays a large role in shaping relationships with others and determining one's behavior, including media usage. As previously stated, intersectionality does not call for a complete dismissal of dominant categories, so they are very much a part of the discussion on identities. Racial identity is shaped by one's daily experiences as an individual, by history, and by society, and can be either a voluntary self-designation or one that is prescribed to them by others. In this way, one's racial identity varies across individuals. It can be based on "perceived similarities in the personal characteristics of members," how much being a group member matters to the person's sense of self, and how aware the person is that society treats all group members similarly (Davis & Gandy, 1999). Additionally, racial ethnicity is situation-bound; people can slip in and out of their group membership depending on the setting (see Clement, Baker, Josephson, & Noels, 2005).

As Harris (2004) noted, "[popular culture and media] images are critical in constructing and/or challenging lived reality and perceptions of that reality" (p. 189). In other words, media can and have been strong guiding forces in how African Americans negotiate the world, sometimes with both positive and negative results. To the extent that media can shape and influence one's identity, the identity they hold is a factor in determining just how much of a role media plays in their lives.

Individuals with high levels of ethnic identity or in-group racial identity have a higher motivation to protect the interests and status of their ethnic group, exhibit higher self-esteem in regards to their ethnic group, and are, in some cases, less likely to be impacted by the negative images presented of their in-group (Rivadeneyra, Ward, & Gordon, 2007; Stroman, 1986). This outcome is usually the case when positive group images are infrequent, provoking either a favorable intergroup comparison or more thoughtful media content selection in an effort to avoid threats to one's self-image (Mastro, 2009). Young viewers with weaker ethnic identity tend to be adversely affected, while those with stronger identification levels are less affected by the lack of ethnic minority visibility and the level of negativity that permeates the representations present (Rivadeneyra et al., 2007).

Other studies, however, have revealed that effects of media images are primarily moderated by the strength of ethnic identification (Appiah, 2002; Zhang, Dixon, & Conrad, 2009). In their examination of the effects of rap music on body image, Zhang et al. (2009) found the most pronounced negative effects among listeners who reported weaker ethnic identification. There was a positive relationship between low ethnic identification and body dissatisfaction, increased drive for thinness and increased tendencies toward bulimic behaviors.

Racial Standpoint

In addition to racial identity strength, an individual's racial location also shapes interpretations (Orbe & Harris, 2008). Racial location is the position in which an individual is placed in a social classification system where access and power are dependent on racial and ethnic membership (Hallstein, 2000). This location is very much impacted by the intersection of multiple social categories. Racial standpoint is a distinguishing concept which speaks to an individual's awareness of race politics in everyday life. This is derived through collective engagement and conversations about race. Grounded in standpoint theories, both racial location and racial standpoint suggest that individuals' perspectives are shaped by their social location and their education on the issue of race. Our understanding of race depends on our experience with race. Those who only interact with individuals of similar backgrounds will see the world differently from people with diverse experiences. By extension they will also see general-market and ethnic media differently, and thus be influenced differently (Kinefuchi & Orbe, 2008).

Research in this area argues that although Whites have a racial location, usually privileged, Whites' resistance to racial discourse inhibits the formulation of a racial standpoint (Martin, Krizek, Nakayama, & Bradford, 1996). In Kinefuchi and Orbe's (2008) exploration of reactions to the film *Crash*, the authors found that White viewers were more likely to view the issue of race demonstrated in the film as separate from their lived experiences and a societal problem that did not concern them. In contrast, African American viewers identified more strongly with the message in the film. Both interpretations are argued to derive from racial location. However, an interpretation that challenges dominant ideologies about race in the film is argued to be a racial standpoint. Thus, African Americans can evaluate media messages based on their racial location or their consciousness about the social and political construction of race, African American women on the basis of ethnicity, gender, and in some instances class.

Future Directions

While a host of research has examined the relationship between mass media and African Americans, there still remain areas that are under-researched, namely, the consumption and effects of Black-oriented media and the role that multiple layered identities play in these outcomes. Future scholarship should consider the expanding and defining role of ethnic media in the African American community by examining usage and group representation. Some argue that ethnic media are no longer ethnic, given producers' multicultural aims and since out-group members can access this specialized form of media. Recent studies have revealed African Americans' concerns about Black-oriented programming reinforcing stereotypes in Whites' minds (Banjo, 2008). However, Banjo (2011) found that Whites high in cultural competence are presumably able to enjoy and relate to Black entertainment without reinforcing supremacist ideology. Newer research has the potential to challenge dominant constructions by introducing complex and multiple layered identities.

As illustrated by the previous sections in this chapter, not only are identities themselves complex, but so too are the various factors that influence them. As media technology and content continue to evolve, so too should the way in which scholars discuss the impact of such a ubiquitous outlet, particularly when it comes to the area of social identities. One could argue that even now, as media allow for more venues and opportunities for the sharing of opinions but also for interpersonal and parasocial contact, that individuals' sense of self are becoming even more complex than what was observed a decade ago. The influx and consistent consumption of media materials give media representations the power to create mutually shared realities—even multiple realities for one individual if we acknowledge that identities are fluid and multiple in nature. Scholars can begin to better understand media's effects and influence on shaping social reality, but also begin to get a better sense as to how media can become a powerful tool in redefining social realities.

References

Abrams, D., & Hogg, M. A. (1990). An introduction to the social identity approach. In D. Abrams & M. A. Hogg (Eds.), *Social identity theory: Constructive and critical advances* (pp. 1–9). New York: Harvester Wheatsheaf.

Abrams, J. R. (2008). African Americans' television activity: Is it related to perceptions of out-group vitality? *Howard Journal of Communications, 19*, 1–17.

Abrams, J. R., & Giles, H. (2007). Ethnic identity gratifications selection and avoidance by African Americans: A group vitality and social identity gratifications perspective. *Media Psychology, 9*, 115–134.

Allen, R. L. (2001). A culturally based conception of the Black self-concept. In V. H. Milhouse, M. K. Asante, & P. Nwosu (Eds.), *Transcultural realities: Interdisciplinary perspectives on cross-cultural relations* (pp. 161–185). Thousand Oaks, CA: Sage.

Anthias, F., & Yuval-Davis, N. (1983). Contextualizing feminism: Ethnic, gender and class divisions. *Feminist Review, 15*, 62–75.

Appiah, O. (2002). Black and White viewers' perception and recall of occupational characters on television. *Journal of Communication, 52*(4), 776–793.

Arbitron, Inc. (2009). Black radio today: How America listens to radio. Retrieved from http://www.Arbitron.com

Bandura, A. (2009). Social cognitive theory of mass communication. In J. A. Bryant & M. B. Oliver (Eds.), *Media effects: Advances in theory and research* (pp. 94–124). New York: Routledge.

Banjo, O. (May 2008). *For us only? Hostile media perception in the presence of a White audience*. Paper presented at the annual International Communication Association. Montreal, Canada.

Banjo, O. (2011). What are you laughing at? Examining predictors of Whites' enjoyment of Black entertainment. *Journal of Broadcasting and Electronic Media, 55*(2), 137–159.

Barnes, E. J. (1980). The Black community as the source of positive self-concept for Black children: A theoretical perspective. In R. L. Jones (Ed.), *Black psychology* (pp. 166–192). New York: Harper & Row.

Barnum, A. J., & Zajicek, A. M. (2008). An intersectional analysis of visual media: A case of diesel advertisements. *Social Thought and Research, 29*, 105–128.

Bogle, D. (1974). *Toms, coons, mulattoes, mammies & bucks: An interpretive history of Blacks in American films*. London: Bantam.

Byrne, B. (1984). The general/academic self-concept nomological network: A review of construct validation research. *Review of Educational Research, 54*(3), 427–456.

Carter, T., & Allen, R. (2004). An examination of mainstream and Black media's influence on the self-concept of African Americans, In G. Meiss & A. Tait (Eds.), *Ethnic media in America: Images, audiences, and transforming forces* (pp. 27–32). Dubuque, IA: Kendall Hunt.

Children Now. (2004). *Fall prime time diversity report 2003–2004*. Oakland, CA: Author.

Clement, R., Baker, S. C., Josephson, G., & Noels, K. A. (2005). Media effects on ethnic identity among linguistic majorities and minorities: A longitudinal study of bilingual setting. *Human Communication Research, 31*(3), 399–422.

Cole, E. R., & Omari, S. R. (2003). Race, class and the dilemmas of upward mobility for African Americans. *Journal of Social Issues, 59*(4), 785–802.

Collins, P. H. (1993). *Black feminist thought: Knowledge, consciousness and the politics of empowerment*. New York: Routledge.

Dates, J., & Stroman, C. (2001). Portrayals of families of color on television. In J. A. Bryant (Ed.), *Television and the American family* (pp. 207–225). Mahwah, NJ: Erlbaum.

Davis, J. L., & Gandy, O. H. (1999). Racial identity and media orientation: Exploring the nature of constraint. *Journal of Black Studies, 29*(3), 367–397.

Dixon, T. L. (2006). Psychological reactions to crime news portrayals of black criminals: Understanding the moderating roles of prior news viewing and stereotype endorsement. *Communication Monographs, 73*, 162–187.

Dixon, T. L. (2007). Black criminals and White officers: The effects of racially misrepresenting law breakers and law defenders on television news. *Media Psychology, 10*, 270–291.

Dixon, T. L. (2008a). Crime news and racialized beliefs: Understanding the relationship between local news viewing and perceptions of African Americans and crime. *Journal of Communication, 58*(1), 106–125.

Dixon, T. L. (2008b). Network news and racial beliefs: Exploring the connection between national television news exposure and stereotypical perceptions of African Americans. *Journal of Communication, 58*(2), 321–337.

Dixon, T. L., & Linz, D. (2000a). Overrepresentation and underrepresentation of African Americans and Latinos as lawbreakers on television news. *Journal of Communication, 50*, 131–154.

Dixon, T. L., & Linz, D. (2000b). Race and the misrepresentation of victimization on local television news. *Communication Research, 27*, 547–573.

Edison Research/Arbitron. (2010). *Twitter usage in America: 2010*. Retrieved from http://www.edisonresearch.com/home/archives/2011/05/the_social_habit_2011.php

Entman, R. M., & Rojecki, A. (2000). *The Black image in the White mind*. Chicago, IL: University of Chicago Press.

Fujioka, Y., Ryan, E., Agle, M., Legapsi, M., & Toohey, R. (2009). The role of racial identity in responses to thin media ideals. *Communication Research, 36*(4), 451–474.

Fuller, A. (2004). What difference does difference make? Women race ethnicity, social class, and social change. *Race, Gender & Class, 11*(4), 8–29.

Gabbadon, N. (2006, June). *Let's get it on: Sexual content in African American situation comedies*. Paper presented at the annual meeting of the International Communication Association. Dresden, Germany.

Gerbner, G., Morgan, M., Gross, L., Signorielli, N., & Shanahan, J. (2002). Growing up with television: Cultivation processes. In J. Bryant & D. Zillmann (Eds.), *Media effects: Advances in theory and research* (2nd ed., pp. 43–67). Hillsdale, NJ: Erlbaum.

Giles, H., Bourhis, R. Y., & Taylor, D. M. (1977). Towards a theory of language in ethnic group relations. In H. Giles (Ed.), *Language, ethnicity, and intergroup relations* (pp. 307–348). London: Academic Press.

Graves, S. B. (1999). Television and prejudice reduction: When does television as a vicarious experience make a difference? *Journal of Social Issues, 55*, 707–727.

Greenberg, B., & Collette, L. (1997). The changing faces of TV: A demographic analysis of network television's new seasons, 1966–1992. *Journal of Broadcasting & Electronic Media, 41*, 1–13.

Greenberg, B., Mastro, D., & Brand, J. (2002). Minorities and the mass media: Television into the 21st century. In J. Bryant & D. Zillman (Eds.), *Media effects advances in theory and research* (2nd ed., pp. 333–357). Mahwah, NJ: Erlbaum.

Hallstein, D. L. O. (2000). Where standpoint stands now: An introduction and commentary. *Women's Studies in Communication, 23*, 115.

Harris, T. M. (2004). Interrogating the representation of African American female identity in the films *Waiting to Exhale* and *Set It Off*. In R. L. Jackson (Ed.), *African American communication and identities: Essential readings* (pp. 189–196). Thousand Oaks, CA: Sage.

Harwood, J., & Roy, A. (2005). Social identity theory and mass communication research. In J. Harwood & H. Giles (Eds.), *Intergroup communication: Multiple perspectives* (pp. 189–212). New York: Peter Lang.

Hazel, V., & Clarke, J. (2007). Race and gender in the media: A content analysis of advertisements in two mainstream Black magazines. *Journal of Black Studies, 39*(5), 5–21.

Hodges, J. (1996, May 13). Black, White teens show similarity in TV tastes, *Advertising Age*, 24.

Iyengar, S. (1991). *Is anyone responsible?* Chicago, IL: University of Chicago Press.

Iyengar, S. (1996). Framing responsibility for political news. *American Academy of Political and Social Science, 546*, 59–70.

Jackson, L., von Eye, A., Fitzgerald, H. E. Zhao, Y., & Witt, E. A. (2010). Self-concept, self-esteem, gender, race and information use. *Computers in Human Behavior, 26*, 323–328.

Johnson, M. (2010). Incorporating self-categorization concepts into ethnic media research. *Communication Theory, 20*, 106–125.

Johnson, M. A., David, P., & Huey, D. (2004). Looks like me? Body image in magazines targeted to U. S. Latinas. In A. Tait & G. Meiss (Eds.), *Ethnic media in America: Images, audiences, and transforming forces*. Dubuque, IA: Kendall Hunt.

Kean, L. B., & Prividera, L. C. (2007). Communicating about race and health: A content analysis of print advertisements in African American and general readership magazines. *Health Communication, 21*, 289–297.

Kinefuchi, E., & Orbe, M. (2008). Situating oneself in a racialized world: Understanding student reactions to *Crash* through standpoint theory and context-positionality frames. *Journal of International and Intercultural Communication, 1*, 70–90.

Lichter, R., Lichter, L. S., Rothman, S., & Amundson, D. (1987). Prime-time prejudice: TV's images of Blacks and Hispanics. *Public Opinion, 10*, 13–16.

Maher, J. K., Herbst, K. C., Childs, N. M., & Finn, S. (2008). Racial stereotypes in children's' television commercials. *Journal of Advertising Research, 48*(1), 80–93.

Martin, J., Krizek, R., Nakayama, T., & Bradford, L. (1996). Exploring whiteness: A study of self-labels for White Americans. *Communication Quarterly, 44*(2), 125–144.

Mastin, T., & Campo, S. (2006). Conflicting messages: Overweight and obesity advertisements and articles in Black magazines. *Howard Journal of Communication, 17*(4), 265–298.

Mastro, D. E. (2003). A social identity approach to understanding the impact of television messages. *Communication Monographs, 70*(2), 98–113.

Mastro, D. E. (2009). Effects of racial and ethnic stereotyping. In J. A. Bryant & M. B. Oliver (Eds.), *Media effects: Advances in theory and research* (pp. 325–341). New York: Routledge.

Mastro, D. E., & Behn-Morawitz, E. (2005). Latin representation on primetime television. *Journalism and Mass Communication Quarterly, 82*, 110–130.

Mastro, D. E., & Greenberg, B. S. (2000). The portrayal of racial minorities on prime time television. *Journal of Broadcasting & Electronic Media, 44*(4), 690–703.

Mastro, D., Tamborini, R., & Hullett, C. (2005). Linking media to prototype activation and subsequent activation and subsequent celebrity attraction: An application of self-categorization theory. *Communication Research, 32*, 323–348.

McDermott, S. T., & Greenberg, B. S. (1984). Black children's esteem: Parents, peers, television. *Communication yearbook, 8,* 164–177.

Merskin, D. (2007). Three Faces of Eva: Perpetuation of the hot-Latina stereotype in Desperate Housewives. *Howard Journal of Communication, 18,* 133–151.

Messineo, M. J. (2008). Does advertising on Black Entertainment Television portray more positive gender representations compared to broadcast networks? *Sex Roles, 59,* 752–764.

Milkie, M. (1999). Social comparisons, reflected appraisals, and mass media: The impact of pervasive beauty images on Black and White girls self-concept. *Social Psychology Quarterly, 62*(2), 190–210.

Miller, P., & Kemp, H. (2006). *What's Black about it?* Ithaca, NY: Paramount Market.

Morgan, M., Shanahan, J., & Signorielli, N. (2009). Growing up with television: Cultivation processes. In J. A. Bryant & M. B. Oliver (Eds.), *Media effects: Advances in theory and research* (pp. 34–49), New York: Routledge.

Motion Picture Association of America. (2009). *Theatrical market statistics 2009.* Retrieved from http://www.mpaa.org

Nakano Glenn, E. (1999). The social construction and institutionalization of gender: An integrative framework. In M. M. Ferree, J. Lorber, & B. Hess (Eds.), *Revisioning gender* (pp. 3–43). London: Sage.

New California Media. (2005, June). The ethnic media in America: The giant hidden in plain sight. Retrieved from http://meldi.snre.umich.edu/node/7222

Nielsen Media Research. (2005). *TV audience special study: African American audience.* Retrieved from http://www.nielsen.com

Nielsen Media Research (2007). African-American TV usage and buying power highlighted by Nielsen. New York: Author.

Nielsen Media Research (2011). State of the media: March 2011 U.S. TV trends by ethnicity. New York: Author.

Orbe, M., & Harris, T. M. (2008). *Interracial communication: Theory into practice* (2nd ed.). Thousand Oaks, CA: Sage.

Pew Research Center. (2010). *Mobile access 2010.* Retrieved from http://www.pewinternet.org/Reports/2010/Mobile-Access-2010.aspx

Project for Excellence in Journalism. (2009). *State of the news media: An annual report on American journalism.* Retrieved from http://www.stateofthemedia.org/2009/narrative_ethnic_africanamerican.php?media=11&cat=3

Project for Excellence in Journalism. (2010). *State of the news media: An annual report on American Journalism.* Retrieved from http://www.stateofthemedia.org/2010/

Renz, B. (2006). The role of ethnic media. In G. Meiss & A. Tait (Eds.), *Ethnic media in America: Building a system of their own* (pp. 15–33). Dubuque, IA: Kendall Hunt.

Rivadeneyra, R., Ward L. W., & Gordon, M. (2007). Distorted reflections: Media exposure and Latino adolescents' conceptions of self. *Media Psychology, 9,* 261–290.

Screen Actors Guild. (n.d.). *2007 & 2008 Casting data reports.* Retrieved from http://www.sagaftra.org/files/sag/documents/2007-2008_CastingDataReports.pdf

Shields, S. A. (2008). Gender: An intersectionality perspective. *Sex Roles, 59*, 301–311.

Squires, C. (2009). *African Americans and the media.* Cambridge, England: Polity Press.

Stroman, C. A. (1986). Television viewing and self-concept among Black children. *Journal of Broadcasting & Electronic Media, 30*(1), 87–93.

Tirodkar, M., & Jain, A. (2003). Food messages on African American television shows. *American Journal of Public Health, 93*(3), 439–441.

Townsend, T. G. (2008). Protecting our daughters: Intersection of race, class and gender in African American mothers' socialization of their daughters' heterosexuality. *Sex Roles, 59*, 429–442.

Trepte, S. (2006). Social identity theory. In J. Bryant & P. Vorderer (Eds.), *Psychology of entertainment* (pp. 255–272). Mahwah, NJ: Erlbaum.

Turner, J. C. (1985). Social categorization and the self-concept: A social cognitive theory of group behavior. In E. J. Lawler (Ed.), *Advances in group processes: Theory and research* (Vol. 2, pp. 77–122). Greenwich, CT: JAI.

UCLA Center for African American Studies. (2003). *Prime time in black and white: Not much is new for 2002.* Los Angeles, CA: Author.

Viswanath, K., & Arora, P. (2000). Ethnic media in the United States: An essay on their role in integration, assimilation, and social control. *Mass Communication & Society, 3*(1), 39–56.

Wade-Gayles, G. (1997). *No crystal stair: Visions of race and gender in black women fiction.* Cleveland, Ohio: The Pilgrim Press.

Ward, L. M. (2004). Wading through the stereotypes: Positive and negative associations between media use and black adolescents' conceptions of self. *Developmental Psychology, 40*(2), 284–294.

Warner L. R. (2008). A best practices guide to intersectional approaches in psychological research. *Sex Roles, 59*, 454–463.

Zhang, Y., Dixon, T. L., & Conrad, K. (2009). Rap music videos and African American women's body image: The moderating role of ethnic identity. *Journal of Communication, 59*(2), 262–278.

Chapter 9

Rebooting Identities
Using Computer-Mediated Communication to Cope with a Stigmatizing Social Identity

Katie Margavio Striley and Shawn King

Ian Bates has become an Internet sensation and a role-model for online gaming "geeks." Bates is an avid World of Warcraft player, the most popular online role-playing game in the world. Face-to-face social interactions are difficult for Bates because he has Asperger's syndrome. Bates has immersed himself in the fantasy world of World of Warcraft as a way to cope with being different, and has become an expert on even the smallest game details. At a gaming convention, Blizzcon, Bates questioned game designers about a character omitted from the beta version of a new game installment. The designers were unaware of this mistake and promised to fix the oversight. Bates gained Internet stardom when a YouTube video surfaced of his convention question. To geeks everywhere, Bates has become known as "The Red Shirt Guy," a name created both as an inside joke for geeks and his appearance on YouTube wearing a red shirt. Bates' question was so popular and helpful to game designers that a World of Warcraft character, Wildhammer Fact Checker, was created in honor of Bates. YouTube volunteered to give Bates a share of online revenue, and Bates decided to donate the proceeds to an Asperger's syndrome foundation. Through online social media, Bates has turned two stigmatized identities, Asperger's syndrome and being a gaming geek, into a source of pride. Online, Bates has found the acceptance and social support he has lacked in face-to-face interactions.

Our chapter incorporates a variety of theoretical perspectives to explore the importance and implications of engaging in computer-mediated communication (CMC) to cope with *stigmatized*, or *out-group* social identities (often referred to as negative social identities). We argue that CMC allows marginalized and stigmatized individuals to form and maintain *desired* or *in-group* social identities (often referred to as positive social identities). Our aims are twofold. First, we seek to broaden the context of CMC. Computer-mediated communication research has often focused on the average person, but marginalized individuals also use CMC for a specific type of identity formation and maintenance.

Second, we attempt to broaden the theoretical understanding of CMC. Current theory is ill-equipped to understand the rapidly changing context of CMC (Scott, 2009) and its influence on identity management. We begin by examining how communication creates the self and the stigmatized social identity, and then explore CMC's ability to destroy negative social identities and re-form positive social identities, and finally we investigate future directions and new agendas for CMC scholars.

The formation of the self cannot occur in isolation (Berger & Luckmann, 1966; Blumer, 1969; Cooley, 1902; Goffman, 1959; Mead, 1934). Human genes allow for "the potential to develop into humans, but without contact, this potential cannot be realized" (Stewart, 2002, p. 10). The social identity perspective asserts that social identities are formed and maintained through social interaction (Tajfel & Turner, 1979). Humans are motivated to view themselves positively by maintaining positive self-identities (Foels, 2006; Hogg & Reid, 2006; Schmidt, Branscombe, Silvia, Garcia, & Spears, 2006); therefore, most individuals will seek out interactions that enhance their self-image (Steele, 1988; Tesser, 1988). However, what happens when interactions with others serve to create a self that the individual views as negative? Members of marginalized or stigmatized populations experience such identity threats (Blanz, Mummendey, Mielke, & Klink, 1998; Mummendey, Kessler, Klink, & Mielke, 1999) and must enact coping strategies to restore a positive sense of self (Blanz et al., 1998). Many individuals utilize CMC to cope with undesirable social identities. Some may choose to escape into online anonymity and disassociate from their stigmatized identity, and others, like Ian Bates, may seek out online social support to find pride in their identity.

Communication and the Creation of Self

The communication theory of identity conceptualizes identity *as* communication rather than as a byproduct of communication (Jung & Hecht, 2004). Communication with others is essential for the creation of self (Cooley, 1902; Jung & Hecht, 2004; Mead, 1934; Ting-Toomey, 1986). Identities are asserted, defined, and agreed upon in conversations (Ting-Toomey, 1999). From birth, humans depend on others for self-definition because identities are created and molded during communicative interaction (Jackson, 2002). Through feedback, identities are confirmed, rejected, and disconfirmed by others (Watzlavick, Beavin, & Jackson, 1967).

For Cooley (1902), self-concepts are formed through others' appraisals where others serve as mirrors in which we view ourselves. Similarly, Mead (1934) argued that self-concepts are formed through observing others' communicative responses and adjusting ourselves accordingly.

Human consciousness arises from the interplay between the individual and the environment. Identity formation becomes a social process because "selves can only exist in definite relationships to other selves" (Mead, 1934, p. 164). Blumer (1969) posited that the self is a process defined *within* the interaction. Communication both facilitates the self-view and provides individuals with information that is later utilized to form a self-view. Goffman (1959) theorized the production of identity through everyday social life. For Goffman, collectives create a set of acceptable roles for individuals to perform, and individuals are socialized to know which roles are appropriate to enact. Goffman argued that "a performance is 'socialized,' molded, and modified to fit into the understanding and expectations of the society in which it is presented" (p. 35). For Goffman, identity is a performance which is maintained through the cooperation of multiple social actors. Finally, Berger and Luckmann (1966) argued that once identity is crystallized it is shaped and reshaped by social relations.

The Past and Present of CMC

Communication technology influences the formation and maintenance of identity by offering new frontiers for identity exploration. New communication technologies often change how humans think, interact, and view themselves (Ong, 1982). Often, new communication technologies are met with skepticism and distrust as individuals attempt to ascertain the effects of the technology. Early computer-mediated communication research was characterized and shaped by concerns about the social effects of this new technology (Lee, 2009). Researchers raised concerns about the effects on face-to-face communication (Jacobson, 1999), the authenticity of online identity (Stone, 1995), and the social and psychological effects (Kraut et al., 1998). Some media theories challenged the ability of CMC to facilitate interpersonal goals. For example, media richness theory contended that rich mediums, those high in cue systems, immediate feedback, personalized messages, and linguistic variety, were more effective facilitators of emotional and relational goals (Daft & Lengel, 1984). Insofar as identity goals are personal and emotional, media richness theory predicts that lean mediums, such as text-based CMC, would not effectively gratify identity goals.

Empirical results only partially supported these early assumptions about CMC and newer theories have emerged to explain the discrepancy. For instance, social information processing theory (SIP) (Walther, 1992) contends that relational goals can be facilitated through CMC, because visual cues are filtered out. Although it may take longer, people adapt to the absent cues and make substitutions. Computer-mediated communication can actually feel hyperpersonal and foster stronger personal bonds than face-to-face interactions (Walther, 1992, 1997). Our chapter adopts Walther's hyperpersonal argument. Therefore, we believe CMC might effectively offer marginalized individuals new possibilities to form and maintain positive social identities.

Recent CMC research has taken up issues of anonymity, identity, and the blurring of realities. Computer-mediated communication has become so integrated into the lives of some Americans that it has earned its place as a serious sphere of academic inquiry. Turkle (1995) even suggested "people can get lost in virtual worlds" (p. 268). Baym (2009) argued that the boundaries between the virtual and non-virtual world are becoming blurred as we integrate technology into our lives, even suggesting that "online and offline are not different entities to be contrasted" (p. 720).

CMC and the Creation of Self

Computer-mediated communication can have profound identity implications for users, and has a long history of identity scholarship (Scott, 2009) with a strong theoretical background (D'Urso, 2009). Turkle (1995) argued that cyberspace allows for the construction and reconstruction of identity and the ability to take on multiple identities. When individuals enter virtual worlds they begin to post narratives that construct identity (Sanderson, 2010). Online contexts allow users to perform identity online (Palomares & Lee, 2010; Sanderson, 2010). Virtual environments also may allow for more identity control. For instance, Palomares and Lee (2010) argued that users have more control over identity cues they share with others. Sanderson (2010) posited that online identity performances might conform to idealized notions of how users want others to see them. Gonzales and Hancock (2008) suggested a strong link exists between self-presentation and the creation of self-concept. The Internet is an arena for self-presentation, thus mediated self-presentation can construct the self.

Uses-and-gratifications theory states that media users are active members driven by specific goals (McQuail, Blumler, & Brown, 1972) and media are utilized to achieve these goals (Katz, 1959). Uses-and-gratification theory has traditionally been at the forefront of new communication technologies (Ruggiero, 2000); it was utilized when radio (Herzog, 1944), newspaper (Berelson, 1949), and CMC (Boneva, Kraut, & Frohlich, 2001) became popularized. Computer-mediated communication provides users with a two-way channel which provides an opportunity to present and receive appraisals about the self. Additionally, the means by which identities are presented and appraised through CMC might be particularly attractive to those with identity anxiety. Receiving feedback about identity is a potentially traumatic event: negative appraisals can lead to negative self-concepts which can lead to depression and poor mental health, whereas perceived inaccurate appraisals "engender fear that [individuals] may not know themselves after all" (Swann, Pelham, & Krull, 1989, p. 783). Therefore, some people may distance themselves from face-to-face interactions when an undesired appraisal is perceived (Tesser, 2003) and utilize CMC when face is potentially threatened (O'Sullivan, 2000).

The role of both communication and CMC in the creation of the self having been discussed, we will shift our focus to formation of the stigmatized and marginalized self and the potential of CMC to provide opportunities for individuals to redefine themselves or find self-acceptance online.

Social Identity Theory

Communicative interactions create both personal and social identities (Tajfel & Turner, 1979). Personal identities are akin to Mead's "I"; they are the identity of the individual "at rest." Social identities are drawn from group membership; essentially, individuals have a repertoire of identities they may pull from depending on the social context. Social identity is similar to Goffman's (1959) "roles" and Berger and Luckmann's (1966) "identity types." During communicative interaction, values about social identities are exchanged (Heckt, Jackson, & Ribeau, 2003). Some social identities come to be viewed more or less positively than others. Some identities are socially accepted, rejected, or disconfirmed. Social identity theory (SIT) (Tajfel & Turner, 1979) illuminates the creation and maintenance of social identity, the process by which identities become negative, and negative identities are stereotyped.

According to SIT, social identity formation is a three-step process: individuals categorize themselves and others, identify with their categories, and compare categories. The human brain is prone to categorization as a means to efficient operation (Foels, 2006). Individuals categorize according to perceived group membership. Categories are compared to existing templates from past experiences, called schemas (Markus, 1977). When one individual encounters another, she subconsciously places that person into an existing schema. Once individuals are categorized, they identify with their group memberships. Social identity becomes an internalized aspect of the self (Tajfel & Turner, 1986). Individuals begin to view themselves "interchangeably with other group members" (Plataw, Byrne, & Ryan, 2005, p. 606). Finally, they begin to compare social categories. Humans are motivated to have a positive self-image (Schmidt et al., 2006) and will value their own social category above others (Foels, 2006; Hogg & Reid, 2006). This in-group bias will lead to a more positive social identity, which will lead to an enhanced self-image.

Figure 9.1 Identity cues enmeshed within text.

Social Identity Model of Deindividuation

Computer-mediation communication researchers have recognized SIT as an important theory. The extension of SIT into cyberspace (Wang, Walther, & Hancock, 2009) prompted the articulation of a new theory: the social identity model of deindividuation (SIDE; Spears & Lea, 1992). Before SIDE, researchers assumed a lack of visual cues allowed individuals to escape into online anonymity, which implied that individuals would rely less on social identity and more on personal identity. However, SIDE states that individuals communicating online may actually rely more on social identity because they actively search for more subtle social cues. For instance, Shaw (1994) found that online interactants could ascertain physical location, ethnic identity, and social information based on spelling. Word choices, like "ya'll" or "yins" could reveal geographic location; "moxie," "frenemy," or "ginormous" might suggest age; "dawg," "aint," or "phat" could indicate ethnicity. In Figure 9.1, Mickey tries to convince Rachel of his superior intelligence, but his bad typing betrays him.

Once group differences are uncovered online, the anonymity of CMC might serve to highlight these differences (Spears, Lea, Corneliussen, Postmes, & Haar, 2002). Thus, CMC might depersonalize individuals and make them more aware of a shared or disparate group identity (Lea, Spears, & DeGroot, 2001; Postmes & Spears, 1998). Deindividuation is a focal shift away from the self and towards the group. Essentially, the online environment tends to obscure interpersonal differences and heighten group salience (E. Lee, 2007). The social identity model of deindividuation has become a leading theory in CMC research; however, scholars should be careful to avoid being blinded by SIDE (Scott, 2009)—it simply illuminates one aspect of CMC, there are other theoretical possibilities left to explore.

Effects of Social Identification

Social identity theory offers one explanation for systems of stigma, stereotyping, and oppression. When social identity is triggered, individuals respond to each other based on group membership rather than personal identity (Goar, 2007), resulting in depersonalization (Goar, 2007; Hogg & Reid, 2006). Then, some group differences are oversimplified, stereotyped, and perceived negatively. Once a difference has been associated with a negative attribute, individuals who do not possess the difference separate themselves from those who do; an "us" and "them" mentality is created (Link & Phelan, 2001). The comparison of categories and attribution of value creates high-status and low-status groups. Individuals marked as different experience a social status loss; they exist at the nadir of the social hierarchy. Individuals are communicatively informed of the worth of their ascribed social categories (Scott, 2007). Knowing the worth of their categories will lead individuals to perceive their self-image as either positive or negative (Blanz et al., 1998; Hogg & Reid, 2006). Members of low-status groups are often considered marginalized or stigmatized (Harrington, 2004).

Stereotypes and stigmas are persistent and resist change (Harrington, 2004). The tendency to categorize (stereotype) gives humans the advantage of operating quickly in complex social contexts (Macrea & Bodenhausen, 2000); categorization allows the brain to run on "autopilot" and frees it to focus on other concerns. The result, however, is that humans tend to make snap judgments that conform to existing beliefs (Nickerson, 1998) and often ignore information that discredits existing cognitive schemas (Edwards & Smith, 1996). Johnson (2006) calls this tendency for adherence to preformed cognitive schemas following "paths of least resistance." According to Johnson, falling mindlessly into a habit is easier than creating new behavioral or cognitive patterns. Ultimately, the combination of placing people into groups and valuing some groups over other groups creates a social hierarchy where those on the bottom are stigmatized.

Stigma and Marginalization

Stigma is inherently a social process (Link & Phelan, 2001; Reeders, 2008; Yang et al., 2007), constituted and reconstituted in communication (Goffman, 1963; Kleinman & Hall-Clifford, 2009; Major & O'Brien, 2005). Collectives negotiate conceptualizations of what it means to be "normal" or "deviant." Individuals are socialized into epistemological and ontological orientations that conceive of stigma as naturally occurring (Yang et al., 2007); perceptions of stigma become "objectivated" (Berger & Luckmann, 1966) and are rarely questioned. Therefore, Goffman (1963) said, "the normal and the stigmatized are not persons but rather perspectives" (p. 138). The stigmatized are the "social remainder" (Reeders, 2008, p. 30), discounted by the rest of society (Goffman, 1963). Stigma can be immediately apparent or concealed; the individual with a visible stigma is termed "discredited" by

Goffman, and the individual with a hidden stigma is "discreditable." The discredited must learn to manage social tensions, whereas the discreditable must learn to manage social information.

Stigma and marginalization carry a number of adverse health effects. Physical effects of social rejection can include increased blood pressure (Zadro & Williams, 2006), nerve responses that mimic physical pain (Eisenberger, Lieberman, & Williams, 2003; Zadro & Williams, 2006), and anxiety (Eisenberger et al., 2003). Psychological effects can include the loss of a sense of well-being (Diener, 2005), impaired cognitive functioning (Williams, 2001), lower self-esteem (Vandevelde & Miyahara, 2005), a lack of belonging (Sommer, Williams, Ciarocco, & Baumeister, 2001), hopelessness, and a sense of despair (Williams, 2001). Since people want to maintain a positive social identity, members of low-status groups face an identity crisis.

Coping Strategies

Members of low-status groups enact identity management strategies to cope with their consigned social positions (Blanz et al., 1998; Mummendey et al., 1999; Tajfel & Turner, 1979, 1986). Blanz et al. (1998) suggested those with negative social identities adopt individual or collective strategies that are either cognitive or behavioral. Individual strategies benefit the individual, such as exiting the low status group and hiding a social stigma. Collective strategies include a group attempt to raise group status, such as challenging the social hierarchy. Behavioral responses are changes in action, whereas cognitive responses are mental restructuring techniques where an individual changes her perspective on a situation. For instance, Striley (2010) found that some gifted peer groups utilize the collective cognitive strategy of valuing intellect over popular culture; gifted children redefined high status within their peer groups and rejected nongifted peers. Goffman (1963) observed that individuals can hide a stigmatized identity by utilizing disidentifiers and attempt to "pass" as a member of another group.

Co-cultural theory (Orbe, 1998) provides an overarching view of how those without power communicate to cope with negative social identities. Marginalized group members may attempt to *assimilate* into dominant culture and minimize their marginalized identity; *separate* themselves from dominant culture and revel in their low-status group; or attempt to *accommodate* both dominant culture and their marginalized group by assuming dual membership. We maintain that individuals who accept their marginalized identity or have high in-group esteem are more likely to enact separation tactics; those who reject their stigmatized identity or have low in-group esteem are more likely to enact assimilation tactics;

finally, those who accept their stigmatized identity but also recognize the value of dominant culture will enact accommodating tactics.

CMC and Stigma

Computer-mediated communication can provide a safe haven for those with negative social identities and foster the adoption of identity management coping strategies. Online networks provide a valuable opportunity for social inclusion, which may improve the lives of stigmatized or marginalized individuals (Notly, 2009). Computer-mediated communication provides a virtual channel for individuals with similarities to come together and share collective grievances and identity (Spears et al., 2002); these opportunities for empowerment create space for collective resistance against an out-group authority (Spears et al., 2002). Computer-mediated communication often facilitates status neutrality, democracy, and support networks (Spears & Lea, 1994) and allows minority groups to voice their dissent (Spears et al., 2002). Notley (2009) found that Australian teens utilized social networks both to find inclusion and express themselves. Online inclusion gave teens a sense of security and social support. Computer-mediated communication might be particularly helpful for those at risk for offline social exclusion. We focus here specifically on how individuals can utilize CMC to enact separation and assimilation identity tactics in order either to shed an unwanted identity or come to accept a stigmatizing identity.

Anonymity and Assimilation Tactics

Computer-mediated communication can give marginalized and stigmatized individuals an opportunity to create and maintain a positive self view. Self-enhancement theory (Steele, 1988; Tesser, 1988) states that individuals desire to be viewed positively by themselves and others. Therefore, some marginalized individuals might desire to adopt assimilation tactics and shed their marginalized identity. Assimilation tactics might be more plausible in CMC than face-to-face communication because visually recognizable identity cues, such as race, gender, and sexuality, are less immediately apparent, and can be strategically managed. Individuals who choose assimilation can escape into online anonymity (Lea & Spears, 1992). Individuals can strategically choose anonymity by deciding when and if to disclose information; or medium design can privilege anonymity, such as multiuser games like World of Warcraft. Although SIDE posits that even in the absence of visual cues users may detect identity clues, SIDE theorists have found that individuals strategically manipulate cues to express or hide identity (Spears et al., 2002).

A lack of social cues affords individuals an opportunity to elicit a positive perception from others. A strong connection exists between the amount of cues filtered out of a self-presentation and the valence of the perception of the self-presentation. For instance, romantic partners are more attracted to each other when communicating via CMC (Walther, 1997), and the less cues the better. Individuals who incorporate photographs in their online self-presentations are perceived as less attractive than those who only present themselves textually (Walther, Sloveck, & Tidwell, 2001). Groups communicating via text form greater group identities than groups communicating via video conference (Lea, Spears, & deGroot, 2001). The more a couple communicates via lean mediums, the more they idealized their relationship (Stafford & Merolla, 2007). Long-distance couples tend to idealize their relationship more than those who are geographically close (Stafford, Merolla, & Castle, 2006; Stafford & Reske, 1990) because of the increase in filtered mediums (Stafford & Merolla, 2007).

Computer-mediate communication's anonymity and control over message production (Walther, 1997) provides an attractive opportunity to escape a stigmatized identity. Computer-mediated communication filters out many cues and allows for greater strategic control over message design. Therefore, marginalized and stigmatized individuals could readily adopt assimilation tactics online by denying their low-status identity and adopting a higher-status identity. Users who seek conformity to dominant social groups can strategically conceal their identity though online anonymity. Users may even employ disidentifiers (Goffman, 1963) in an attempt to distance themselves from the unwanted identity. Some scholars view inaccurate online self-presentations as a form of deception (Donath, 1999; Donn & Sherman, 2002). However, Orbe (1998) argued that co-cultural communication strategies are neither positive nor negative, they are simply responses that those without power have developed to cope with their social status.

Self-Verification, Social Support, and Separation Tactics

Marginalized individuals can employ assimilation tactics to deny an unwanted identity and create a more positive online identity as discussed above. However, despite the desire to maintain a positive self-view and the opportunity to do so through CMC, a growing body of research suggests that many individuals want to be viewed accurately online. For instance, Mitja et al. (2010) found that Facebook users' presentations reflected their actual selves rather than an idealized self. Ellison, Heino, and Gibbs (2006) found that many online daters fought the desire to portray unrealistically positive self-images and portrayed themselves realistically. Therefore, some marginalized and stigmatized individuals will desire accurate perceptions, even if perceptions are not perceived positively by others. Marginalized individuals may choose to employ separation tactics and seek verification of a negative social identity.

Self-verification theory (Swann, 1983), in contrast to self-enhancement theory, argues that people desire congruent perceptions of themselves from others. Self-verification theorists believe even those with negative social identities seek identity verification because individuals are highly opposed to shedding their self-concept (Swann, 1987; Swann, Hixon, Stein-Seroussi, & Gilbert, 1990; Swann, Pelham, & Krull, 1989). Accurate identity perceptions from others are linked to a host of positive emotional and psychological outcomes, including higher self-esteem, pride, happiness (Cast & Burke, 2002), greater self-efficacy, self-worth (Stets & Burke, 2005), higher perceived competency, and greater authenticity (Burke, 2004). People often strategically select verifying contexts (Swann, Pelham, & Krull 1989) and abandon nonverifying contexts (Swann, 2005). Computer-mediated communication provides identity verification because of the presence of feedback and the ability to negotiate identity.

Computer-mediated communication can be utilized both to garner accurate identity verification from others and to enhance self-image. Simply because society has deemed a particular identity as negative does not mean those who exist within that social category must view themselves negatively. Some marginalized individuals might choose to employ separation tactics (Orbe, 1998) and seek online social support from others with a similar social identity. In this way, stigmatized individuals can learn to embrace their identities and find pride in their social status. Online camaraderie may lead individuals to accept their social identity and engage in cognitive restructuring (Blanz et al., 1998); a negative social identity can become a positive one to the marginalized individual. Individuals with a particular stigma may even come together and engage in collective coping strategies such as attempting to redefine the social hierarchy or convincing mainstream society to accept their particular stigma. Thus, one does not need to shed a negative social identity to have high self-esteem.

Stigmatized individuals may find it difficult or embarrassing to find similarly stigmatized individuals in face-to-face interactions, which may lead them to seek CMC for social support. Additionally, people often prefer online support groups over face-to-face groups (Wright, 2000), in part because they prefer to receive support from weak interpersonal ties rather than strong ties (Constant, Sproull, & Kiesler, 1996; Walther & Boyd, 2002; Wright & Bell, 2003; Wright & Query, 2004). This preference may become particularly salient within sensitive or problematic circumstances (Parks, Adelman, & Albrecht, 1987; LaGaipa, 1990;

Granovetter, 1973; Wills & Fegan, 2001). Members of online support groups value the social distance, anonymity, interaction management, and access provided by CMC (Walther & Boyd, 2002).

Identity Disclosure

One identity management tactic particularly salient to CMC is identity disclosure. When the desire to be viewed accurately outweighs the desire to be viewed positively, an individual might be driven to voluntarily self-disclose. Bergart (2003) suggested that the inner conflict and isolation of being untrue to oneself drives individuals to disclose. Additionally, the presence of others with the same social identity could drive individuals to disclose. Goffman (1963) suggested three ways individuals disclose marginalizing identities: voluntarily parading a stigma symbol, offering fleeting evidence of group status, and bluntly communicating their stigma nonchalantly, "supporting the assumption that those present are above such concerns while preventing them from trapping themselves into showing that they are not" (p. 101).

Computer-mediated communication offers opportunities to self-disclose in ways not found in face-to-face interactions (McKenna & Bargh, 1998). Self-disclosure through CMC is filtered and controlled, which can be advantageous to marginalized and stigmatized individuals. Because of the ability to control self-disclosure, the risks of online disclosure may be reduced (Derlega, Metts, Petronio, & Margulis, 1993). Individuals tend to disclose differently and more often online than in face-to-face communication (Joinson, 1998).

In summary, communication is essential to the construction of identity. The self is not formed in isolation, but within a social context. Individuals desire a self that is viewed positively by themselves and others. However, due to the human proclivity to categorize and compare social categories, some individuals will inevitably be forced to the bottom of the social hierarchy. Bottom dwellers become stigmatized and marginalized and face an identity crisis because they desire in-group status but are cast into an out-group position. Computer-mediated communication offers these individuals a unique opportunity to cope with their consigned social positions. Individuals might choose to utilize Orbe's (1998) assimilation tactics and strategically escape into online anonymity to conceal a negative social identity. Conversely, individuals may choose to be viewed accurately and engage in separation tactics by strategically revealing their marginalized identity and seeking out like-others online. In this chapter, we have examined the role of communication and CMC in the creation of self and identity, we then explored the role of CMC in rebooting negative social identities and transforming them into positive identities. We end by investigating several future directions and new horizons for CMC research.

Future Directions

Computer-mediated communication scholars should address the needs of marginalized and stigmatized individuals and CMC's potential alleviation of social identity crises. Little research has attempted to dissect how those without power communicate online. The context of CMC has enormous liberating potentials for users. Particular attention should focus on how children at risk for social exclusion can find inclusion online. Additionally, researchers should further examine the notions of escaping into online anonymity as an assimilation tactic and seeking out social support to find like-minded others.

Future CMC research should consider the role of the continually evolving nature of computer-related technology in social identity formation and maintenance. Many CMC theories are based on a *cues-filtered-out* perspective (see Walther, 1992), but this cannot explain the appeal of CMC in its entirety. As technology has evolved, cues are continually being *filtered-in* to CMC through pictures, video conferencing, and video integration. Users seem to desire more cues in CMC. For instance, emoticons developed in e-mail communication; the incorporation of pictures may partially explain Facebook's success and Friendster's failure; YouTube has profited greatly from video communication; Skype, which attempts to incorporate virtually all the same cues as face-to-face communication, is wildly popular. The increase in cues has added to the popularity of these online social media.

Theories about CMC need to be able to adapt to rapidly changing communication technologies. Computer-mediated communication is a much richer context than accounted for in many CMC theories; therefore, new theories are needed. Baym (2009) cautioned that chasing the next new CMC innovation is futile and will be quickly outdated unless it is linked to history and a strong theoretical framework. Yet, as Scott (2009) mentioned, CMC scholars still need theories capable of keeping up with new CMC innovations. Walther (2009) lamented that a dramatic lack of progress in CMC research is due to a lack of articulating theoretical boundaries. Additionally, CMC theories must be diversified, and while theories like SIDE and SIP offer important insights, they should not monopolize research endeavors.

In today's society, mediums other than computers are being utilized for what scholars call computer-mediated communication. For example, modern cell phones embody early CMC researchers' conceptualization of computers. Therefore, CMC scholars should consider the role of mediated communication beyond computers. Ultimately, CMC scholarship has great potential to illuminate the role of media in the formation of social identities; however, scholars' current conceptions of CMC may be problematic and new agendas and directions for CMC must be articulated and realized.

References

Baym, N. K. (2009). A call for grounding the face of blurred boundaries. *Journal of Computer-Mediated Communication, 14*, 720–723.

Bergart, A. M. (2003). Group work as an antidote to the isolation of bearing an invisible stigma. *Social Work with Groups, 26*, 33–43.

Berger, P. L., & Luckmann, T. (1966). *The social construction of reality: A treatise in the sociology of knowledge.* Garden City, NY: Anchor Books.

Berleson, B. (1949). What missing the newspaper means. In P. F. Lazarsfeld & F. M. Stanton (Eds.), *Communication research* (pp. 111–129). New York: Duell, Sloan & Pearce.

Blanz, M., Mummendey, A. L., Mielke, R., & Klink, A. (1998). Responding to negative social identity: A taxonomy of identity management strategies. *European Journal of Social Psychology, 28*, 697–729.

Blumer, H. (1969). *Symbolic interactionism: Perspective and method.* Englewood Cliffs, NJ: Prentice-Hall.

Boneva, B., Kraut, R., & Frohlich, D. (2001). Using email for personal relationships. *American Behavioral Scientist, 45*, 530–549.

Burke, P. J. (2004). Identities and social structure: The 2003 Cooley-Mead award address. *Social Psychology Quarterly, 67*(1), 5–15.

Cast, A. D., & Burke, P. J. (2002). A theory of self-esteem. *Social Forces, 80*, 1041–1068.

Constant, D., Sproull, L., & Kiesler, S. (1996). The kindness of strangers: The usefulness of electronic weak ties for technical advice. *Organization Science, 7*(2), 119–135.

Cooley, C. H. (1902). *Human nature and the social order.* New York: Scribner's.

Daft, R. L., & Lengel, R. H. (1984). Information richness: A new approach to managerial behavior and organization design. In B. M. Staw & L. L. Cummings (Eds.), *Research in organizational behavior* (Vol. 6, pp. 191–233). Greenwich, CT: JAL.

Derlega, V. J., Metts, S., Petronio, S., & Margulis, S. T. (1993). *Self-disclosure.* London: Sage.

Diener, E. (2005). The nonobvious social psychology of happiness. *Psychological Inquiry, 16*(4), 162–167.

Donath, J. S. (1999). Identity and deception in the virtual community. In M. A. Smith & P. Kollock (Eds.), *Communities in cyberspace* (pp. 29–59). New York: Routledge.

Donn, J., & Sherman, R. (2002). Attitudes and practices regarding the formation of romantic relationships on the Internet. *CyberPsychology & Behavior, 5*(2), 107–123.

D'Urso, S. (2009). The past, present, and future of human communication and technology research: An introduction. *Journal of Computer-Mediated Communication, 14*, 708–713.

Edwards, K., & Smith, E. E. (1996). A disconfirmation bias in the evaluation of arguments. *Journal of Personality and Social Psychology, 71*, 5–24.

Eisenberger, N. I., Lieberman, M. D., & Williams, K. D. (2003). Does rejection hurt? An FMRI study of social exclusion. *Science, 302*, 290–292.

Ellison, N. Heino, R., & Gibbs, J. (2006). Managing impressions online: Self-presentation processes in the online dating environment. *Journal of Computer-Mediated Communication, 11*, 415–441.

Foels, R. (2006). In-group favoritism and social self-esteem in minimal groups: Changing a social categorization into a social identity. *Current Research in Social Psychology, 12*(3), 38–53.

Goar, C. D. (2007). Social identity theory and the reduction of inequality: Can cross-cutting categorization reduce inequality in mixed-race groups? *Social Behavior and Personality, 35*, 537–550.

Goffman, E. (1959). *The presentation of self in everyday life.* Garden City, NY: Doubleday Anchor.

Goffman, E. (1963). *Stigma: Notes on the management of spoiled identity.* New York: Simon & Schuster.

Gonzales, A. L., & Hancock, J. T. (2008). Identity shift in computer-mediated environments. *Media Psychology, 11*, 167–185.

Granovetter, M. (1973). The strength of weak ties. *American Journal of Sociology, 78*, 1360–1380.

Harrington, E. R. (2004). The social psychology of hatred. *Journal of Hate Studies, 3*(49), 49–82.

Hecht, M. L., Jackson, R. L., & Ribeau, S. A. (2003). African American communication: Exploring identity and culture. *European Review of Social Psychology, 4*, 85–111.

Herzog, H. (1944). What do we really know about day-time serial listeners? In P. Lazarsfeld & F. Stanton (Eds.), *Radio research 1942–1943* (pp. 3–33). New York: Duel, Sloan & Pearce.

Hogg, M. A., & Reid, S. A. (2006). Social identity, self-categorization, and the communication of group norms. *Communication Theory, 16*, 7–30.

Jackson, R. L. (2002). Cultural contracts: Toward understanding of identity negotiation. *Communication Quarterly, 50*, 359–367.

Jacobson, D. (1999). Impression formation in cyberspace: Online expectations and offline experiences in text-based virtual communities. *Journal of Computer-Mediated Communication, 5*(1). http://jcmc.indiana.edu/vol5/issue1/jacobson.html

Johnson, A. G. (2006). *Privilege, power, and difference* (2nd ed.). Boston, MA: McGraw-Hill.

Joinson, A. N. (1998). Causes and implications of disinhibited information on the Internet. In J. Gackenbach (Ed.), *Psychology and the Internet* (pp. 43–60). San Diego, CA: Academic Press.

Jung, E., & Hecht, M. (2004). Elaborating the communication theory of identity: Identity gaps and communication outcomes. *Communication Quarterly, 52*(3), 265–283.

Katz, E. (1959). Mass communication research and the study of culture. *Studies in Public Communication, 2*, 1–6.

Kleinman, A., & Hall-Clifford, R. (2009). Stigma: A social, cultural and moral process. *Journal of Epidemial Community Health, 63*, 418–419.

Kraut, R., Lundmark, V., Patterson, M., Kiesler, S., Mukopadhyay, T., & Sherlis, W. (1998). Internet paradox: A social technology that reduces social involvement and psychological well-being? *American Psychologist, 53*, 1017–1031.

LaGaipa, J. L. (1990). The negative effects of informal support systems. In S. Duck & R. C. Silver (Eds.), *Personal relationships and social support* (pp. 122–139). Newbury Park, CA: Sage.

Lea, M., Spears, R., & de Groot, D. (2001). Knowing me, knowing you: Anonymity effects on social identity processes within groups. *Personality and Social Psychology Bulletin, 27*, 526–537.

Lee, E. (2007). Deindividuation effects on group polarization in computer-mediated-communication: The role of group identification, public-self-awareness, and perceived argument quality. *Journal of Communication, 57*, 385–403.

Lee, S. J. (2009). Online communication and adolescent social ties: Who benefits more from Internet use? *Journal of Computer-Mediated Communication, 14*, 509–531.

Link, B. G., & Phelan, J. C. (2001). Conceptualizing stigma. *Annual Review of Sociology, 27*, 363–385.

Macrae, C. N., & Bodenhausen, G. V. (2000). Social cognition: Thinking categorically about others. *Annual Review of Psychology, 51*, 93–120.

Major, B., & O'Brien, L. T. (2005). The social psychology of stigma. *Annual Review of Psychology, 56*, 393–421.

Markus, H. (1977). Self-schemata and processing information about the self. *Journal of Personality and Social Psychology, 35*, 63–78.

McKenna, K. Y. A., & Bargh, J. A. (1998). Coming out in the age of the Internet: Identity "demarginalization" through virtual group participation. *Journal of Personality and Social Psychology, 75*(3). 681–694.

McQuail, D., Blumler, J. G., & Brown, J. (1972). The television audience: A revised perspective. In D. McQuail (Ed.), *Sociology of mass communication* (pp. 135–165). Harmondsworth, England: Penguin.

Mead, G. H. (1934). *Mind, self and society*. Chicago, IL: University of Chicago Press.

Mitja, D. B., Juliane, M. S., Simine, V., Giddis, S., Schmukle, S. C., Egloff, B., & Gosling, S. D. (2010). Facebook profiles reflect actual personality, not self-idealization. *Psychological Science, 21*, 372–374.

Mummendey, A., Kessler, T., Klink, A., & Mielke, R. (1999). Strategies to cope with negative social identity: Predictions by social identity theory and relative deprivation theory. *Journal of Personality and Social Psychology, 76*, 229–245.

Nickerson, R. S. (1998). Confirmation bias: A ubiquitous phenomenon in many guises. *Review of General Psychology, 2*, 175–220.

Notley, T. (2009). Young people, online networks, and social inclusion. *Journal of Computer-Mediated Communication, 14*, 1208–1227.

Ong, W. (1982). *Orality and literacy*. New York: Routledge.

Orbe, M. P. (1998). *Constructing co-cultural theory: An explication of culture, power, and communication*. Thousand Oaks, CA: Sage.

O'Sullivan, P. B. (2000). What you don't know won't hurt me: Impression management functions of communication channels in relationships. *Human Communication Research, 26*, 403–441.

Palomares, N. A., & Lee, E. (2010). Virtual gender identity: The linguistic assimilation to gendered avatars in computer-mediated-communication. *Journal of Language and Social Psychology, 29*, 5–23.

Parks, M. R., Adelman, M. B., & Albrecht, T. L. (1987). Beyond close relationships: Support in weak ties. In T. L. Albrecht, M. B. Adelman, & Associates (Eds.), *Communicating social support* (pp. 126–147). Newbury Park, CA: Sage.

Platow, M. J., Byrne, L., & Ryan, M. K. (2005). Experimentally manipulated high in-group status can buffer personal self-esteem against discrimination. *European Journal of Social Psychology, 35*, 599–608.

Postmes, T., & Spears, R. (1998). Deindividuation and anti-normative behavior: A meta-analysis. *Psychological Bulletin, 123*, 238–259.

Reeders, D. (2008). Solutions to stigma. *HIV Australia, 7*(3), 29–49.

Ruggiero, T. E. (2000). Uses and gratifications theory in the 21st century. *Mass Communication and Society, 3*, 3–37.

Sanderson, J. (2010). "The nation stands behind you": Mobilizing social support on 38pitches.com. *Communication Quarterly, 58*, 188–206.

Schmidt, M. T., Branscombe, N. R., Silvia, P. J., Garcia, D., M., & Spears, R. (2006). Categorizing at the group level in response to intragroup social comparisons: A self-categorization theory integration of self-evaluation and social identity motives. *European Journal of Social Psychology, 36*, 297–314.

Scott, C. R. (2007). Communication and social identity theory: Existing and potential connections in organizational identification research. *Communication Studies, 58*, 123–138.

Scott, C. R. (2009). A whole-hearted effort to get it half-right: Predicting the future of communication technology scholarship. *Journal of Computer-Mediated Communication, 14*, 753–757.

Shaw, P. (1994). Spelling, accent and identity in computer-mediated communication. *English Today, 24*(2), 42–49.

Spears, R., & Lea, M. (1992). Social influence and the influence of the "social" in computer-mediated communication. In M. Lea (Ed), *Contexts of computer-mediated communication* (pp. 30–65). Hemel Hempstead, UK: Harvester Wheatsheaf.

Spears, R., & Lea, M. (1994). Panacea or panopticon? The hidden power in computer-mediated communication. *Communication Research, 21*, 427–459.

Spears, R., Lea, M., Corneliussen, R. A., Postmes, T., & Haar, W. (2002). Computer-mediated communication as a channel for social resistance: The strategic side of SIDE. *Small Group Research, 33*, 555–574.

Stafford, L., & Merolla, A. J. (2007). Idealization, reunions, and stability in long-distance dating relationships. *Journal of Social and Personal Relationships, 24*, 37–54.

Stafford, L., Merolla, A. J., & Castle, J. (2006). When long-distance relationships become geographically close. *Journal of Social and Personal Relationships, 23,* 901–919.

Stafford, L., & Reske, J. R. (1990). Idealization and communication in long-distance premarital relationships. *Family Relations, 39,* 274–279.

Steele, C. M. (1988). The psychology of self-affirmation: Sustaining the integrity of the self. In L. Berkowitz (Ed.), *Advances in experimental social psychology* (pp. 261–302). New York: Academic Press.

Sommer, K. L., Williams, K. D., Ciarocco, N. J., & Baumeister, R. F. (2001). When silence speaks louder than words: Explorations into the intrapsychic and interpersonal consequences of social ostracism. *Basic and Applied Social Psychology, 23(4),* 225–243.

Stets, J. E., & Burke, P. J. (2005). Identity verification, control, aggression in marriage. *Social Psychology Quarterly, 2,* 160–178.

Stewart, J. (2002). *Bridges not walls.* Boston, MA: McGraw-Hill.

Stone, A. R. (1995). *The war of desire and technology at the close of the mechanical age.* Cambridge: MIT Press.

Striley, K. M. (2010). *Socially disabled: Identity management strategies of low-status peer groups.* Unpublished manuscript.

Swann, W. B., (1983). Self-verification: Bringing social reality into harmony with the self. In J. Suls & A. A. Greenwald (Eds.), *Psychological perspectives on the self* (pp. 33–66). Hillsdale, NJ: Erlbaum.

Swann, W. B. (1987). Identity negotiation: Where the two roads meet. *Journal of Personality and Social Psychology, 53,* 1038–1051.

Swann, W. B. (2005). The self and identity negotiation. *Interaction Studies: Social Behaviour and Communication in Biological and Artificial Systems, 6,* 69–83.

Swann, W. B., Hixon, J. G., Stein-Seroussi, A., & Gilbert, D. T. (1990). The fleeting gleam of praise: Cognitive processes underlying behavioral reactions to self-relevant feedback. *Journal of Personality and Social Psychology, 59,* 17–26.

Swann, W. B., Pelham, B. W., & Krull, D. S. (1989). Agreeable fancy or disagreeable truth? Reconciling self-enhancement and self-verification. *Journal of Personality and Social Psychology, 57,* 782–791.

Tajfel, H., & Turner, J. C. (1979). An integrative theory of intergroup conflict. In W. G. Austin & S. Worchel (Eds.), *The social psychology of intergroup relations* (pp. 33–47). Monterey, CA: Brooks Cole.

Tajfel, H. & Turner, J. C. (1986). The social identity theory of intergroup behavior. In S. Worchel (Ed.), *Psychology of intergroup relations* (2nd ed., pp. 7–24). Chicago, IL: Nelson-Hall.

Tesser, A. (1988). Toward a self-evaluation maintenance model of social behavior. In L. Berkowitz (Ed.), *Advances in experimental social psychology* (pp. 181–227). New York: Academic Press.

Tesser, A. (2003) Self-evaluation. In M. R. Leary & J. P. Tangney (Eds.), *Handbook of self and identity* (pp. 275–290). New York: Guilford Press.

Ting-Toomey, S. (1986). Interpersonal ties in intergroup communication. In W. B. Gudykunst (Ed.), *Intergroup communication* (pp. 114–126). Baltimore, MD: Edward Arnold.

Turkle, S. (1995). *Life on the screen: Identity in the age of the Internet*. New York: Simon & Schuster.
Vandevelde, L., & Miyahara, M. (2005). Impact of group rejections from physical activity on physical self-esteem among university students. *Social Psychology of Education, 8*, 65–81.
Walther, J. B. (1992). Interpersonal effects in computer-mediated interaction: A relational perspective. *Communication Research, 19*, 52–90.
Walther, J. B. (1997). Group and interpersonal effects in international computer-mediated collaboration. *Human Communication Research, 23*, 342–369.
Walther, J. B. (2009). Theories, boundaries, and all of the above. *Journal of Computer-Mediated Communication, 14*, 748–752.
Walther, J. B., & Boyd, S. (2002). Attraction to computer-mediated social support. In C. A. Lin & D. Atkin (Eds.), *Communication technology and society: Audience adoption and uses* (pp. 153–188). Cresskill, NJ: Hampton.
Walther, J. B., Sloveck, C., & Tidwell, L. C. (2001). Is a picture worth a thousand words? Photographic images in long-term and short-term virtual teams. *Communication Research, 28*, 105–134.
Wang, Z., Walther, J. B., & Hancock, J. T. (2009). Social identification and interpersonal communication in computer-mediated communication: What you do versus who you are in virtual groups. *Human Communication Research, 35*, 59–85.
Watzlavick, P., Beavin, J. H., & Jackson, D. D. (1967). *Pragmatics of human communication: A study of interactional patterns, pathologies, and paradoxes*. New York: Norton.
Williams, K. D. (2001). *Ostracism: The power of silence*. New York: Guilford Press.
Wills, T. A., & Fegan, M. F. (2001). Social networks and social support. In A. Baum, T. Revenson, & J. E. Singer (Eds.), *Handbook of health psychology* (pp. 209–234). Mahwah, NJ: Erlbaum.
Wright, K. B. (2000). Social support satisfaction, on-line communication apprehension, and perceived life stress within computer-mediated support groups. *Communication Research Reports, 17*, 139–147.
Wright, K. B., & Bell, S. B. (2003). Health-related support groups on the Internet: Linking empirical findings to social support and computer-mediated communication theory. *Journal of Health Psychology, 8*, 39–54.
Wright, K. B., & Query, J. L., Jr. (2004). Online support and older adults: A theoretical examination of benefits and limitations of computer-mediated support networks for older adults and possible health outcomes. In J. F. Nussbaum & J. Coupland (Eds.), *Handbook of communication and aging research* (2nd ed., pp. 499–519). Mahwah, NJ: Erlbaum.
Yang, L. H., Kleinman, A., Link, B. G., Phelan, J. C., Lee, S., & Good, B. (2007). Culture and stigma: Adding moral experience to stigma theory. *Social Science & Medicine, 64*, 1524–1535.
Zadro, L., & Williams, K. D. (2006). How do you teach the power of ostracism? Evaluating the train ride demonstration. *Social Influence, 1*(1), 81–104.

Chapter 10

Conceptualizing the Intervening Roles of Identity in Communication Effects

The Prism Model

Maria Leonora (Nori) G. Comello

This chapter reviews conceptualizations of identity from the social identity perspective and other psychological perspectives on the self. Across these various models, identity is characterized as dependent on context and as composed of multiple components, with the components varying in both accessibility and weight as a function of contextual stimuli. Within a media-effects framework that links communication with behavioral effects, these features allow identity to serve both as a moderator of communication effects and as a mediator of communication effects—and on occasion even at the same time. The metaphor of a prism is offered to help conceptualize these dual and sometimes simultaneously occurring roles. Implications for the design and evaluation of persuasive communication campaigns and efforts are discussed.

Identity Is Multifaceted

Identity is a multifaceted construct. Depending on one's theoretical perspective, identity can be conceptualized as shifting or stable, as nonconscious or deeply reflective, and as everything else in between. Other dimensions of the concept "identity" can be considered as well (see Baumeister, 1998; Swann & Bosson, 2010). Furthermore, the relationship between identity and communication offers additional facets to examine. Within the scope of empirical mass communication research, for example, identity can be conceptualized as a predictor or as an outcome of communication. Perhaps most interesting, however, are the intervening roles that identity may play in presumed causal paths between communication and behavior.

Two possible intervening roles are explored here: the potential for identity to serve (a) as a variable that can influence the effect of communication on behavior (i.e., as a moderator of communication effects, altering its impact) and (b) as a conduit for the effects of communication on behavior (i.e., as a mediator of communication effects, explaining its impact). Although the roles may appear similar at first glance, they are conceptually distinct processes. It is also argued that these intervening roles can occur simultaneously, given the right conditions, adding measurably to the complexity, but also to the richness of any analysis of the impact of communication on behavior. To aid in conceptualization of this configuration of influences, the metaphor of a prism is used to bring to light the many-faceted nature of the ordinary communication context.

A prism is a transparent body with nonparallel planes used to refract or disperse a beam of light. Because the prism serves in one sense as a conduit of light, the prism can be thought of as a mediator of the effect of the light source. Thus, a prism placed in the beam of a flashlight may carry the light and we may observe the effect on a ceiling or floor. At the same time, the prism refracts the light by sending it out at different, yet predictable, angles. In this sense, the prism can be said to moderate the effect of the light source, because the effect depends on the angles of the planes. Drawing the connection to identity, the light source could be seen as the mediated message or as any communication event, and the prism could represent identity, with different angles serving as different aspects of self.

To the best of my knowledge, there is no work that has examined the roles of identity as mediator and moderator in a single model, nor is there any work from quantitative communication research that uses the metaphor of a prism to describe identity. Yet the model is precisely what is suggested about the role of identity by influential conceptualizations of identity. The model thus contributes to theory-building by integrating propositions about the roles of identity from these perspectives and by developing them in the context of mass communication and persuasive message effects.

Conceptualizations of Identity

In laying the conceptual foundation for the prism model, I draw primarily from two theoretical frameworks—the social identity perspective based on the work of Henri Tajfel, John Turner, and their colleagues (see reviews by Abrams & Hogg, 2004; Hogg & Reid, 2006) and the multiple-selves perspective of William James (1890/1981). These perspectives were chosen because each has had considerable impact on the study of communication or behavior influence. For example, the social identity perspective has been developed within a mass communication framework by Harwood and Roy (2005), and the multiple-selves perspective has inspired fruitful lines of research in psychology involving behavior prediction based on discrepancies between identity components (Higgins, 1987) and "possible selves" as a motivational guide (Markus & Nurius, 1986). Although the social identity and multiple-selves frameworks may appear to be distinct, they share similar conceptualizations of identity that deserve to be discussed in tandem and that together inform the development of the prism model.

Social Identity Perspective

The social identity perspective encompasses approaches to studying identity that are guided by the insight that behavior is strongly influenced by the alignment of people in terms of social category memberships (Abrams & Hogg, 2004, p. 100). Serving as complementary approaches to studying identity within this perspective are self-categorization theory, which focuses on the cognitive processes of categorization of self and others (Turner, 1987), and social identity theory, which emphasizes the relational aspects of internalizing and enacting group memberships (Tajfel & Turner, 1986). The root conceptualization of self is that it consists of multiple representations. On one dimension, the self can be thought of as multiple in terms of levels of abstraction, from the personal to increasingly inclusive social groups. On this dimension, the self can be thought of as occupying the center of larger social categories; a person who identifies with a group extends the self outward to the boundaries of the social group and becomes an interchangeable member of the group, at which point the "I" becomes "we" (Brewer & Gardner, 1996).

The self can also be thought of as multiple in terms of the number of social groups with which a person can identify. The theory posits that there are as many self-representations as there are groups to which a person belongs, and identification with one or another is dependent on frame of reference. A collection of stimuli (people, for instance) will be categorized as a group to the extent that the differences between the people in the group are judged to be less than the differences between the group and other people on a given dimension. Groups are valued on the extent to which they maximize differences, or to the extent to which they provide both a sense of belonging within an in-group and differentiation from relevant out-groups (Brewer, 1991).

Of more relevance to this paper, however, is how a category becomes salient in memory and therefore capable of guiding behavior. Adapting the work of Jerome Bruner (1957) on categorization, Turner (1987) proposed that the salience of a categorization is a function of the relative accessibility of that categorization and the "fit" between the categorization and some stimulus input. Whereas accessibility of a categorization refers to the extent of readiness of an individual to apply a category to a given object, fit refers to the congruence between an object and the category.

As a general example of category salience, imagine that you are seated along the first baseline at a baseball game. In such a setting, all things related to baseball would likely be top-of-mind. Consequently, if you were to see an object hurtling toward your head, you would be more prepared to think and act as if it were a baseball than you would be in other situations. However, your likelihood of perceiving a baseball would be higher if the object were, for example, an orange instead of a shoe, because the set of attributes describing an orange would share more in common with the set describing a baseball (i.e., spherical and of a certain size) than would the set describing a shoe. Thus, the accessibility of the category and the congruence of the stimulus with the category jointly determine the likelihood of categorization.

Similar reasoning can be applied to categorizations of people. For example, if you have just returned from a trip to Hawaii, you might be more motivated to find connection between Hawaii and people you might encounter. You might think that a person wearing a tropical floral print shirt, for example, was from Hawaii more readily than you would ordinarily, and you may even strike up a conversation in hopes of finding out where the person resides. Similar to the previous example, the salience of the social category (person from Hawaii) is a function of the accessibility of all things related to Hawaii, as well as the match between the person's shirt and that category.

The same reasoning can even be applied to categorizations of the self. Although one might think that human capabilities of introspection would make the self easier to categorize than other people or objects, the self is also subject to fuzzy or conflicting definitions with regard to an issue. For example, young people may vacillate between thinking of themselves as being primarily attached to family or peer group, and certain situations may bring out one identity over another. Likewise, health issues are often mired in competing self-cognitions, particularly when the health issue involves approaching or avoiding pleasurable behaviors (e.g., "I am a healthy person" and "I love rich desserts"). However, a trip to the gym may increase motivation to perceive the self as healthy, and to the extent that one's activities at the gym are a reasonable fit to the workout desired ("Great, I made it through yoga"), then one is likely to categorize the self as healthy, at least for the time being. It has also been observed that people often think of themselves in terms of attributes that make them unique in a particular setting (McGuire & McGuire, 1988). Thus, if one's exercise class at the gym were attended by people who were all overweight by 100 pounds, whereas one had only a 10-pound excess of weight to shed after the holidays, one's self-concept as a healthy person may be more accessible, at least in that context.

Multiple-Selves Perspective

The observation of potentially conflicting self-views provides a good segue to the conceptualization of self which is offered by psychologist and philosopher William James (1890/1981). James proposed (as did the originators of the social identity perspective) that the self is composed of multiple components and that the accessibility of components is context dependent. However, James's view of multiplicity is distinctive in that it addresses directly the possibility that views of self can be in conflict. For example:

> I am often confronted by the necessity of standing by one of my empirical selves and relinquishing the rest. Not that I would not, if I could, be both handsome and fat and well dressed, and a great athlete, and make a million a year, and be a wit, a bon-vivant, and a lady-killer, as well as a philosopher; a philanthropist, statesman, warrior, and African explorer, as well as a "tone-poet" and saint. But the thing is simply impossible. The millionaire's work would run counter to the saint's; the bon-vivant and the philanthropist would trip each other up; the philosopher and the lady-killer could not well keep house in the same tenement of clay. (James, 1890/1981, p. 295)

The selves of James are also therefore arranged in a hierarchy, with certain selves capable of preempting conflicting selves when there is competition for scarce resources (see Comello, 2009, for further discussion of James's view of self and multiplicity within the self-system).

The Jamesian view of self is also noteworthy in that it addresses the role of persuasive communications in identity-relevant appeals. With respect to the differing values of selves, James (p. 297) asserts, "The first care of diplomats and monarchs and all who wish to rule or influence is, accordingly, to find out their victim's strongest principle of self-regard, so as to make that the fulcrum of all appeals." This assertion appears strikingly similar to the notion of "fit" proposed by Bruner (1957), cited in Turner (1987), within the social identity perspective, in that the stimulus (i.e., the advocated behavior in a persuasive message) must seem congruent with an accessible identity.

Likewise, with respect to the context dependence of the self, James singles out persuasive appeals as a source of self-concept activation. Specifically, James (p. 297) claims that in order to be effective, persuasive attempts must first activate the appropriate self: "Neither threats nor pleadings can move a man unless they touch some one of his potential or actual selves." A contemporary theory of self that draws inspiration from the notion of activated self-concept and that lends itself to the study of media effects is the active-self account of prime-to-behavior effects (Wheeler, DeMarree, & Petty, 2007; see also Comello, 2009). The active-self account posits that the self-system guides behavior. The features of the self that guide behavior are those that are currently in the active self-concept, which can shift rapidly in response to external inputs such as primed constructs. The authors propose that the activation of stereotypes, traits, and related constructs can influence behaviors by affecting temporarily active self-representations in ways that are either consistent or inconsistent with the primed constructs (Wheeler et al., 2007, p. 235). Thus, exposure to messages or media content could temporarily increase the accessibility of a particular self-view, which could then influence behavior.

To summarize, the conceptualizations of self that are proposed by the social identity perspective and by William James include assumptions of multiple components of self, differing accessibility of components, and different values ascribed to components. In addition, the Jamesian view of self identifies persuasive communication as a source of self-concept activation and as a means to link an advocated behavior to a valued self. However, the process of persuasion (in other words, of categorizing an object in a desired manner) is essentially the same: one must make accessible a desired view of self and also link the advocated behavior with that self-view. From a causal modeling standpoint, accessibility and fit are different processes with different graphical representations. Whereas accessibility is best represented by the process of mediation, fit is best described by moderation. We now turn to definitions of mediation and moderation, including examples of how identity has been studied in each. It is important to note, however, that this paper is not intended to be a comprehensive technical account of moderation and mediation. Readers are referred to more technical works for further background and explanation (e.g., Baron & Kenny, 1986; Hayes, 2005; MacKinnon, 2008; Preacher, Rucker, & Hayes, 2007).

Moderation and Mediation

Baron and Kenny (1986) were among the first to clarify the role of intervening variables (also known as third variables) in social science research by drawing a distinction between moderating and mediating roles. In the moderator function, the intervening variable partitions the focal independent variable into different levels of effectiveness. In other words, the effectiveness of the focal independent variable depends on the level of the moderator. These relationships are represented by Figure 10.1, in which identity moderates the influence of communication on behavior.

In contrast, when the variable is a mediator, the variable serves as the explanatory mechanism through which the focal independent variable is able to influence the outcome. In media effects research, for example, the mediator might be a psychological state through which a given message has its effects on behavior (O'Keefe, 2003). Thus, the mediator is both an outcome of communication and an influence on the target behavior, as shown in Figure 10.2.

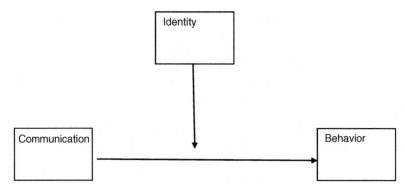

Figure 10.1 Identity as a moderator of the effect of communication on behavior.

The bulk of research in which identity is conceptualized as an intervening variable has focused primarily on moderation of message effects. For example, three identity-related constructs that have been shown to moderate communication effects are group identification, self-affirmation, and the congruence of a message with self-concepts. In terms of group identification, Reid and Hogg (2005) demonstrated that the third-person effect (i.e., the tendency to believe that other people are more influenced by media than they are themselves (Davison, 1983) depends on perceived similarity to a group of "others." For instance, perceived influence of the Jerry Springer Show was moderated by self-similarity to the group "trailer trash," with a large discrepancy between perceived effects on self and others for those who viewed themselves as low in similarity to trailer trash, and no discrepancy for those who were similar. Group identification has also moderated the effects of communication variables in health contexts, such as the stronger effect of media dependency on safe sex attitudes for men with high versus low identification

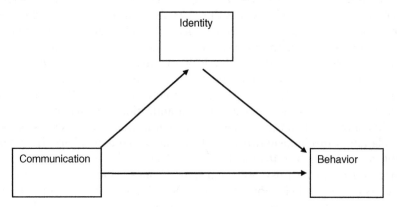

Figure 10.2 Identity as a mediator of the effect of communication on behavior.

with the gay community (Morton & Duck, 2000), and the effectiveness of appeals in reducing risky behaviors as a function of whether or not the risky behavior is linked to an undesirable social identity (Berger & Rand, 2008).

Similarly, levels of self-affirmation (i.e., reflecting on the values one holds most dear) can change the effectiveness of health message effects (Steele, 1988). When people experience self-affirmation, they will be more likely (compared to those not affirmed) to accept a health message, to perceive themselves at higher risk, and to show stronger intentions to act in accordance with the health message (Sherman, Nelson, & Steele, 2000). Further, affirmed participants are more likely to recall less risk-disconfirming information and to feel more personal control over the behavior at a one-week follow-up (Reed & Aspinwall, 1998). Self-affirmation assumes a multifaceted self with a built-in compensatory mechanism, such that threats to one aspect can be remedied by reinforcing another aspect. Thus, a persuasive health message that delivers a threat is more likely to be accepted by someone who has experienced affirmation (even in an unrelated self-aspect) than would a person who has not been affirmed. Given that most professional communicators aim to tailor messages to intended audiences, a number of studies have explored the impact of matching messages to recipient self-concepts. Congruence of advertisement with self-concept was shown to moderate message effects on evaluations of ad, brand, and self (Chang, 2002). In addition, messages were more likely to lead to greater self-referencing and positive affect when the message was congruent (versus incongruent) with a person's ideal self-schema (Chang, 2005). Other aspects of the self have also been recruited as targets for persuasive-ad matching. For example, matching ads to a person's level of extroversion increases the effects of argument quality on attitudes and behavioral intentions (Wheeler, Petty, & Bizer, 2005). Similarly, matching messages to a person's regulatory focus (promotion or prevention) results in more positive attitudes toward the topic and greater intentions to perform the advocated behavior (Cesario & Higgins, 2008).

These studies show that identity-relevant constructs can change the communication-behavior relationship, as depicted in Figure 10.1. It should be noted, however, that if identity moderates the effect of communication, it is also the case that communication moderates the effect of identity on behavior. The two variables are said to interact or to moderate each other, because the effect of one depends on the value of the other. Thus, Figure 10.3 is statistically equivalent to Figure 10.1, and the selection of which model to use is a matter of theoretical or practical focus.

The moderation examples cited thus far correspond to Figure 10.1, but it is also helpful to think of the alternative configuration provided in Figure 10.3, in which communication is the moderator. The rationale

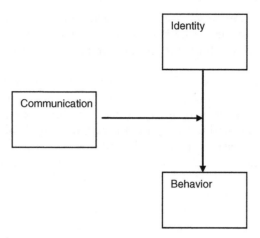

Figure 10.3 Communication as a moderator of the effect of identity on behavior (statistically equivalent to Figure 10.1).

for doing so has been demonstrated in the political (Nelson, Oxley, & Clawson, 1997) and health (Fishbein & Yzer, 2003) arenas with respect to beliefs, but I argue that the same rationale applies to self-concepts, a point to which I will return. Both sets of authors argue that the assumption behind many persuasive efforts is that a message is going to introduce new information that will result in changes in beliefs about outcomes and other cognitions, which will in turn lead to the desired behavior change. The authors observe, however, that many people are already familiar with arguments about political and health issues, so there may be little that a persuasive message can change with respect to belief, but what *can* be increased is the weight carried by a belief in the prediction of other outcomes. In other words, a message may strengthen the association between a belief and a behavior-relevant outcome. Whereas Nelson and colleagues (1997) refer to this as a framing effect, Fishbein and Yzer (2003) use the term *media priming*. It is important to distinguish this definition of media priming from another conceptualization of media priming as heightened accessibility of a construct (Roskos-Ewoldsen, Roskos-Ewoldsen, & Carpentier, 2003).

It has been proposed that the change-in-weight route to persuasion is particularly important when there are several competing beliefs about an issue, as may be the case when a person sorts through various arguments for and against a political candidate. Likewise, health issues may be attended by competing beliefs, such as beliefs that marijuana use will make one more popular but will also put one's health at risk. A key assertion of the model is that communication may have an impact on behavior not necessarily by changing means in a measured psychological state, but rather by increasing the correspondence between the psychological state and the behavior-relevant outcome.

An example of this somewhat nonobvious means of exerting influence is provided by Fishbein and Yzer (2003, p. 177) with data from a prevention campaign promoting antimarijuana beliefs. In the condition that demonstrates priming of a belief by exposure to antimarijuana messages, the mean of belief expectancy ("Marijuana trial damages your brain cells") does not change from baseline, but there is an increase in its regression weight as a predictor of attitude. This condition is distinguished from other possible outcomes of the media intervention changing the mean of the belief but not its predictive strength, and the intervention changing both mean of the belief and its weight as a predictor of attitude.

Let us now shift the focus back to identity. From a multiple selves perspective, the media priming model is quite compelling. It can be argued that self-concepts represent beliefs about the self, and that self-concepts have attached value, consistent with the propositions of identity theorists; furthermore, it can be argued that one can have competing beliefs about the self (e.g., James, 1890/1981), including a self-concept consistent with an advocated behavior and potentially opposing self-concepts. Thus, efforts to introduce "new" self-concepts consistent with the advocated behavior may fail to demonstrate effects, because the self is already there. Because this situation is analogous to that described earlier with respect to beliefs, the mechanism for media effects via priming described in that context could readily apply to studies of media effects on identity and behavior. For example, a person may have coexisting self-concepts about being a smoker and being a health-conscious person, perhaps because she has been trying to quit or because she does other things to promote health. If the person is conflicted about whether to have a cigarette, both concepts are likely to be equally accessible in memory. However, if the person happened to see an attractive person smoking on a TV show, that image might increase the weight of the smoker self-concept in predicting smoking, relative to the weight without exposure to the image.

Mediation

Whereas moderation is about the conditions under which a message (or an identity) will have effects, mediation addresses the extent to which changes in identity (as a nonmanipulated variable) can be said to explain the effects of communication on behavior. Although demonstration of moderation certainly has value, it has been argued that demonstration of mediation is an even more important consideration from a message design perspective, because doing so substantively informs message design and evaluation (see O'Keefe, 2003; Slater, 2006; Tao & Bucy, 2007).

Mediation is sometimes explored in studies guided by social cognitive theory (Bandura, 1986) because the theory makes explicit the reciprocally determining links among personal factors, behavior, and the environment. Thus, any number of three-variable mediation models could be examined. The one that would be most congruent with the study of mediation of communication effects via identity would be a model in which environment (exposure to communication) influences personal factors (self-relevant cognitions), which in turn influences behavior. A key construct within social cognitive theory is self-efficacy, which is the belief that one is able to enact a particular behavior. Numerous studies across multiple issues have demonstrated that communication activities or content can affect levels of self-efficacy, which can then affect behavior. For example, a campaign that promoted healthy heart behaviors increased self-efficacy, which in turn increased adoption of health behaviors (Maibach, Flora, & Nass, 1991). In the domain of adolescent health, exposure to TV sexual content increased sexual intercourse initiation via increases in safe-sex self-efficacy (Martino, Collins, Kanouse, Elliott, & Berry, 2005).

As already mentioned, the active-self account (Wheeler et al., 2007) seems ideally suited to guide studies exploring the mediating role of identity because it postulates that people have a variety of views they can hold about themselves, but only the self-views that have been activated will have an effect on behavior and on antecedents to behavior. However, the active-self account studies to date have generally only manipulated self-view accessibility and have not directly measured it. For example, in one study, accessibility of a self-concept as an African American is manipulated by asking participants to write an essay describing a day in the life of either Tyrone Walker or Erik Walker. Writing as Tyrone is intended to activate a self-view as an African American, with the result of higher scores on a measure of anger among participants who tended to look inward for guidance on how to behave (i.e., low scores on self-monitoring scale). The authors argue that the finding of higher anger among those participants is consistent with an activated self-concept as an African American.

It is somewhat curious that empirical tests of an activated self mechanism would not measure self-concept activation so that it could be studied as a mediator (for a discussion of this issue, see Wheeler, DeMarree, & Petty, 2008, pp. 1044–1055). Although there is evidence that communication effects on behavior are mediated by self-relevant variables such as self-efficacy (as noted above) and self-ratings on traits (Galinsky, Wang, & Ku, 2008), on the whole, studies have not focused on mediation by a more global self-concept. However, a study by Comello and Slater (2011), which was guided by the notion of activated self-concept, found preliminary evidence for such a mechanism. In an evaluation of drug prevention ads representing different themes, the authors showed that the ads that had proven most effective in the field were also more successful at eliciting a self-concept as a nonuser in the lab. Furthermore, the effect of the ads on behavioral willingness to use drugs was carried through (i.e., was mediated by) self-concept as a nonuser. Moreover, this relationship held in the presence of a competing potential mediator.

In summary, the literature shows that identity has been studied as a moderator and as a mediator in presumed causal paths between communication and behavior. The majority of work appears to focus on moderation rather than mediation, perhaps because of the relative ease of manipulating rather than measuring self-concept accessibility. The prism model, though, is about the potential for identity to serve simultaneously as a mediator and a moderator in a single model, which is a configuration suggested by the social identity perspective and the Jamesian view of the self. Next we turn to what such a model would look like and how it could be studied.

Combining Moderation and Mediation: The Prism Model

If you have ever picked up a prism, you would likely describe it as a multifaceted, transparent object. Depending on the light available, you might turn the prism this way and that to catch the light in such a way as to create pleasing patterns on the opposite wall. It is a fitting metaphor for the mediating and moderating roles of identity because the prism, strategically turned, serves as a conduit for light in one sense, while at the same time refracting the light by sending it out at different angles. Drawing the connection to identity, the light source could be seen as the media message or as any communication event, and the prism could be identity, with different angles serving as different aspects of self.

To the best of my knowledge, there is no work on identity that has examined the roles of identity as mediator and moderator in a single model, nor do I know of any work using the metaphor of a prism to describe identity. Although there has been work from a critical-theory perspective that suggests that identity can be thought of as a crystal, the metaphor was offered as an alternative to thinking about identities in terms of static dichotomies (Tracy & Trethewey, 2005) and not in terms of intervening roles of identity, as intended here. There is also a PRISM model of personality and identity but the word serves as an acronym and not as a metaphor (Wood & Roberts, 2006).

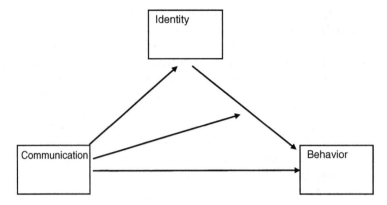

Figure 10.4a Prism model—version a.

The metaphor of a prism is also well suited in that the visual representations of the moderating and mediating roles of identity also happen to resemble prisms. There are two alternative views, given the two different ways of conceptualizing the interaction between communication and identity. They are represented above in Figure 10.4a and below in Figure 10.4b. Figure 10.4a combines elements of Figure 10.2 (mediation) and Figure 10.3 (moderation, with communication as the moderator), whereas Figure 10.4b combines elements of Figure 10.2 (mediation) and Figure 10.1 (moderation, with identity as the moderator).

In both versions, the self-concept variable is positioned between communication and behavior in the classic mediator configuration, and there is also interaction depicted between communication and identity. Whereas the first version places emphasis on the moderation of the identity–behavior link by communication, the second version places emphasis on the moderation of the communication–behavior link by identity.

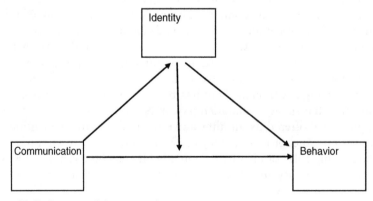

Figure 10.4b Prism model—version b.

These models are mathematically identical (they would be represented by the same regression model). Conceptually, however, the models are distinct and can provide useful ways to think about the relationships that might exist among the variables.

For example, let us return to the proposition of the social identity perspective that the accessibility of a social category and the fit between a stimulus and the category will together influence behavior. The example offered was being at a baseball game and experiencing an object hurtling toward you. The situational context of being at the baseball game would lead to increased *accessibility* of baseball-related categories, and the degree to which the object shared the same attributes as a baseball (its *congruence*) would determine how easily it was categorized as a baseball. Translating this example to an identity- and communication-effects context, it is assumed that communication can serve as both context provider and stimulus input. In other words, communication has the potential to increase accessibility of a social category via contextual cues, and then to provide input that will be judged as congruent or not with that category. Finally, as a whole, the communication is intended to have an effect on an outcome related to behavior.

As suggested by William James and other identity theorists, the mechanism through which this occurs is via identity activation. This set of relationships seems best represented by Figure 10.4a in which accessibility mediates the effect of communication on behavior, and the strength of that indirect effect is dependent on features of the communication stimulus that make it congruent with that identity. Consider, for example, the targeting of health campaigns to ethnic and cultural groups. Typically, such campaigns embed visual or other cues to increase the salience of a cultural identity; ad copy might then talk about the adoption of the advocated behavior as a matter of cultural pride (see Resnicow, Baranowski, Ahluwalia, & Braithwaite, 1999). Increasing exposure to the campaign may well be linked to increases in performance of the behavior, with the effect mediated by increased accessibility of the cultural identity. This indirect effect might be stronger with exposure to messages that are more successful than others at forging a link between the cultural identity and performance of the behavior.

This causal configuration has been referred to as a conditional indirect effect, or the changing strength of an indirect effect at different values of the moderator (see Preacher et al., 2007). Although the authors observe that there is often some confusion about what is meant by a conditional indirect effect, such a causal configuration should not be viewed as an out-of-the-ordinary case in the social sciences. Rather, it is often of theoretical interest to know whether a mediation effect remains constant across different contexts, groups of individuals, or other values of the predictor variables (Preacher et al., 2007, p. 186).

For example, the knowledge gap effect (Tichenor, Donohue, & Olien, 1970) could be described in terms of conditional indirect effects, in which education influences learning via media exposure (i.e., effect of education on learning is mediated by media exposure), but people who are more educated tend to learn more from the media sources to which they are exposed than are those who are lower in education.[1] Thus, the strength of the indirect effect of education on learning through media depends on the level of education itself. Likewise, in terms of identity, the strength of the indirect effect of communication through identity could depend on the type of communication itself, as suggested in the example above on the cultural targeting of health campaigns.

While Figure 10.4a appears to represent the Bruner-inspired formula of accessibility and fit, other theoretical models are better represented by Figure 10.4b, which shows identity being influenced and in turn influencing behavior (identity as a mediator), while at the same time moderating the communication–behavior link. This version lends itself to models that focus on changes in media effects. For example, the reinforcing spirals model (Slater, 2007) proposes that media selection and a set of attitudes, intentions, and behaviors are mutually reinforcing over time. That is, each is prospectively predictive of the other, with the relationship growing stronger over time until the identity being reinforced is stable, given competing pressures. If the mechanism through which media selectivity affects behaviors is identity, and if the strength of the media selectivity–behavior relationship also depends on level of social identification, then the model resembles the conceptualization in the second version of the prism model in Figure 10.4b, which emphasizes changes in the communication–behavior relationship depending on level of identity.

Although the model captures both mediation and moderation, it is not always the case that both processes will operate in a persuasive appeal. The degree to which one or the other is included is likely to depend on the situation, but the model includes both in order to encourage thinking about the potential roles and the strategies that might be implied in different situations.

For example, a message designer should consider which self-concepts are associated with a particular behavior, whether those self-concepts are well-defined, and whether they are in competition with other self-concepts. Given that behavior change is a process, this could vary by stage in the process, with correspondingly different strategies recommended by the prism model. Let us consider the development of a nonsmoker identity in someone who is a regular smoker but who wants to quit. In the early stages, self-concept as a nonsmoker is still ambiguous and is likely in conflict with identity as a smoker. At this stage, it is probably most important for behavior-change efforts to keep this new identity "top of mind" (i.e., to increase accessibility) by providing frequent reminders of that identity, of successful quitting strategies, and of values reinforced by quitting. It is also important for behavior-change efforts to encourage contact with other nonsmokers for greater support of this emerging identity within the framework of a concrete social reference group. At this stage, another possibility would be to forge a connection between nonsmoking and an identity that already is highly accessible, such as being a responsible parent or an athlete. In this case, the strategy would be to ensure that messages fully evoked that identity and tightly linked nonsmoking with this identity.

Over time, as the person begins to develop a more elaborated view of self as a nonsmoker, along with consistent attitudes, intentions, and social connections, a more chronic sense of self as a nonsmoker should emerge. However, quitting can be a rocky road, and if the person has succumbed to old habits along the way, these could keep the smoker self-view alive and kicking. Perhaps a self-view as a failure could develop and compete with the nonsmoker self-view, as well. Messages could aim to increase the weight (i.e., value) given to self-view as a nonsmoker and to the social group of nonsmokers to increase identification as a nonsmoker over competing concepts. Strategies could include drawing attention to successes, linking efforts to other positive self-concepts, and presenting nonsmokers in an exceedingly attractive light. Another option might be to design communication that integrated competing self-concepts by acknowledging them as a natural part of the change process. This could be accomplished perhaps by a narrative describing the experience of another person who has undergone a similar process and who has ultimately achieved success in quitting.

Although the examples above highlight different situations that call for accessibility-increasing strategies or value-increasing strategies, the implication of the prism model is that both can be implemented and have effects simultaneously. A smoking prevention campaign aimed at youth, for example, could link nonsmoking to an identity of being rebellious against powerful industries and deceptive marketing tactics, similar to the approach of the truth campaign (Evans, Wasserman, Bertolotti, & Martino, 2002). Young people may already have an autonomous self-concept, given the developmental importance of achieving competence and self-sufficiency in young adulthood. The campaign might then make such a self-concept more accessible, relative to other possible self-concepts. But beyond simply increasing accessibility, the campaign might also elevate and glamorize an autonomous self-concept and give it more importance as a predictor of nonsmoking, relative to other possible predictors.

After all, there are many competing views that young adults might have about themselves. On the one hand, they might value autonomy and rebellion against business, but without a persuasive message that specifically linked autonomy with nonsmoking, an autonomous self-concept might not be applied systematically in decisions regarding smoking; consequently, if one were inclined to test mediation, there might not be any measurable indirect effect of communication through that self-view. But with a message that tightly linked autonomy with nonsmoking, there could be a very strong indirect effect. Thus, increasing exposure to the campaign might lead to higher levels of accessibility, and at higher levels, the correspondence between an autonomous self-view and a nonsmoker self-view would be stronger than the correspondence at lower levels.

Although the model is described using statistical terms, it is hoped that the model will have heuristic value even for those who are not inclined to conduct quantitative research to test proposed relationships. Once again, the larger purpose is to foster appreciation of the complex intervening roles of identity and to suggest questions that can be asked prior to the design of any persuasive appeal. However, for those wishing to explore model-inspired possibilities in quantitative research, a few notes are in order.

In terms of operationalizations, the identity variable would have to be measured rather than manipulated if it is to serve as both an outcome and a predictor (in other words, as a mediator). A promising approach is to use reaction times to categorize self as consistent or not in terms of a given attribute, similar to the "me/not-me" task that has been used in social psychology (Markus, 1977). In this task, the quickness to respond indicates the accessibility of a given category in memory. Although the measure was originally used to show whether a person was schematic or aschematic with respect to an attribute, in recent work the measure has proven to be sensitive to the effects of media exposure (Comello & Slater, 2011).

In terms of analysis techniques, statistical tools exist to explore models such as those represented in Figures 10.4a and 10.4b. For example, a macro designed for this purpose (MODMED version 3.1; Hayes, 2011) is available for use with computer statistical packages (SPSS and SAS). Preacher and colleagues (2007) describe several models incorporating both moderation and mediation that can be tested with the macro. The configuration they identify as Model 1 is exactly the configuration of Figure 10.4a here, which is mathematically identical to Figure 10.4b, as noted earlier. The macro could be used to evaluate the effectiveness of message strategies that differ in how they frame an advocated behavior as consistent with a given self-view, with the key question of whether the strength of the indirect effect will vary as a function of message type. Future research formally would hypothesize and test these ideas.

Conclusion

This paper has attempted to synthesize the conceptualizations of identity across leading theoretical frameworks: the social identity perspective and the multiple-selves perspective of William James and other theorists. What has emerged is a view of identity as context-sensitive, complex, and as composed of multiple components. As these components shift in both accessibility and weight in response to stimuli, then so too can behavior-related outcomes. In a causal model of media effects, this conceptualization of identity suggests a dual function as both a moderator and mediator of communication effects on behavior.

A prism was offered as a metaphor for the relationships among the variables, because of the capability of a prism (strategically turned to catch the light just so) to serve as both a conduit and refractor of light. These are strikingly similar to the functions proposed for identity; serendipitously, the conceptual models of the relationships among communication, identity, and behavior proposed by the prism model also happen to resemble a prism visually. It is argued that such a model integrates the time-honored propositions of Bruner (1957) about category salience and of William James (1890/1981) about the activated-self mechanisms underlying persuasive message effects. The model is intended to generate more careful thinking about the multiple roles of the self, especially when there are conflicting self-concepts regarding an issue. In such cases, the model suggests that increasing the salience or the value of the desired identity (that is, the identity that would be congruent with the advocated behavior) is a promising route to successful persuasion.

Future research should test the model empirically, using statistical tools designed to assess conditional indirect effects. Although the model can certainly be made more complex with the addition of other variables and other possible causal configurations, it is hoped that the basic prism model illuminates key propositions and will serve as a useful starting point in defining new agendas for research in mass communication and identity.

Note

1. Andrew Hayes is acknowledged for making this observation in an unpublished document. General acknowledgements: I am grateful to Michael Slater, Robert Arkin, and Kenneth DeMarree for valuable feedback on this chapter.

References

Abrams, D. & Hogg, M. A. (2004). Metatheory: Lessons from social identity research. *Personality and Social Psychology Review, 8*(2), 98–106.

Bandura, A. (1986). *Social foundations of thought and action: A social cognitive theory.* Englewood Cliffs, NJ: Prentice-Hall.

Baron, R. M., & Kenny, A. (1986). The moderator-mediator variable distinction in social psychological research. *Journal of Personality and Social Psychology, 51*(6), 1173–1182.

Baumeister, R. F. (1998). The self. In D. T. Gilbert, S. T. Fiske, & G. Lindzey (Eds.), *Handbook of social psychology* (4th ed., pp. 680–740). New York: McGraw-Hill.

Berger, J. A., & Rand, L. (2008). Shifting signals to help health: Using identity-signaling to reduce risky health behaviors. *Journal of Consumer Research, 35*(3), 509–518.

Brewer, M. B. (1991). The social self: On being the same and different at the same time. *Personality and Social Psychology Bulletin, 17*(5), 475–482.

Brewer, M. B., & Gardner, W. (1996). Who is this "we"? Levels of collective identity and self representations. *Journal of Personality and Social Psychology, 71*, 83–93.

Bruner, J. S. (1957). On perceptual readiness. *Psychological Review, 64*(2), 123–152.

Cesario, J., & Higgins, E. T. (2008). Making message recipients "feel right": How nonverbal cues can increase persuasion. *Psychological Science, 19*, 415–420.

Chang, C. (2002). Self-congruency as a cue in different advertising-processing contexts. *Communication Research, 29*(5), 503–536.

Chang, C. (2005). Ad–self-congruency effects: Self-enhancing cognitive and affective mechanisms. *Psychology and Marketing, 22*(11), 887–910.

Comello, M. L. G. (2009). William James on "possible Selves": Implications for studying identity in communication contexts. *Communication Theory, 19*(3), 337–350.

Comello, M. L. G., & Slater, M. D. (2011). The effects of drug-prevention messages on the accessibility of identity-related constructs. *Journal of Health Communication, 16*(5), 458–469. doi:10.1080/10810730.2010.546485

Davison, W. P. (1983). The third-person effect in communication. *Public Opinion Quarterly, 47*(1), 1–15.

Evans, W., Wasserman, J., Bertolotti, E., & Martino, S. (2002). Branding behavior: The strategy behind the truth campaign. *Social Marketing Quarterly, 8*(3), 17–29.

Fishbein, M., & Yzer, M. C. (2003). Using theory to design effective health behavior interventions. *Communication Theory, 13*(2), 164–183.

Galinsky, A. D., Wang, C. S., & Ku, G. (2008). Perspective-takers behave more stereotypically. *Journal of Personality and Social Psychology, 95*, 404–419.

Harwood, J., & Roy, A. (2005). Social identity theory and mass communication research. In J. Harwood & H. Giles (Eds.), *Intergroup communication: Multiple perspectives* (pp. 189–211). New York: Lang.

Hayes, A. F. (2005). *Statistical methods for communication science.* Mahwah, NJ: Erlbaum.

Hayes, A. F. (2011). MODMED version 3.1. School of Communication, The Ohio State University. Available at http://www.afhayes.com/spss-sas-and-mplus-macros-and-code.html

Hogg, M. A., & Reid, A. (2006). Social identity, self-categorization, and the communication of group norms. *Communication Theory, 16*(1), 7–30.

James, W. (1981). The consciousness of self. In *The principles of psychology* (Vol. 1, pp. 279–379). Cambridge, MA: Harvard University Press. (Original work published 1890)

Maibach, E., Flora, J. A., & Nass, C. (1991). Changes in self-efficacy and health behavior in response to a minimal contact community health campaign. *Health Communication, 3*(1), 1–15.

MacKinnon, D. P. (2008). *Introduction to statistical mediation analysis*. New York: Erlbaum.

Markus, H. R. (1977). Self-schemata and processing information about the self. *Journal of Personality and Social Psychology, 35*, 63–78.

Markus, H. R., & Nurius, P. (1986). Possible selves. *American Psychologist, 41*(9), 954–969.

Martino, S. C., Collins, R. L., Kanouse, D. E., Elliott, M., & Berry, S. H. (2005). Social cognitive processes mediating the relationship between exposure to television's sexual content and adolescents' sexual behavior. *Journal of Personality and Social Psychology, 89*(6), 914–924.

McGuire, W. J. & McGuire, C. V. (1988). Content and process in the experience of self. In L. Berkowitz (Ed.), *Advances in experimental social psychology* (Vol. 21, pp. 97–144). New York: Academic Press.

Morton, T. A., & Duck, J. M. (2000). Social identity and media dependency in the gay community: The prediction of safe sex attitudes. *Communication Research, 27*(4), 438–460.

Nelson, T. E., Oxley, Z. M., & Clawson, R. A. (1997). Toward a psychology of framing effects. *Political Behavior, 19*(3), 221–246.

O'Keefe, D. J. (2003). Message properties, mediating states, and manipulation checks: Claims, evidence, and data analysis in experimental persuasive message effects research. *Communication Theory, 13*(3), 251–274.

Preacher, K. J., Rucker, D. D., & Hayes, A. F. (2007). Addressing moderated mediation hypotheses: Theory, methods, and prescriptions. *Multivariate Behavioral Research, 42*(1), 185–227.

Reed, M. B., & Aspinwall, L. G. (1998). Self-affirmation reduces biased processing of health-risk information. *Motivation & Emotion, 22*(2), 99–132.

Resnicow, K., Baranowski, T., Ahluwalia, J. S., & Braithwaite, R. L. (1999). Cultural sensitivity in public health: Defined and demystified. *Ethnicity & Disease, 9*(1), 10–21.

Reid, S. A., & Hogg, M. A. (2005). A self-categorization explanation for the third-person effect. *Human Communication Research, 31*(1), 129–161.

Roskos-Ewoldsen, D., Roskos-Ewoldsen, B., & Carpentier, F. R. D. (2002). Media priming: A synthesis. *Media effects: Advances in theory and research* (2nd ed., pp. 97–120). Mahwah, NJ: Erlbaum.

Sherman, D. A. K., Nelson, L. D., & Steele, C. M. (2000). Do messages about health risks threaten the self? Increasing the acceptance of threatening health messages via self-affirmation. *Personality & Social Psychology Bulletin, 26*(9), 1046–1058.

Slater, M. D. (2006). Specification and misspecification of theoretical foundations and logic models for health communication campaigns. *Health Communication, 20*(2), 149–157.

Slater, M. D. (2007). Reinforcing spirals: The mutual influence of media selectivity and media effects and their impact on individual behavior and social identity. *Communication Theory, 17*(3), 281–303.

Steele, C. (1988). The psychology of self-affirmation: Sustaining the integrity of the self. *Advances in Experimental Social Psychology, 21*, 261–302.

Swann, W. B., & Bosson, J. K. (2010). Self and identity. In S. T. Fiske, D. Gilbert, & G. Lindzey (Eds.), *Handbook of social psychology* (5th ed., Vol. 1, pp. 589–628). Hoboken, NJ: Wiley.

Tajfel, H., & Turner, J. C. (1986). The social identity theory of intergroup behavior. In S. Worchel & W. Austin (Eds.), *Psychology of intergroup relations* (pp. 7–24). Chicago, IL: Nelson.

Tao, C., & Bucy, E. P. (2007). Conceptualizing media stimuli in experimental research: Psychological versus attribute-based definitions. *Human Communication Research, 33*(4), 397–426.

Tichenor, P. J., Donohue, G. A., & Olien, C. N. (1970). Mass media flow and differential growth in knowledge. *The Public Opinion Quarterly, 34*(2), 159–170.

Tracy, S. J. & Trethewey, A. (2005). Fracturing the real-self fake-self dichotomy: Moving toward "Crystallized" organizational discourses and identities. *Communication Theory, 15*(2), 168–195.

Turner, J. C. (1987). A self-categorization theory. In J. C. Turner, M. A. Hogg, P. J. Oakes, S. D. Reicher, & M. S. Wetherell (Eds.), *Rediscovering the social group* (pp. 42–67). Oxford, England: Basil Blackwell.

Wheeler, S. C., Demarree, K. G., & Petty, R. E. (2005). The roles of the self in priming-to-behavior effects. In A. Tesser, J. V. Wood, & D. A. S. Stapel (Eds.), *On building, defending and regulating the self: A psychological perspective* (pp. 245–271). New York: Psychology Press.

Wheeler, S. C., DeMarree, K. G., & Petty, R. E. (2007). Understanding the role of the self in prime-to-behavior effects: The active-self account. *Personality and Social Psychology Review, 11*(3), 234–261.

Wheeler, S. C., DeMarree, K. G., & Petty, R. E. (2008). A match made in the laboratory: Persuasion and matches to primed traits and stereotypes. *Journal of Experimental Social Psychology, 44*(4), 1035–1047.

Wheeler, S. C., Petty, R. E., & Bizer, G. Y. (2005). Self-schema matching and attitude change: Situational and dispositional determinants of message elaboration. *Journal of Consumer Research, 31*, 787–797.

Wood, D., & Roberts, B. W. (2006). Cross-sectional and longitudinal tests of the personality and role identity structural model (PRISM). *Journal of Personality, 74*(3), 779–810.

Index

Page numbers in italics refer to figures

A
Acculturation, 67–68
Adolescence, social identity, 6–17
  coping mechanisms, 7–8
  future directions, 17
  impact on behavior, 8–10
  importance, 6–7
  peer crowd identification, 7–8
Advertising, 134–136
African Americans
  ethnic media, 128–129
  identity
    advertising, 134–136
    group vitality, 139–140
    media effects, 136–143
    media's impact on self-concept, 138
    racial identity, 140–141
    racial standpoint, 141–142
    self-categorization theory, 137–138
    self-esteem, 138–139
    social identity theory, 137
  Internet access, 128
  intersectionality, 129–131
  media
    class, 130–131
    film, 132–134
    future research directions, 142–143
    news media, 131–132
    television, 132–134
    use by, 127–128
Alternative media, 115–116
Anti-Muslim rhetoric, Fox News, 101–102
Arab American media, 115
Asian Americans

identity, 22–39
  belief in their own agency, 32
  concerns about lasting impacts, 31
  frustration, 29–30
  future-directed optimism, 34–36
  future directions, 39
  in-depth interviews, 25–38
  media representation perceptions, 27–38
  optimistic cultural logic, 31–32
  positive images and racial identity, 36–38
  racial identity views, 26–27
  resistance strategies, 33–34
  seeking humanizing range of representations, 29
media
  audience reception, 23–24
  belief in their own agency, 32
  concerns about lasting impacts, 31
  frustration, 29–30
  future-directed optimism, 34–36
  identity, 23–24
  media representation perceptions, 27–38
  optimistic cultural logic, 31–32
  positive images and racial identity, 36–38
  race, 23–24
  resistance strategies, 33–34
  seeking humanizing range of representations, 29
self-esteem, 22
stereotypes, 22
Assimilation
  benchmarks, 67
  Latinos, 68

Audience reception studies, Asian American identity, 23–24

B
Biased optimism, 24–25
Bicultural identity, 27
Bilingual press, 72–76
  conversion from Spanish-only to bilingual, 62
  counternarratives, 73–74
  cross-cultural transformations, 73
  Latinos, 62–63, 72–76
    business-model perspective, 75
    future directions, 76–77
  reasons for choosing, 73–74
Black, *see* African American
Brewerton, George Douglas, 96–97
Browne, John Ross, 97–99, 100

C
Category salience, 170–171
Cigarettes
  media, 15–16
  social identity, 15–16
Class, media, 130–131
Class identity, Mexico, 96
Code-switching, 63
Communication
  mediation, 173–179, *174*
  moderation, 173–177, *174, 175*
Conditional indirect effect, 181–182
Content assessment, 86
Contrapuntal reading, 85
Counternarratives, 43
  bilingual newspaper, 73–74
  critical race theory, 46–47
Critical race theory
  counternarratives, 46–47
  Latina/o-oriented press, 43–44, 45–47
  principles, 46–47
  social identity, 43–44, 45–47
Cultural contrapuntal reading, future research, 101
Cultural proximity, Spanish-language press, 71–72

D
Dana, Richard Henry Jr., 88–89
Davis, William Watts Hart, 89–90
Dehumanizing discourse, 113–114
Diversity, media, 54–55

E
Ethnic media, African Americans, 128–129

F
Film
  African American identity, 132–134
  peer communities, 14
Fox News, anti-Muslim rhetoric, 101–102

G
Gregg, Josiah, 94–95
Group identity, 107–108
Group vitality, 139–140

H
Hijab, 107, 113

I
Identity
  African Americans
    group vitality, 139–140
    media effects, 136–143
    media's impact on self-concept, 138
    racial identity, 140–141
    racial standpoint, 141–142
    self-categorization theory, 137–138
    self-esteem, 138–139
    social identity theory, 137
  Asian Americans, 22–39, 23–24
    belief in their own agency, 32
    concerns about lasting impacts, 31
    frustration, 29–30
    future-directed optimism, 34–36
    future directions, 39
    in-depth interviews, 25–38
    media representation perceptions, 27–38
    optimistic cultural logic, 31–32
    positive images and racial identity, 36–38
    racial identity views, 26–27
    resistance strategies, 33–34
    seeking humanizing range of representations, 29
  conceptualizations, 169–170
  identity activation, *180*, 181
  intersectionality, 129–131

Latinos, 64–67
  cultural identities, 65
  ethnic identities, 65
  racial identities, 65
  socioeconomic status, 65–66
media
  African Americans, 127–128, 136–143
  relationship, 1
  mediation, 173–177, *174*, 177–179
  as mediator and moderator, 169–185
  moderation, 173–177, *174, 176*
  multifaceted, 168–169
  prism model, 170–185
    identity as mediator and moderator, 179–185, *180*
Internet access, African Americans, 128
Intersectionality, 52–56
  African Americans, 129–131
  emergent groups, 130
  identity, 129–131
  stereotypes, 129–131
Islam, media-constructed identity
  alternative media, 115–116
  American Muslim identity, 112
  Arab American media, 115
  audience responses, 117–119
  communication theories guiding research, 111
  content type analyzed, 110
  current research agendas, 108, 109
  dehumanizing discourse, 113–114
  documentaries, 116–117
  future research agendas, 119–122
  gendered nuances, 113
  Iranian Muslim identity, 113
  methodologies, 110
  multiculturalism, 115
  multiple self-identities, 115
  Muslim-oriented media, 114–116
  nationalities of studied Muslims, 109–110
  negative connotations, 112
  Orientalism, 111
  overview of research, 108
  Shari'ah law, 114
  terrorism, 112, 117–118
  traditional general-market news media, 111–114
  Turkish Muslims, 118–119

J
James, William, 171
Jihad, 107

K
Kendall, George Wilkins, 95

L
Language, Latinos, 63–64
  code-switching, 63
Latina/o-oriented press, 66–72, *see also* Bilingual press
  critical race theory, 43–44, 45–47
  growth, 45
  social identity, 43–44, 43–58, 45–47, 62–77
    acculturation, 44–45
    counternarratives, 43
    counternarratives of population growth, 48–49
    framing and counternarrative, 45–48
    framing diversity as burden or benefit, 54–55
    framing narratives center on fear, 51
    general-market news mostly ignores Latina/os, 44–45
    general-market news unitary approach to identity, 56–57
    general-market *vs.* Latina/o-oriented newspaper coverage, 44–58
    language shapes social identity, 50
    Latina/o lived experience, 46–47
    Otherness, 51
    pluralism, 44–45
    reader loyalty, 45
    Sotomayor nomination, 52–56
    test of framing intersectionality, 52–54
    thematic immigration coverage, 51–52
    "wise Latina" reclaimed in counternarrative, 55–56
Latina/os
  assimilation, 68
  bilingual press, 62–63, 72–76
    business-model perspective, 75
    future directions, 76–77
  choosing news sources, 69

Latina/os (*continued*)
  identity, 64–67
    cultural identities, 65
    ethnic identities, 65
    racial identities, 65
    socioeconomic status, 65–66
  language, 63–64
    code-switching, 63
    loss or retention of Spanish, 64
  media, 68–76, 82–102
    cultural contrapuntal reading, 85–88
    future research, 101–102
    mass media othering of Mexicans, 82–102
    methodology, 85–88
    nineteenth-century press, 83–85
    process of Othering, 83
    theory, 85–88
  in the newsroom, 69
  stereotypes, 82–102
  transnational activities, 67–68

M
Manifest destiny, mass media Othering of Mexicans, 82–102
Media, *see also* Specific type
  African Americans
    advertising, 134–136
    class, 130–131
    film, 132–134
    future research directions, 142–143
    news media, 131–132
    television, 132–134
    use by, 127–128
  Asian Americans
    audience reception, 23–24
    belief in their own agency, 32
    concerns about lasting impacts, 31
    frustration, 29–30
    future-directed optimism, 34–36
    identity, 23–24
    media representation perceptions, 27–38
    optimistic cultural logic, 31–32
    positive images and racial identity, 36–38
    race, 23–24
    resistance strategies, 33–34
    seeking humanizing range of representations, 29
  cigarettes, 15–16
  diversity, 54–55
  identity
    African Americans, 127–128, 136–143
    Asian Americans, 23–24
    relationship, 1
    Latinos, 68–76, 82–102
      cultural contrapuntal reading, 85–88
      future research, 101–102
      mass media Othering of Mexicans, 82–102
      methodology, 85–88
      nineteenth-century press, 83–85
      process of Othering, 83
      theory, 85–88
  manifest destiny, mass media Othering of Mexicans, 82–102
  Mexico
    future research, 101–102
    mass media Othering of Mexicans, 82–102
  peer crowd identification, 10–16
    consequences, 15–16
    content defining, 13–14
    creating and providing access to social categories, 11–12
    increasing salience, 14–15
    influencing desirability of social categories, 13
  social identity, 1–5
  stereotypes, 82–102
Media-constructed identity, 107–122
  benefits, 107–108
  Muslims
    alternative media, 115–116
    American Muslim identity, 112
    Arab American media, 115
    audience responses, 117–119
    communication theories guiding research, 111
    content type analyzed, 110
    current research agendas, 108, 109
    dehumanizing discourse, 113–114
    documentaries, 116–117
    future research agendas, 119–122
    gendered nuances, 113
    Iranian Muslim identity, 113
    methodologies, 110
    multiculturalism, 115

multiple self-identities, 115
Muslim-oriented media, 114–116
nationalities of studied Muslims, 109–110
negative connotations, 112
Orientalism, 111
overview of research, 107–108
Shari'ah law, 114
terrorism, 112, 117–118
traditional general-market news media, 111–114
Turkish Muslims, 118–119
Mediation
 communication, 173–179, *174*
 identity, 173–177, *174*, 177–179
 prism model, identity as mediator and moderator, 179–185, *180*
Mexicanism, 86
Mexico
 media
  future research, 101–102
  mass media Othering of Mexicans, 82–102
  Northern observers in the Borderlands, 88–94
  poor Mexicans *vs.* Mexican elites, 82–83
  race, 94–99
  religion, 82, 88–94, 100, 101
  Southern views of Mexicans, 94–99
Moderation
 communication, 173–177, *174*, *175*
 identity, 173–177, *174*
 prism model, identity as mediator and moderator, 179–185, *180*
Moderator, identity, *176*
Multiculturalism, 115
Multiple-selves perspective, prism model, 169, 171–173
Muslims
 media-constructed identity
  alternative media, 115–116
  American Muslim identity, 112
  Arab American media, 115
  audience responses, 117–119
  communication theories guiding research, 111
  content type analyzed, 110
  current research agendas, 108, 109
  dehumanizing discourse, 113–114
  documentaries, 116–117
  future research agendas, 119–122
  gendered nuances, 113
  Iranian Muslim identity, 113
  methodologies, 110
  multiculturalism, 115
  multiple self-identities, 115
  Muslim-oriented media, 114–116
  nationalities of studied Muslims, 109–110
  negative connotations, 112
  Orientalism, 111
  overview of research, 107–108
  Shari'ah law, 114
  terrorism, 112, 117–118
  traditional general-market news media, 111–114
  Turkish Muslims, 118–119
 Serbia, 112, 118
 stereotypes, 107

N
News media, African American identity, 131–132

O
Optimistic bias, 24–25
Orientalism, 86, 87, 111
Othering
 characterized, 87
 means of detecting, 87–88
 representations deconstructed, 87

P
Peer communities, cinema, 14
Peer crowd identification, 7–8
 media, 10–16
  consequences, 15–16
  content defining, 13–14
  creating/accessing social categories, 11–12
  increasing salience, 14–15
  influencing desirability of social categories, 13
 social identity theory, 8
Prism model, 169
 accessibility-increasing strategies, 181–184
 identity, 170–185
  as mediator and moderator, 179–185, *180*
  mediation, identity as mediator and moderator, 179–185, *180*

Prism model (*continued*)
  moderation, identity as mediator and moderator, 179–185, *180*
  multiple-selves perspective, 169, 171–173
  social identity, 169
  value-increasing strategies, 181–184

R
Race
  Mexico, 94–99
  stereotypes, 94–99
Racial identity, 140–141
Racial location, defined, 141–142
Racial standpoint, 141–142
Reinforcing spirals model, 182
Religion
  Mexico, 82, 88–94, 100, 101
  stereotypes, 82, 88–94, 100, 101
Richardson, Albert Deane, 92–94, 99–100, 101

S
Self, 170
  active-self account, 172–173
  categorizations, 171
  context dependence, 172
  Jamesian view, 171–173
  persuasive message, 172
Self-esteem, 138–139
  Asian Americans, 22
Serbia, Muslims, 112, 118
Shari'ah law, 114
Social categories
  creation, 11–12
  desirability, 12–13
Social identity
  adolescence, 6–17
    coping mechanisms, 7–8
    future directions, 17
    impact on behavior, 8–10
    importance, 6–7
    peer crowd identification, 7–8
  characterized, 1
  cigarettes, 15–16
  critical race theory, 43–44, 45–47
  defined, 86
  importance, 6–7
  Latina/o-oriented press, 43–44, 43–58, 45–47, 62–77
    acculturation, 44–45
    counternarratives, 43
    counternarratives of population growth, 48–49
    framing and counternarrative, 45–48
    framing diversity as burden or benefit, 54–55
    framing narratives center on fear, 51
    general-market news mostly ignores Latina/os, 44–45
    general-market news unitary approach to identity, 56–57
    general-market *vs.* Latina/o-oriented newspaper coverage, 44–58
    language shapes social identity, 50
    Latina/o lived experience, 46–47
    Otherness, 51
    pluralism, 44–45
    reader loyalty, 45
    Sotomayor nomination, 52–56
    test of framing intersectionality, 52–54
    thematic immigration coverage, 51–52
    "wise Latina" reclaimed in counternarrative, 55–56
  mass media, 1–5
  prism model, 169
  salience, 14–15
Social identity theory, 137
  peer crowd identification, 8
Sotomayor Supreme Court nomination, 52–56
Spanish-language press, 70–72
  characteristics, 71
  cultural proximity, 71–72
  daily newspapers, 43–58
  economic and political development, 72
Stereotypes, 108
  Asian Americans, 22
  intersectionality, 129–131
  Latinos, 82–102
  mass media, 82–102
  Muslims, 107
  race, 94–99
  religion, 82, 88–94, 100, 101
Strategic formation, 87
Strategic location, 87

T
Taylor, Bayard, 90–91, 93
Television, African American identity, 132–134
Terrorism, 112, 117–118
Third-person effect, 24–25
Turkish Muslims, 118–119

U
Unrealistic optimism, 224

W
Women
　Afghan women, 116
　Muslim identities, 113, 116, 117

Taylor & Francis
eBooks
FOR LIBRARIES

ORDER YOUR FREE 30 DAY INSTITUTIONAL TRIAL TODAY!

Over 23,000 eBook titles in the Humanities, Social Sciences, STM and Law from some of the world's leading imprints.

Choose from a range of subject packages or create your own!

- ▶ Free MARC records
- ▶ COUNTER-compliant usage statistics
- ▶ Flexible purchase and pricing options

- ▶ Off-site, anytime access via Athens or referring URL
- ▶ Print or copy pages or chapters
- ▶ Full content search
- ▶ Bookmark, highlight and annotate text
- ▶ Access to thousands of pages of quality research at the click of a button

For more information, pricing enquiries or to order a free trial, contact your local online sales team.

UK and Rest of World: **online.sales@tandf.co.uk**
US, Canada and Latin America:
e-reference@taylorandfrancis.com

www.ebooksubscriptions.com

A flexible and dynamic resource for teaching, learning and research.